Fielding's

CALIFORNIA The Mission Trail

Current Fielding Titles

Red Guides—updated annually

FIELDING'S BERMUDA AND THE BAHAMAS 1988
FIELDING'S CARIBBEAN 1988
FIELDING'S ECONOMY EUROPE 1988
FIELDING'S EUROPE 1988
FIELDING'S MEXICO 1988
FIELDING'S PEOPLE'S REPUBLIC OF CHINA 1988
FIELDING'S SELECTIVE SHOPPING GUIDE TO EUROPE 1988

Blue Guides—updated as necessary

FIELDING'S AFRICAN SAFARIS
FIELDING'S CALIFORNIA
FIELDING'S EUROPE WITH CHILDREN
FIELDING'S FAMILY VACATIONS USA
FIELDING'S FAR EAST
FIELDING'S HAVENS AND HIDEAWAYS USA
FIELDING'S LEWIS AND CLARK TRAIL
FIELDING'S LITERARY AFRICA
FIELDING'S MOTORING AND CAMPING EUROPE
FIELDING'S SPANISH TRAILS IN THE SOUTHWEST
FIELDING'S WORLDWIDE CRUISES 3rd revised edition

Fielding's CALIFORNIA The Mission Trail

by

Lynn V. Foster

Fielding Travel Books
c/o William Morrow & Company, Inc.
105 Madison Avenue, New York, N.Y. 10016

Library of Congress
Library of Congress Cataloging-in-Publication Data

Foster, Lynn V.
Fielding's California : the mission trail, San Diego to San Francisco / Lynn Foster.
p. cm.
Bibliography: p.
Includes index.
ISBN 0-688-04756-4
1. California—Description and travel—1981- —Guide-books.
2. Spanish mission buildings—California—Guide-books. I. Title.
F859.3.F66 1988 87-30163
917.94'0453—dc19 CIP

Printed in the United States of America
First Edition
1 2 3 4 5 6 7 8 9 10
BOOK DESIGN BY BERNARD SCHLEIFER

For my mother

Acknowledgments

My heartfelt thanks are due to Larry Foster for his photographs and assistance while traveling, to Randy Ladenheim for her editing, to Theresa McEleney for maps and Jeanne Gaz for the typed manuscript. In addition, thanks are most certainly due to the following organizations for generously enabling me to carry out the research so essential to a travel book:

California Office of Tourism
Greater Los Angeles Visitors & Convention Bureau
Greater Ventura Visitors & Convention Bureau
Long Beach Area Convention & Visitors Council
Monterey Peninsula Visitors & Convention Bureau
San Diego Convention & Visitors Bureau
San Francisco Convention & Visitors Bureau
San Jose Convention & Visitors Bureau
Santa Barbara Conference & Visitors Bureau
Sonoma County Convention & Visitors Bureau

CONTENTS

LIST OF MAPS

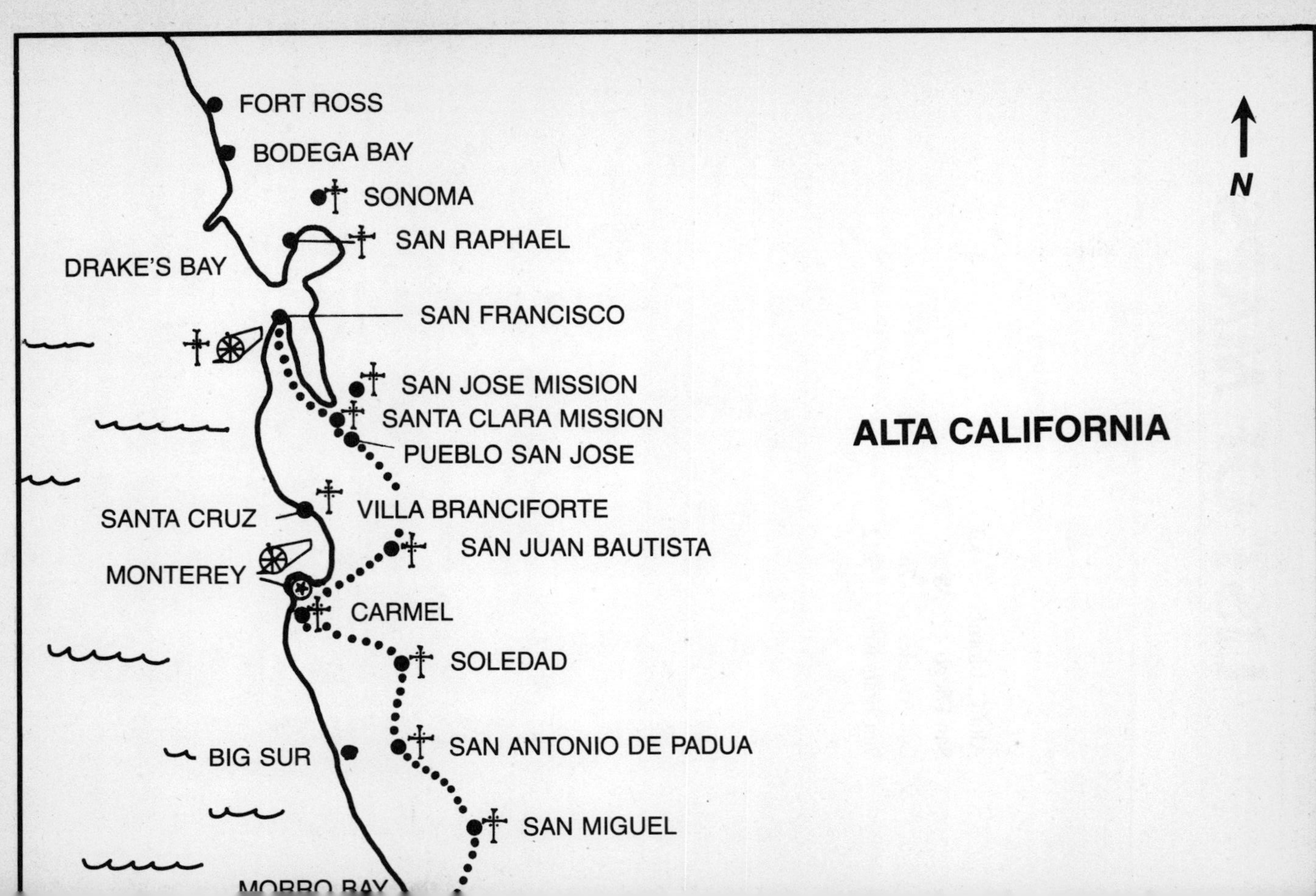
N
ALTA CALIFORNIA
FORT ROSS
BODEGA BAY
SONOMA
SAN RAPHAEL
DRAKE'S BAY
SAN FRANCISCO
SAN JOSE MISSION
SANTA CLARA MISSION
PUEBLO SAN JOSE
VILLA BRANCIFORTE
SANTA CRUZ
SAN JUAN BAUTISTA
MONTEREY
CARMEL
SOLEDAD
SAN ANTONIO DE PADUA
BIG SUR
SAN MIGUEL

DRAWN BY THERESA McELENEY

INTRODUCTION

Fielding's California: The Mission Trail is full of practical information to help you enjoy your trip to California, from listings of hotels and restaurants to descriptions of driving routes and outdoor activities. But first and foremost it is a living history guide to California. The Spaniards were the first Europeans to discover the Pacific coast, the first to describe Big Sur and San Francisco Bay, the first to settle Los Angeles and Monterey. From their diaries and those of Yankee traders, French emissaries and English settlers, we learn about life along the old mission trail called the Camino Real. Through these eyewitness accounts you are guided along the magnificent coast past the great sights of this state, through not only Disneyland and redwood forests, but also through Santa Barbara, so redolent of pastoral California, into the Spanish capital of Monterey, and to the old towns of San Diego and Los Angeles as well as to quiet valleys where missions still stand, and along country roads to the ranches of the Mexican dons.

How To Use This Guide

In planning your trip, you'll want to refer to the "Practical Tips for California Travel" chapter as well as the "Suggestions," "Accommodations," and "Restaurant" sections that appear toward the end of each destination chapter. Also, you might check the star-ratings of historical sights to include an extra day here and there for a special detour. If you can't find a particular place in the contents, just check the index. And if an occasional Spanish word or a colloquial expression is new to you, check the glossary. The historical backgrounds to each sightseeing chapter are there to increase your enjoyment of the local sights and culture, and each is written to stand on its own so that you don't have to read the entire book just to visit one place. The "Early California" chapter, however, provides an overview of the history in case you want a better framework for understanding the days of the explorers and missions. At the end of the book is a listing of sources for the quotations in this book, provided not just to properly acknowledge the authors, editors, and translators who have made these historical works accessible, but also to enable you to read more about California if you wish to do so.

Star-Rated Historical Sights

There are 21 missions, numerous ranches, adobes, and historical exhibits to choose from in California. Some are mere replicas with nothing much to see; others are elaborate buildings and complexes with excellent exhibits accompanying them. To distinguish between them I have rated them on a scale of zero to three stars. The star ratings for these sights certainly involve a lot of my own personal prejudices, and even I would probably re-rank some of them given another visit. Nonetheless, I have starred the historical sights in the hope that it will prove useful to you in your travels.

★★★ An exceptional example of a mission or adobe; or an exceptionally large amount to see.

★★ A particularly interesting mission, adobe, or museum; or a fair amount to see.

★ A mission, adobe, or museum of some interest.

No Star Not much to see; recommended only if part of some larger complex such as an old town or path of history tour.

Prices

Throughout the book price categories are given for hotels and restaurants. The categories for hotels are based on a double room for two people (without tax) during peak season. Often a hotel adds extra fees for tennis and other facilities, so you should check to see exactly what is included in the price quoted to you by a hotel.

Hotel Categories

Very Expensive—$120 plus
Expensive—80–120
Moderate—40–80
Inexpensive—40 and under

Restaurant Categories

The categories for restaurants are based on a dinner with entree, and either appetizer or dessert for one person (without tax or tip).

Expensive—$25 plus
Moderately Expensive—15–25
Moderate—8–15
Inexpensive—8 and under

Updates

I have checked and rechecked the information contained in this book, but without doubt there are bound to be some typographical errors along the way and without doubt some restaurants will change hands, some hotels will close, and some museums will change their hours or even their locations between press time and your visit. While I can't be responsible for the inaccuracies that result from these constant changes, I will make an ongoing effort to keep abreast of them. Your comments and suggestions would be most welcome and helpful. Write to me: c/o Fielding Travel Books, William Morrow & Company, 105 Madison Avenue, New York, NY 10016.

EARLY CALIFORNIA

The surf, rough and forbidding was breaking over the rocks along the shore. But Umai looked past the breakers, out across the ocean and she saw where the rim of the sky meets the water. And she thought she would like to ride the ocean . . .

YUROK STORY *(Kroeber)*

Vast was the ocean that encircled the world and, for the Yurok of California, led to the Land-Beyond-the-World. For the Spaniards, too, the seas encompassed the globe, but for them they led to the Orient, land of cinnamon and clove, silk and porcelain, ivory and jade. The Spaniards rode the ocean seeking a Western route to these Asian lands and instead encountered the New World. Diverted by conquest, the Spaniards nonetheless soon made their way to the Philippines, exploring the great Pacific from Mexico and establishing the Manila trade that would bring riches to Madrid for 250 years. For most of these years, the Yurok and other native Californians would be left undisturbed. Only the coast of California would be explored and probed, tested for the shelter of a safe harbor, but hardly bothered with. English pirates, too, would stop ashore. And Russian entrepreneurs with their Aleut otter hunters would occasionally explore to the north. But for decades the riders of the Pacific paid scant attention to Umai and the land called California.

Know that on the right hand of the Indies there is an island called California, very close to the side of the Terrestial Paradise; and it was peopled by black women, without any men among them, for they lived in the fashion of Amazons.

LAS SERGAS DE ESPLANDIAN
16TH-CENTURY SPANISH NOVEL
(*Caughey*)

Many have believed it only appropriate that California received its name from a legendary land. After all, something has always beckoned, if not the tawny coast then the towering redwoods or benign climate. Even the earliest inhabitants were attracted from many regions, bringing with them their various languages and customs. Around the time the Spanish conquered the land, California was one of the most densely settled areas of what is now the United States, with 300,000 people speaking about 135 distinct languages, Algonquit from the Atlantic seaboard being one. These peoples lived comfortably off the land and sea (see "Land of the Chumash: The Santa Barbara Region"), harvesting acorns to make into mush, fishing the sea and rivers alike, and hunting small game.

. . . no one will die of hunger, because the field and the sea has the table always set for them.

PADRE NARCISCO DURAN, 1839
(Engelhardt)

Little was needed in the way of clothes, though a tattoo added interest, a bear skin cape granted status, and abalone shells wealth. Little was needed in the way of housing either. A reed hut served very well: when it became dirty it could be burnt; when a new location was desired, it could be carried. California supported the good life for millennia before the arrival of Europeans. Yet its naming was no more than a mistake, a confusion by the explorer Hernando de Alarcon in 1541 who thought the name of an island off La Paz in Baja was the name for the entire peninsula. A year later when Cabrillo explored further north, he extended the mistake to upper California.

Early Explorers

Juan Rodriguez Cabrillo, 1542

By the time Cabrillo sailed from Mexico in 1542, De Soto had already lost his life at the Mississippi River, Ponce de Leon had died in Florida seeking the Fountain of Youth, and Coronado was just returning to Mexico from the Southwest, sick and disillusioned. Yet the Pacific remained to be explored for a route to the Orient. Perhaps, just perhaps there would be discovered the Straits of Anian, leading from the Atlantic to the Pacific and then to China, or even the California of the Amazons where everything, including "the harness of the wild beasts they tamed to ride,'' was made of gold. Still, the lure of legendary lands was diminishing and Cabrillo would discover the last of Spain's American possessions.

Sailing around the tip of Baja, and pushing north on the coast, Cabrillo entered the unknown and turbulent Pacific. He explored the sea against all odds, his small vessels encountering terrible storms and tacking near a coast plagued with dangerous currents and erratic winds. Time and again they were blown out to sea. Time and again gales forced them back and the sea washed over them like rocks. And at times

> . . . *there was a sea so high that they became crazed.*
>
> CABRILLO EXPEDITION, 1543

Cabrillo didn't discover the Anian Straits, but then no one ever would. He did chart the California coast, discover the shelter of San Diego Bay, the Santa Barbara Channel, and other points north to at least Mendocino. And he claimed the entire region for Spain before dying of an injury from a fall while on one of the Channel Islands.

Spain seemed little interested in its new possession. With Cabrillo's feat, the Crown had completed its incredible explorations of the hemisphere from Chile to Oregon, from Argentina to California. Having assured itself that no fabled lands had been overlooked, Spain concentrated on reaping for itself the known riches of gold in Peru, silver in Mexico, and the long sought after trade with China. Even in 1565 when a safe return from Manila to Acapulco took the galleons along the California coast, little attention was paid to Cabrillo's discovery. Each year, though, California would be glimpsed or at least remembered from the great Manila galleons if nowhere else. Sixty years would lapse before Spain, against its wishes, would once again focus on its Pacific coast possession, and by then Cabrillo's accomplishments would be so forgotten that a new explorer could rename the harbors, bays, and islands of California, names that this time would endure.

Sebastian Vizcaino, 1602

Until 1579 Spain totally dominated the Pacific. So uncontested was its possession that the annual galleons used every inch of gun space to instead pack on the riches of Peru and the Philippines.

As no other ships but ours have ever been sighted on this voyage, which is through so remote regions, they have always sailed with little or no artillery . . .

BISHOP SALAZAR OF THE PHILIPPINES 1587
(Richman)

But other powers, England foremost among them, sought their own opportunities to contest Spain's hegemony. So in 1579 Sir Francis Drake captured the first Pacific galleon (see "Point Reyes National Seashore") and soon after the pirate Cavendish robbed the Manila galleon—"the richest ship to leave" the Philippines.

Suddenly vulnerable Spain decided to establish a port of call where its ships could find safety and supplies. If the Hawaiian islands had been discovered, certainly the safe harbor would have been established there. Instead, a few of the Manila galleons were ordered to more closely explore California for a site on their return to Acapulco, but the ungainly vessels crashed to shore—that of Cermeno at the same spot where Drake had landed. Finally in 1602 the expedition of Sebastian Vizcaino followed Cabrillo's route around Baja and encountered the same turbulent headwinds of the California coast.

The seas were very high so that we could neither run nor lie by at sea. All the men had fallen sick, so that there were only two sailors who could climb to the main topsail.

SEBASTIAN VIZCAINO, 1603

At one point the stormy sea so pitched the ship that its keel seemed to stand on end. Although suffering much, Vizcaino accomplished little more than to rename what Cabrillo had already discovered. He did probably find a bay of his own, however, named it Monterey, and heartily recommended it "as the best port that could be desired" for the galleon.

Conquest

So glowing was Vizcaino's report on Monterey Bay that Captain Gaspar de Portola overlooked the real Monterey on his expedition to settle it (see "The Capital City of Monterey"). By then the Yurok had already enjoyed another 160 years free of the riders of the sea while Spain disentangled itself from European intrigues and wars. And Portola's instructions were not simply to establish a port of call at Monterey. After so many years Spain had decided to fund and create another colony, one that would grow into 21 missions, 4 presidio towns, and 3 pueblos. It was a late colony at that, one that would still be struggling with its very foundations while to the east another colony fought for its independence from England. It would be Spain's last colony, one founded not for gold or silver, but in reaction to foreign threats.

The Russians have several times made attempts to open a route to America and have recently carried out their intentions through navigating in the northern part of the Pacific . . . The King has ordered me to inform your grace of the danger so that the governor named for [Baja] California can be made alert . . . thwarting them [the Russians] however possible.

MARQUES DE GRIMALDI, 1768
(Treutlein)

Like all the other great powers of the time, the Russians were trading with China, too. Only they traded sea otter pelts hunted in the northwest Pacific, valuable pelts that brought the Russians to Alaska and occasionally even to the mainland of America (see "Foreign Threats: San Francisco Bay"). The English, too, were threatening a greater presence in the Pacific as they crossed Canada in pursuit of the Anian Straits they called the Northwest Passage. The French eventually would become attracted to the region as well.

California is no less attractive than Virginia on the other side of the continent except that it is farther from Europe. Proximity to Asia should make up for that.

COMTE DE LAPEROUSE, 1797

There was nothing to stop these powers from seizing unoccupied California, nothing then to prevent them from disrupting Spain's most valuable trade in the Pacific or even, perhaps, interfering with the silver mines in northern Mexico. Nothing except the occupation and fortification of California.

. . . the King gave orders to guard that part of his dominions from all invasion and insult.

MIGUEL COSTANSO, 1769

The Portola Expedition, 1769

Two centuries in the New World had created a Spain experienced in conquest. No longer did troops wear the steamy metal armor of the Coronado expedition or the 30-pound weight of chain mail. Years of frontier struggle had proven leather jackets sufficient against Indian arrows, double-ply shields against their spears. And years of Indian warfare had proven the sword inferior to spiritual conquest in achieving a lasting peace.

. . . better results have always been obtained by acquisitions that have been made gently by means of the missionaries than by those obtained by force of arms.

VICEROY ANTONIO MARIA
BUCARELI 1772
(Treutlein)

Not only was the new California colony's success dependent on peace with the Indians, it required their active participation—as wives to the leather jacket soldiers, as laborers and farmers, and as arms bearing citizens against foreign invasion. So in 1769 Gaspar de Portola, governor of Baja California, would lead an expedition north to Alta California that would include not only three ships' crew, but also a land force of leather jackets and Franciscan missionaries. He would lead this expedition north not just to found the initial presidios, or forts, at San Diego and Monterey, but also to found the first missions.

. . . take his Royal order . . . that the said establishments be supported and supplied that they will not decline, but will rather grow by means of the voluntary conversion of the Indians.

ROYAL INSTRUCTIONS, 1773
(Treutlein)

A number of the leaders of the expedition were recent arrivals from Spain. One, Padre Junipero Serra, was destined to become the founder of California's first nine missions. His lack of experience deterred him not at all from making the commitment to a life on the frontier. Even though he couldn't walk at times due to an injury, his zeal for Christianizing Indians enabled him to endure the long journey to San Diego, and eventually to Monterey.

I shall not turn back. They can bury me wherever they wish and I shall gladly be left among the pagans, if it be the will of God.

FRIAR JUNIPERO SERRA, 1769

With him from Catalonia was Fray Juan Crespi, who was about to become a great explorer of California and the Pacific. These members of the expedition best exemplified the pioneering spirit of the early missionaries (see ''Along the Camino Real: The Padres''), and both would remain in the new colony until their deaths.

While most of the leaders and all of the missionaries on the expedition were Spaniards of the ''nasty white color'' described by a Gabrileno Indian, most of the leather jackets were not. Years of living on the frontier of Mexico where few Spaniards, much less senoritas, could be found had led to more than a change of attire. Since only five Spaniards on the expedition remained in California, the colonizer of the new province would be this Mexican frontiersman, predominantly Indian in descent, sometimes with a trace of Black, and with more Spanish culture than genes. These *gente de razon,* or ''people of reason'' as they called themselves, would be responsible for the creation of the province of California. Much like Sergeant Jose F. Ortega, the scout of Portola's expedition who blazed the way from San Diego to Monterey, and who must have been the first to discover San Francisco Bay, these soldier-settlers would survive near starvation before going on to found the forts and towns of California. Eventually their families would inherit their land, like Ortega's Rancho El Refugio (see ''Land of the Chumash: Santa Barbara Region'') and prosper as *Californio* aristocrats.

About 300 individuals made up the expedition. Fewer than half would survive the journey. Of the three supply ships, one was forever lost to the sea and the other two, miscalculating their course, rode the sea too long only to arrive at San Diego with scurvy-ridden crews. The land divisions forged their way through the unknown desert of Baja, stumbled over and down unending ravines, and finding little wood with which to cook, they burnt the poles of tents in order to make their tortillas. Enduring months at sea and in the wilderness, the expedition reunited at San Diego. Nine hundred miles by land from the settlement at Loreto in Baja, over 1500 miles by sea and land to the capital of New Spain at Mexico City, the expedition reunited in ill-health, low on supplies, and with barely enough energy to make their way further to Monterey (see "The First Colony: San Diego").

Our position here is what you can well imagine. But we are not dead yet, thank God.

SERRA, 1770

Yet they not only founded the presidio at Monterey, they explored much of California and discovered the great bay of San Francisco (see that chapter). The Spaniards remained, ending the millennia during which California belonged just to the Yurok and their neighbors.

The Camino Real

Struggling their way through hundreds of miles of Baja desert, the colonizers provided the first land route into California, a route that would initially permit cattle to be driven and other supplies to be carried to the new province. The Baja settlements would eventually wither away in that barren land, leaving the Camino Real, or King's Highway, of upper California to flourish on its own as a royal road. It would flourish much like an island road, rarely approachable by land from Mexico because of a sea of warring Apaches to the southeast.

The 600 miles of California's Camino Real (see Alta California map) would wander over time, stretching to meet each new mission, branching to include the presidios and the pueblos at Los Angeles and San Jose, detouring to avoid danger such as Indian attacks on

. . . the arduous slopes of the arroyo of San Juan Bautista . . . not only laborious and very difficult for the mule trains but even for the mail couriers in the rainy season.

GOVERNOR FELIPE DE NEVE, 1782

Despite changes, the King's Highway would retain the basic route blazed by Portola's conquistadors. From San Diego they traveled along the coast to present-day San Juan Capistrano before taking a short cut inland to the area of Los Angeles, where they discovered the bubbling tar pits at La Brea. Returning to the sea at the Santa Barbara Channel, they encountered the joyous hospitality of the Chumash Indians (see "Land of the Chumash'') before continuing north to where the ruggedness of the Santa Lucia Mountains, near Big Sur, temporarily diverted them inland. Then between the magnificence of Point Lobos and Point Pinos they searched for, and eventually recognized Monterey Bay. Continuing even farther north they discovered San Francisco Bay, the natural ending of the Camino Real even after missions were founded as far to the north as Sonoma. Coastal meanderings and mountains occasionally forced the Camino Real inland. But no matter how extensively the Spaniards explored the interior valleys of California, the Camino Real remained within 40 miles or so of the coast, the only region ever settled in Hispanic times and even today the location of most of California's population.

The Camino Real never would be much more than a worn cow path. No bridges spanned the sometimes wild and rough streams that cut through it, no pavement held firm during storms. George Vancouver, visiting in 1792, found the royal highway near San Francisco no better than a marsh in which his horses sank knee deep in mud. When the rains were really bad, the mule trains wouldn't even leave from the capital at Monterey. Years later, the road still had its pitfalls, especially where it ran along the coast.

It is certain that if this narrow strip of sand, on which we had been traveling, had been suddenly invaded by the action of the tide, there would have been no way for us to climb this [cliff] . . .

A. DUHAUT CILLY, 1827

But the loneliness on the road and the fear of attack by unmissionized Indians diminished with the years. It was Padre Serra who, in his desire to be permitted to save as many Indian souls as possible, convinced the government of the need for missions evenly spaced a day's journey (about 35 miles) along the road so that travelers could sleep in security, eat in comfort, and replace their horses with those of the missions. Each new mission, with its contingent of soldiers to protect it, would also absorb heathen *rancherias,* or villages. Serra founded the first nine missions. Friar Fermin Lasuen was later able to fill in the gaps along the road with another nine by arguing they would save the government the expense of providing military escorts for caravans. By 1804 there were nineteen missions. A traveler could journey from San Diego to San Francisco and find the comfort of a mission available each night of the way.

. . . one enjoyed absolute personal security in California, in the towns as well as along the roads and it never occurred to any travelers to fear being assaulted by malefactors on the roads unless it might be by a wild Indian in the most deserted parts.

JOSE ARNAZ, 1840–43

The Camino Real became known not just for its safety, but for its hospitality. With the free trade permitted under Mexico, more than government supply caravans traveled the road. Yankee traders, French visitors, English in the hide and tallow trade, and even Russians from their settlements to the north, would ride the trail from mission to mission to make business arrangements—How many hides for tools and religious adornments? How much tallow for cloth for the neophytes? When to rendezvous on the coast and where? Their travel could sometimes be arduous, but more often than not they were treated to fiestas full of the music of the church orchestra and the traditional dances of the Indian neophytes. And in the absence of fiestas, they always were offered the products of the mission (see "Along the Camino Real: Mission Life")—"no recompense required."

[At San Gabriel Mission] there being so much beef, mutton, pork, and poultry, with fruits, vegetables and wines, that a splendid public table was spread daily . . . Horses to ride on were at their service, and a good bed to sleep on at night.

HUGO REID, 1830s

With the end of the missions, California hospitality became even more lavish, as the great *ranchos* replaced them along the Camino Real. Back then visitors always found food and lodging as well as dances and parlor entertainments with the silk-gowned daughters of the wealthy cattle barons, and the dazzling rodeo displays of their silver-spurred sons (see "The Rancheros of Los Angeles").

The proverbial hospitality of which I had heard so much, and I must admit that there was no exaggeration in what I had been told.

JOSE ARNAZ, 1840s

The Spanish Province, 1769–1822

Spain just barely colonized California in time to protect it. The end of the 18th-century brought many foreign ships to the Pacific on world ''scientific'' expeditions that supplied their governments with enticing information on the profits to be made in China from otter and seal hunting. The expedition of Thomas Cook best publicized the region; those of Laperouse and Vancouver actually landed in California. By the early 1800s others visited, too, among them the Yankee smuggler William Shaler (see ''San Diego'' chapter) and the Russian count Rezanov (see chapter on ''San Francisco Bay''). As much as these foreign visitors amused the isolated colonists of California, they simply further alarmed Spain.

Constantly responding to what it saw as threatening to its possessions, Spain expanded its commitment. In addition to the presidios and settlements at San Diego and Monterey, two more were established at Santa Barbara and San Francisco. In addition to permitting the growth of missions,

The continued livelihood of the natives and the prospects of forming them into prosperous towns of individuals useful to the state, all of this depends on good treatment . . .

VICEROY BUCARELI,
1774 *(Beilharz)*

three civilian *pueblos,* or towns, were established with new settlers from Mexico. These towns—San Jose and Branciforte (now Santa Cruz)—helped populate the region around San Francisco Bay (see ''Along the Camino Real: End of the Missions'') as well as, in the case of Los Angeles, farm the land in order to improve the food supply. Yet all such efforts at defense failed to impress any of the foreign observers. Shaler found the number of Spanish inhabitants not worthy of consideration, and besides, even if they did number almost 2000, they had a harmless nature. The few cannon, the crumbling fort walls were noted by all.

This sketch will be sufficient, without further comment, to convey . . . the unprotected state of the establishment of this port [San Francisco] . . . which must have been formed at considerable expense, [yet] it possesses no other means for its protection than such as . . . a brass three-pounder mounted on a rotten carriage and a similar piece . . . [elsewhere]. Before the presidio there had formerly been two pieces of ordnance, but one of them had lately burst to pieces.

GEORGE VANCOUVER, 1798
(Caughey)

Yet Spain would not lose California to its rivals. The Russians might establish a settlement in Sonoma (see "Foreign Threats: San Francisco Bay"), the pirate Bouchard might attack the provinces (see chapters on "Monterey" and "Santa Barbara"), and the English might toy with occupying what would become Vancouver Island, but California would belong to Spain for over 50 years—until one of its own possessions fought and won independence.

Those 50 years would be ones in which California would survive if not flourish. Neatly organized into four presidio districts in which 20 missions (the last and 21st wouldn't be founded until the Mexican period) and three pueblos were protected by outposts of the militia, the province achieved security against Indian attacks. But the early years sometimes resulted in conditions as dire as those confronted by Portola (see "The Capital City of Monterey" and "The First Colony: San Diego"). The annual supply ships too often arrived late, sometimes not at all, leaving the new colony, its lands barely ready for cultivation, to face starvation. The Manila galleons were ordered to stop, too, but more often they preferred the penalty of a fine to the delay in making profits in Acapulco. To make matters worse, disease decimated those Indians joining the mission (see "Mission Life"). Malnourished and often ill, without any of the basic necessities of daily existence, so began the new province of Álta, or upper, California.

It cuts to the quick to see the Indians so poorly clad without prospects of even a breech-cloth and the soldiers so run down . . .

SERRA, 1781

The colony learned to survive on its own. A bear hunt would stave off hunger and, eventually, the mission crops became more bountiful. The missions themselves became more self-sustaining, wool from their sheep was woven into cloth for the Indian neophytes, leather thongs from the increasing herds of cattle replaced nails in construction, wooden columns replaced stone ones, non-existent choir lofts could be created with trompe l'oeil paintings (see chapters on "The Padres" and "Mission Life"). But gunpowder, iron for tools, weapons and horseshoes, and brocaded vestments in which to say mass could not be replaced by simple ingenuity or hard work.

What Spain failed to provide was eventually received from her competitors. If the Manila galleon didn't find California a profitable stopover, other ships did. Californians discovered English, American, and Russian ships were only too willing to smuggle tea samovars from St. Petersburg, priestly vestments from China, and tools from New England in exchange for re-stocking their ships with grain and otter pelts. After all, they were in the region anyway, hunting otter for trade in China, where the pelts were favored over ermine or even sable. Smuggling, often leading to arrest by Spanish port authorities (see "Santa Barbara" chapter) or even to the firing of cannon (see "San Diego"), became part of the China trade.

For several years past, the American trading ships have frequented this coast in search of furs, for which they have left in the country about 25,000 dollars annually, in specie and merchandize. The government have used all their endeavors to prevent this intercourse, but without effect . . .

WILLIAM SHALER, 1808

Sometimes the smuggling went beyond the bare necessities of giving "something to the hungry" and providing "cloth to the naked soldiers of the King of Spain," as one Yankee put it. Sometimes it included the best from China: black silk handkerchiefs, satin slippers, and jade jewelry. California remained Spain's, but very early on, the province became a land of more opportunity and international diversity than the Crown liked, or even permitted.

With the Mexican war for independence, relations with Spain deteriorated even further. From 1811 till even after Mexican independence, not one supply ship arrived from Mexico. Worse, governors' and commandantes' salaries, soldiers' and padres' income, no longer were received. California suffered. Its presidios further decayed, soldiers revolted, and the missions became pressed to support not just themselves but the entire province (see "End of the Missions" chapter). The missions had, indeed, become productive institutions with a total population of 21,000 Indian neophytes. The neophytes were learning to become good Christian citizens not only by studying their catechism, but also by working as gardeners of orchards and vineyards, farmers of wheat and corn fields, *vaqueros,* or cowboys, of vast herds, weavers and shoemakers, blacksmiths and carpenters, church musicians and *alcaldes,* or overseers. Even the wealth of the missions, however, could not support all of California.

. . . our Indians go barefoot in order that they may provide shoes for the troops and many families. They eat their food without butter . . . They do not taste beans in order to deliver them to the military store . . .

PADRE JUAN AMORO, 1816
(Englehardt)

Such deprivations would eventually lead to the worst Indian revolt in California history (see ''Santa Barbara'' chapter).

The Mexican Colony, 1822–1848

Spain simply receded from California life. The colony that had grown from a few hundred settlers to about 3000 gente de razon, and seven times that number in missionized Indians, had lost all contact with the Crown. California had become so isolated that nearly any rumor could find its believer, even one that Spain had sold the province to the Russians. So when officials in Monterey were notified of Mexican independence—a year after the fact, of course—they found no difficulty in swearing allegiance to the new nation. Especially when it meant their limited smuggling would burgeon overnight into Mexican free trade.

Our Province seems to have become another Cadiz, on a small scale. On Tuesday of this week, seven vessels set sail from the roadstead of Santa Barbara—two English and five Anglo-American—which had lain there at anchor for several days. God bless them and the Russians too! And may He preserve the Californias for the Mexican Empire . . .

PADRE JOSE SENAN, 1822

Hide and Tallow Trade

Free trade stimulated many changes. Overland routes opened from that other Mexican province called New Mexico, and soon Anglo fur trappers also made their way across the continent to the coast. Yet California remained basically a maritime province. And even the nature of that trade changed with the years. Otter had not only been overhunted, their pelts were no longer the royal fur of China. Cattle hides and tallow replaced the soft furs as items of trade. Many hides, usually 40,000 annually, but in one year 200,000, would be collected up and down the coast, from the customs house at the capital of Monterey to San Francisco, from Santa Barbara and San Pedro near Los Angeles, then down to the storage sheds in San Diego before beginning the trip again. Before collecting enough hides to take back to the shoe manufacturers in Boston and England, a sailing brig could spend two years on the coast (see San Diego chapter).

On the arrival of a new vessel from the United States, every man, woman, boy, and girl in the place took a proportionate share of interest as to the qualities of her cargo. If the first inquired for rice, sugar, and tobacco, the later asked for prints, silks, and satins; and if the boy wanted a "Wilson's cook knife," the girl desired that there might be some satin ribbons, and even the Indian, in his unsophisticated style, asked for—"Red handkerchiefs" and "beads."

ALFRED ROBINSON, 1830s

Enjoying their increasing prosperity, the gente de razon grew in number quickly to 4700, and their numbers increased more by the addition of foreign settlers, English captains, Yankee traders, and Scotch merchants who set up shops in the towns and eventually married into the best Californian families. (See chapters on Los Angeles, Santa Barbara, Monterey, and San Francisco.) Others less financially well endowed stayed, too, by jumping ship. Some became beachcombers, others happily married spouses of the locals (see "San Diego"). Life in the towns began to pick up, from the elegant balls of Monterey and Santa Barbara, and the exclusive ones in Los Angeles, to those aboard ship in San Francisco and San Diego (see those chapters).

Upon our arrival the Dieguenos informed us that Pedrorena had given a ball, the best that had ever been seen there up to that time, lasting three days and three nights. Piqued by these words . . . the ship gave one for eight.

ARNAZ, 1841

Secularization, 1834

The missions, too, benefited from free trade. In fact, they were the most active participants. Since only 25 land grants had been made to private individuals by Spain, it was mission cattle that grazed the hills and valleys of California, mission cattle that provided the hides and tallow of trade. When merchants such as Alfred Robinson rode the Camino Real to place his orders, it was the friars who did business with him (see "The Padres" chapter). By 1834 nearly 400,000 head of cattle ranged over California, and all belonged to the missions. And the other products of the missions found their markets, too—the brandy and wine to the pueblos as well as the traders, the mutton and wool from over 100,000 sheep supplied the presidios and government as did the thousands upon thousands of bushels of wheat and corn. By 1834, the Mexican government owed the missions one-half million dollars for supplies. But by then the government would never pay.

. . . may God forbid that free trade should lead to the introduction of free thought.

FRIAR SENAN, 1822

Mexican independence did bring more than free trade. It brought an anti-clerical bias. Arguing that the padres, most of whom were Spaniards, had had enough time to prepare the Indians, Mexico demanded they be freed to assume their rights of citizenship. Such idealism might never have been realized in California if the gente de razon weren't anxious to receive their own land and make what they could out of the hide trade. These forces converged in the early years of the Mexican Republic and by 1834, the missions were no more. Although technically they had been taken from the Franciscans and turned over to the ex-neophytes whose labor had earned them the land, the missions soon became the private ranchos of the gente de razon (see "End of the Missions" chapter). By 1840 the number of private ranchos had grown from 25 to 600; the great age of the Mexican don had begun (see "Los Angeles" chapter). And the number of belligerent Indians living in the wild interior suddenly increased.

U.S. Conquest, 1846–48

The conquest of California did not bother the Californians, least of all the women. It must be confessed that California was on the road to complete ruin.

ANGUSTIAS DE LA GUERRA ORD, 1846

California did prosper under Mexico, but it was no better governed than under Spain. The same distance from Mexican ports to the capital at Monterey made communications just as poor, and prevented Mexico from responding promptly to the growing needs of the province. Secularization of the missions resulted in increasingly numerous and virulent Indian raids on ranches along the Camino Real. The southern cattle ranches made Los Angeles, not the capital at Monterey, the largest and wealthiest California town, and soon the Carrillos and Picos of the south were in power struggles with the Castros, Vallejos and Alvarados of the north. And the land routes into California brought more and more caravans of Anglo-American settlers who illegally farmed Californian soil, mostly in the interior area near Sutter's Mill (see "Foreign Threats: San Francisco Bay").

. . . our people have undoubtedly the same right that other foreigners or even the Californians themselves have, to locate in and enjoy this delightful country . . .

L.W. HASTINGS, 1846

As these problems mounted, Mexico's actions only made them worse. Soldiers were sent to defend the province, but they were convicts sentenced to the California presidios. Their arrival, in "a state of wretchedness and misery unequalled," more often created crime waves than peace. And the order to arrest many of the foreign poachers resulted merely in embarrassing international incidents in which the illegals were reinstated in California. Increasingly preoccupied with foreign threats in Texas and even closer to home, Mexico found itself without the resources to assist, much less govern California. The Californians, having finally gained some semblance of home rule, simply continued their battles, more ritual than real, over whether the north or south would control the governorship and customs house (see "Los Angeles" chapter).

Although I was prepared for anarchy and confusion, I was surprised when I found a total absence of all government in California . . .

CHARLES WILKES, 1845

Much like vultures, foreign powers positioned themselves for a possible takeover of California (see "Monterey" chapter). Conditions were very ripe for a change. Even the Californios realized it.

I did not want to be governor . . . because of the danger of a foreign invasion which was threatening, without resources to prevent it . . .

PIO PICO, 1845

Since Mexico no longer could defend it, Governor Pio Pico believed that independence should be proclaimed and another nation asked for protection. Some Californios favored the French, others the English, and some the Americans. In fact, U.S. Consul Thomas Larkin had been working toward just such a peaceful acquisition of California.

The United States decided the negotiated takeover was taking too long. The more time that passed, the more other contenders, England in particular, would have a chance to win the prize of a port on the Pacific.

We must march from ocean to ocean . . . We must march from Texas straight to the Pacific Ocean, and be bounded only by its roaring wave.

CONGRESSMAN GILES, 1847

So Lt. John Charles Fremont, allegedly without authorization from Washington but with 62 heavily armed soldiers, arrived overland from the Oregon Trail on what he described to Californian authorities as a map-making expedition. He almost immediately provoked a war by raising the U.S. flag near Monterey, but Comandante General Jose Castro ''was not addicted to expose his interesting person to bullets'' and Fremont, with Larkin's urging, retreated. In the area of Sutter's Fort, Fremont successfully stirred up the Anglo poachers into the Bear Flag Rebellion (see ''San Francisco'' chapter). Nearly simultaneously Commodore John Drake Sloat seized California's harbors and raised the U.S. flag (see ''Monterey'' chapter).

I declare to the inhabitants of California that, although I come in arms with a powerful force, I do not come among them as an enemy to California; on the contrary, I come as their best friend, as henceforward California will be a portion of the United States . . .

COMMODORE JOHN D. SLOAT, 1846

It would definitely have been a bloodless takeover if the Californios hadn't been so insulted by the U.S. conquest. Despite the sympathy that many dons had for the Americans—and despite the great increase in the value of real estate promised by Commodore Sloat in his takeover speech—some of their members had been abused by the Bear Flaggers and others offended by the treatment of U.S. forces (see ''Los Angeles'' chapter). While sending for aid from Mexico, the Californios resisted. They regained Los Angeles, defeated American troops at San Pasqual (see "San Diego" chapter), and ambushed the invaders when they could, even capturing Consul Larkin in one of their skirmishes. But no support was coming from beleaguered Mexico. In 1847 Californio resistance ended and the next year the United States acquired both California and Utah, a total of 600,000 square miles of territory, through the Treaty of Guadalupe Hidalgo.

Legacy

The discovery of gold in California inundated the former Hispanic province. From a population that probably reached no more than 15,000 non-Indians by 1848, California grew to hold well over 200,000 people in just four years' time. Swamped by peoples of different culture, the traditions of the *Californio* had little chance of survival. Stripped of their lands by charlatans and bankrupted during the years of drought, the once proud dons lost everything to the newcomers. So rapidly did California change, that the most ardent supporters of the U.S. takeover could bemoan their losses.

I begin to yearn after the time prior to July 1846 and all their honest pleasures . . . Halcyon days they were. We *shall not enjoy their like again.*

THOMAS LARKIN, 1856

Yet much has survived from the days of the Camino Real. The Pacific coast remains rugged and majestic, the *palo colorado,* or redwood, are preserved, the trade with the Orient is still intense. Anglo ranchers may have replaced Mexican dons, but they continue many of their traditions from barbecues and rodeos to the horse farms that proliferate in the Santa Ynez mountains. European varietals may predominate in California vineyards, but it was the padres who first planted the grapes that even today influence wines of Sonoma. And it was their orchards that first brought the orange trees and pomengrantes to the fertile soil of California.

It's not merely the magnificent scenery and traditions that persevere. It is the presidios that have grown into the four cities of San Diego, Santa Barbara, Monterey, and San Francisco, and the first *pueblos,* Los Angeles and San Jose, that remain even today centers of Mexican culture. And missions have grown into pleasant towns like San Luis Obispo, San Juan Capistrano, and San Juan Bautista, each strongly reminiscent of its Hispanic past. Other missions, such as La Purisima, have been completely restored; many continue to function as churches, Carmel and Santa Barbara among them; and others also hold exceptional museums, like San Gabriel. Up and down the Camino Real are the towns and missions of early California, and even the ranches of the dons, like that at Petaluma. From Old Town in San Diego to the Russian settlement at Fort Ross in Sonoma, early California still lives.

THE FIRST COLONY: SAN DIEGO

[We] maintained ourselves for a whole year in these lands at incredible cost of indescribable trouble, fatigue and want, which we do not choose to describe to your Excellency for they are more real than imaginary.

PEDRO FAGES & MIGUEL COSTANSO
1770 *(Geiger)*

Over a century and a half after Vizcaino charted and named the bay here, and more than two centuries after Cabrillo discovered this good port, Spaniards returned to San Diego. They returned both by sea and land, sailor and soldier alike, captains, friars, and Christianized Indians. Making their way north from Baja California, these members of the Portola expedition journeyed across unknown, arid lands and sailed far from the comfort of their supply ports. Unlike those before them, these Spaniards came to conquer and colonize, not just to explore. This time no Vizcaino-style hut erected for mass on San Diego's feast day would suffice, for here would be dedicated the first of California's missions. In 1769 they returned, and for years after the first colony faced extermination and abandonment.

Early in 1769, three ships sailed for San Diego to await the arrival of the land expeditions. The *San Jose,* carrying foodstuffs for the colonists and so hopefully laden with church bells for the missions, never appeared. The *San Antonio,* buffeted by storms, anchored after nearly two months at sea with half its crew down with scurvy. Worse, the *San Carlos,* blown hundreds of miles off course, arrived after 110 days at sea.

. . . its crew and the troops on board—whose fatigue could not be otherwise than excessive on so protracted and laborious voyage in the

depth of winter—arrived in deplorable condition. Scurvy had attacked all without exception.

MIGUEL COSTANSO, 1769

Only four of the *San Carlos* crew could stand. The rest were so afflicted with scurvy that just two would survive. Hospital huts were constructed on the beach; flanked by two ships' cannon they became the first and only buildings at the fort of San Diego. From the land-based hospital, wild herbs and fresh water were collected for the sick, but these were not enough.

Each day, two or three of them died and the whole expedition, which had been composed of more than ninety men, was reduced to only eight soldiers and as many sailors who were in a condition to assist in guarding the ships . . . protecting the camp, and waiting upon the sick.

COSTANSO, 1769

Fortunately for the fledgling colony, the land expedition suffered fewer mishaps. Padre Serra could even say his entire trip "was a very happy one," but the advance company faced more dangers. It forged the route north across several hundred miles of unmapped wilderness and through regions of belligerent Indians.

. . . one village of twenty-nine Indians followed us along the hill-tops, shouting all the time and too often with gestures of wanting to shoot us with their arrows.

FRIAR JUAN CRESPI, 1769

Not a single injury was sustained in battle; however, five Indian auxiliaries starved to death and others deserted rather than continue so arduous a journey. The Spaniards, too, suffered, if less severely.

The beef gave out eleven days before we reached this port, and the soldiers got along with a single dry tortilla . . . This without any seasoning or sauce, and the morning chocolate, which was more like a poor syrup . . . was our only food.

CRESPI, 1769

Despite these hardships, the land companies arrived basically intact after nearly two months on the march.

With their harsh journeys behind them, the various companies of the Portola expedition joyfully reunited in San Diego. They took solace in the apparent fineness of their surroundings: the harbor provided excellent shelter against storms, the river water was fresh, and the surrounding meadows offered pastorage for livestock.

In short, it is a good country—distinctly better than Old California.

FRAY JUNIPERO SERRA, 1769

And the native Dieguenos seemed friendly, their great numbers promising many converts for the mission. Encouraged, even after the loss of more than half of their members, the expedition's survivors built a colony of huts on a hill convenient to the river, and with excellent views over the harbor.

In a few months' time the "humble buildings" of San Diego would be protected by a crude palisade of logs against Diegueno attacks. Fear of attack had become a reality when the *San Antonio* sailed to Mexico for supplies and Governor Portola led part of the expedition further on to Monterey. Left to themselves, the remaining colony appeared too small and vulnerable. Only a few soldiers were well enough to guard the *San Carlos,* still in the harbor, and the community of 40, mostly sick, individuals. Emboldened by this situation, the Dieguenos became increasingly hostile. And they went to outrageous lengths to steal the cloth they so bafflingly coveted.

[They] beg for any rag of clothing; but after different ones on successive occasions had been clothed, on the following day they again presented themselves naked.

COSTANSO, 1769

Some Dieguenos paddled out to the *San Carlos* in the dark of night just to cut its sails for cloth, but they were apprehended. Absolutely determined in their quest, a war party, naked yet painted black and white, appeared armed with bows and arrows. They set about pulling the sheets out from under the sick and even took their clothing.

They broke in all of a sudden; and the only four soldiers present seeing their ugly mood, immediately snatched up their arms. The fight was on.

SERRA, 1769

The Spaniards used their guns for the first time. Four soldiers, protected by leather jackets and shields, were joined by the carpenter and blacksmith against 20 Dieguenos. Others in the camp ran about, trying to glimpse some of the action, only to learn too late about the Indians' accuracy with the bow and arrow. One friar lost a finger; a few others were wounded, including the blacksmith, and one colonist died—Serra's servant.

At the first shot he darted into my hut, spouting much blood . . . He expired on the ground before me bathed in his own blood. And so I was quite a while with him there dead, and my little apartment a pool of blood. Still the exchange of shots—bullets and arrows—went on . . . and there I was with the dead man, thinking it most probable that I would have to follow him.

SERRA

Serra was saved, as was the entire colony, for the Dieguenos had learned the deadliness of Spanish harquebuses. They retreated.

The Dieguenos later made amends. As Friar Serra reported, "We are all, since then, living in peace." Taking no chances, however, the colony barricaded itself in.

Unfortunately, log fortifications provided no protection against starvation. Governor Portola returned from his explorations north after six wearying months and found Padre Serra weak from scurvy, and other sickly members not recovered from their ordeal. His own men, sixty in all, had barely sustained themselves the last days of the march, finding their mules the only source of nourishment. And the *San Antonio* still had not returned from New Spain. Looking over the too few remaining provisions of rice, flour and maize, Portola realized he might have to abandon Alta California.

There was in San Diego a supply . . . sufficient to maintain for several months those who composed the garrison. But with the arrival of sixty additional men, it could not be depended upon . . . and it was to be feared that if the vessels were late in bringing the relief counted upon, the Spaniards would find themselves compelled by hunger to abandon . . . a conquest which, although very successful, had cost so much toil and so many lives.

COSTANSO, 1770

The governor calculated that if provisions weren't received by March 19, the expedition would be forced to withdraw from Alta California on the 20th. From one day to the next, the Spaniards awaited the arrival of the ship. They tried to supplement their ever diminishing supply of tortillas with the fish or fowl traded by the Diegunenos and they prayed each day for relief. The days accumulated until the fateful 19th of March arrived, along with a miracle.

. . . at about three o'clock in the afternoon we saw outside of our desired port a ship which was coming supplied with every kind of provisions . . . at last we let fall our cares for with the ship's arrival we knew that we were provided for and indeed the permanence of the mission of San Diego assured.

CRESPI, 1770 *(Geiger)*

So important was the arrival of the *San Antonio* to the future of the California missions and settlements, that Father Serra celebrated a high mass every month on the nineteenth day for the rest of his life.

Having survived the ravages of scurvy, war, and hunger, the first colony must have considered that divine providence intended its continuation. While most of the expedition left for Monterey, a small group of soldiers and two missionaries settled into their huts on Presidio Hill. Their existence remained far from easy, since food was always scarce in the first years, and supplies practically disappeared.

They say that thus they have passed most of the year, without lard, without tallow, without even a candle . . .

CRESPI, 1772 *(Englehardt)*

Soldier after soldier deserted only to return after finding no place else to go. Often they came back naked, save for their pistols, having bartered their clothes for food in the wilderness. During the difficult years even padres requested their reassignment from San Diego

. . . let those who are to come here as missionaries not imagine that they are coming for any other purpose but to endure hardships for the love of God and for the salvation of souls, for in far-off places such as these . . . it will be necessary in the beginning to suffer many real privations.

SERRA, 1769

Without enough for themselves, the colony had little to offer the Dieguenos—half-starving Spaniards couldn't attract the locally adapted and healthy natives to their lifestyles. In fact, in the first year there was not one conversion. The independent Dieguenos were, as Friar Crespi reported, "too clever, too wide-awake . . . for any Spaniards to get ahead of them." If the padres wished to instruct them in their faith, food was expected in return. If the fathers had nothing to give, the Indians simply didn't appear. Nonetheless the friars, little by little, attracted a following and a few reed huts began to spring up around the stockade.

. . . the entire rancheria, which made war on us . . . is already Christian.

SERRA, 1773 *(Engelhardt)*

Other Indians came, not for the food and security the mission didn't have, but for "their fondness for hearing the neophytes sing." By 1774 the number of neophytes had grown to 79, so the Franciscans decided to move the mission to where it could become more self-supporting for its growing population.

It was determined to move the mission . . . toward the northeast from the presidio . . . This place is more suitable for a population, on account of the facility of obtaining the necessary water and . . . good land for cultivation.

SERRA, 1774 *(Englehardt)*

In a matter of months the new mission had many pole and reed buildings, and even a few of adobe, and the fields were planted with corn and wheat. Looking so permanent, the new mission goaded another attempt by the Dieguenos to rid themselves of the Spaniards. Perhaps dissatisfied with the labor expected of them, and certainly displeased with the interference in their traditional way of life, two neophytes ran away from the mission in order to organize the various Indian rancherias into a plan of attack.

. . . giving as a reason for killing the soldiers that they defended the fathers, and for killing the latter that they wished to make an end of heathenism by making them all Christians.

FRAY FRANCISCO PALOU (1783)

So deep were the feelings of rebellion that in 1776 as many as 70 rancherias united to wage war.

In the quiet of a November night when the presidio soldiers slept soundly, and even those on guard at the mission slumbered, 800 Dieguenos attacked. They set fire to all the reed buildings and incapacitated the neophytes, leaving eleven Spaniards to fend for themselves. Father Jayme, instead of seeking protection, tried calming the rebels and became the first martyr of Alta California.

They stripped him of everything, even the coverings of modesty, and began to fire innumerable arrows into his naked body.

PALOU

The remaining community, protected only by four soldiers, defended itself behind adobe walls. With countless arrows and stones aimed at them, with everything in flames, the Spaniards kept the Dieguenos at bay.

They had reached the point where the powder which the mission had for firing salutes in the principal festivals was all gone. But they succeeded in finding some more.

PALOU

One soldier was dead, the others wounded, and the Spaniards still fought. They fought without relief since the presidial soldiers, just a few miles away, remained asleep, their sentinel oblivious to the raging fires and continuous gunshots. They fought until dawn, when the Dieguenos finally retreated.

It would be a year before the mission was rebuilt and many more years before a dam would enable adequate irrigation of the crops. The years would pass with their hardships, but none would be so eventful as the first seven. The Dieguenos, totally demoralized by their failure to kill the Spaniards, turned peaceful. In 1797, the mission counted 1403 neophytes and briefly won the honor of being the most populous in California. Eventually there were so many converts that an *asistencia,* or branch, had to be constructed at Santa Ysabel. The cattle and sheep herds grew into the thousands, too, and even the rains occasionally cooperated to produce good crops. The gente de razon on Presidio

Hill grew to number almost 200. Only the arrival of a courier from Monterey or the annual supply ship from San Blas disrupted the dull rhythm of the now secure colony's existence.

San Diego's future as a hide depot for foreign traders certainly couldn't have been predicted in 1803 when the Yankee brig *Lelia Byrd* anchored in the harbor. Having smuggled its way along Spain's Pacific coast from Valparaiso to San Blas, the ship sailed into San Diego's waters under the guise of seeking provisions. Too many foreign ships, however, had been using just this pretext as an opportunity to smuggle. Spain had already taken steps to protect its monopoly on trade. A battery of nine pounders had been stationed at the entrance to San Diego's harbor and its commander, Manuel Rodriguez, given the strictest orders on the treatment of foreign vessels: provisions would be granted, but smuggling must stop. Thus the stage was set for the first Anglo-Hispanic culture-clash called "the Battle of San Diego."

Captain William Shaler and his associate Richard Cleveland arrived in San Diego determined to purchase, no matter how illegally, otter skins to trade in China. So firm was their belief in the righteousness of profit and free trade, they never considered themselves smugglers. Rather the Spaniards were obstructionists, their lawful confiscation of goods no more than plunder. As Comandante Rodriguez diligently carried out his orders by inspecting the *Lelia Byrd,* he struck the New Englanders as a vain man who "probably regretted the necessity of leaving on shore his horses." More than likely their irritation resulted from Rodriguez' orders. After granting them their supplies of cattle and chickens, salt and flour,

> *. . . he took leave with characteristic pomp leaving on board five of his escort, as he said, to see that we carried on no contraband trade.*
>
> RICHARD J. CLEVELAND (1842)

Not intimidated by Spanish officialdom, nor seemingly anything else for that matter, Shaler and Cleveland set about negotiating with the guards for otter skins, and they even attempted to bribe Rodriguez who scandalized them by refusing. Finally, in the darkness of their last night in port, some of the crew rowed to the beach to make a rendezvous for the coveted furs. At dawn, Captain Shaler awakened to find his smuggling crew still on the beach and under arrest.

We perceived our men to be so indignant at the treatment of their shipmates, as to be ready for the fight . . .

CLEVELAND

Refusing to submit to Spanish authority, the Americans decided to resist, "hazarding the consequence." With great bravado, Cleveland rescued the prisoners from the beach by "presenting our pistols." Quickly returning to ship, unfurling the sails, and hauling anchor, the Yankees prepared to leave the harbor. Unfortunately they had to pass "within musket-shot" of the cannons on Point Loma, so they forced the five Spanish guards to stand "in the most exposed and conspicuous station." The Spaniards, seeing their friends now held hostage aboard the *Lelia Byrd,* dared fire only a warning shot, but to no avail.

When arrived abreast the fort, several shots struck our hull . . . We now opened our fire and, at the first broadside, saw members, probably of those who came to see the fun, scampering away up the hill at the back of the fort.

CLEVELAND

A few years later Shaler would write that San Diego's battery "does not merit the least consideration as a fortification." Nonetheless neither he nor other foreign captains pulled into the harbor for many years. As for the five Spanish guards, they were dropped ashore just beyond cannon-range. So ended the bloodless Battle of San Diego.

By the 1830s San Diego had more than made its peace with Yankee traders. Under the profitable hide and tallow trade of the Mexican period, the customs house supplanted the cannon's importance on Point Loma, and San Diego flourished as the only hide depot along the coast.

For landing and taking on board hides, San Diego is decidedly the best place in California. The harbour is small and land-locked; there is no surf: the vessels lie within a cable's length of the beach . . . For these reasons it is used by all the vessels in the trade as a depot.

RICHARD HENRY DANA, 1835

Company warehouses lined La Playa, the beach along Point Loma. Here sailors cured the hides, dried and cleaned them, then stored the hides till there were enough for a homeward cargo. Each company storehouse, each ship added to the makeshift colony of sailors and drifters on La Playa. Crowded in with the piles of hides were stray dogs, an ever increasing number of pigs, and "representatives from almost every nation under the sun." The English and Irish joined the French and Tahitians, the Yankees and Italians mingled with the native Chileans and Hawaiian Kanakas. With mere gestures and sailors' songs they found a common language, a camaraderie, for passing their stay at rough and tumble La Playa. For some, the assignment became permanent as the grog house led to what was called "beach-combing," and then to the *calabozo,* or jail. Others, who still had a home to miss, would despair, looking at the enormous warehouses waiting to be stuffed with up to 40,000 hides.

There was scarce a man on board who did not go often into the house, looking round, reflecting, and making some calculation of the time it would require [*to fill it*].

DANA, 1835

Often, two years would pass before capacity was reached. After six weeks of hard labor, from dawn to night "with the exception on Sundays," the hides would be loaded. Then, and only then, would the sailor begin his long voyage home. Soon a new brig would bring others to replace him.

On Sunday leave the sailors would travel down Point Loma to enjoy the social life in town. The town perhaps numbered as many as 500 citizens, many descendants of leather jacket soldiers and their Diegueno wives. With peace and some prosperity, they had left behind the crowded conditions within the crumbling walls of the fort, and built new adobe homes around and about a plaza at the foot of the hill.

The small settlement lay directly below the fort, composed of about forty dark brown-looking huts, or houses, and three or four larger ones white-washed, which belonged to the gente de razon.

DANA

Here festivals were celebrated with bullfights and processions, here homes opened to all for the dancing of a fandango. Even with no special occasion to fill the plaza, Sundays in town always had plenty going on.

The Indians, who always have a holiday on Sunday, were engaged at playing a kind of running game of ball, on a level piece of ground, near the houses . . . Several blue-jackets were reeling about among the houses, which showed that the pulperias [bars] had been well patronized. One or two of the sailors had got on horseback, but being rather indifferent horsemen, and the Mexicans having given them vicious beasts, they were soon thrown, much to the amusement of the people. A half-dozen Sandwich-Islanders [Hawaiians], from the hide-houses . . . were dashing about on the full gallop, hallooing and laughing like so many wildmen.

DANA

Life among the wealthy was a bit more genteel. Not only were the homes of the Carrillos, Estudillos, and Bandinis white-washed, they had wood floors instead of dirt, tiled roofs instead of mud, ballrooms for dancing, and furnishings from China and New England. The ancestry of these finest of San Diegan families was traceable to Spanish *comandantes;* in the case of Juan Bandini it was traceable back to Spain and even further to Italian nobility. To seaman Dana, Don Juan was a "good representation of a decayed gentleman."

He had a slight and elegant figure, moved gracefully, danced and waltzed beautifully, spoke good Castilian, with a pleasant and refined voice and accent, and had, throughout, the bearing of a man of birth and figure.

Such were the rancheros and influential politicians who constituted the upper class of San Diego. In their homes, only the most gentlemanly of the foreign officers were entertained.

I soon became acquainted with several excellent families residing at the place, and received from them much attention. The ladies were mostly quite handsome, particularly those of the families of our friends Bandini and Carrillo.

ALFRED ROBINSON, 1829

Trade led to socializing that soon led to marriages between the Carrillos and Fitches, the Bandinis and Stearns. And Dana's mate Jack Stewart married into "a respectable lower-class family by the name of Muchado [sic]." So strong was the Anglo influence, that even when a Bandini daughter married a Carrillo, the son-in-law "was educated in Boston." By the time Commodore Stockton arrived with his troops in 1846, he found many in the population sympathetic to the American cause, particularly Juan Bandini. While Don Estudillo steadfastly remained neutral and Don Carrillo led the Californio resisters, Don Bandini's daughters sewed an American flag to fly above the plaza. Once the Americans secured San Diego and established its defenses next to the old presidio, Bandini and Stockton joined together to enjoy themselves and provide the only entertainment in town. At Bandini's adobe, Stockton made his headquarters and surrounded himself with the 37 Italian musicians comprising his personally financed *USS Congress* band,

The commodore was accustomed to have the band play during the dinner hour, and to invite the Bandini family and ladies of San Diego to dine with him and listen to the excellent music.

WILLIAM HEATH DAVIS, 1846

On most evenings the band entertained the populace on the town plaza, then retreated to the Bandini ballroom to play the waltzes so enjoyed by the elite.

Don Juan Bandini . . . His house has been thrown open to us, and is the resort of the other society of the place . . . they contrive to have music and dancing every night, the sola diversion *in California. Don Juan, although over sixty, is the most indefatigable and active of the dancers, saying it is* muy inocente.

CAPT. SAMUEL F. DU PONT, 1846

Into this romantic world of the gentry, the reality of the Mexican-American War rudely intruded one December night. Kit Carson and two other messengers interrupted a Bandini ball to announce the desperate circumstances of General Kearney's dragoons in the San Pasqual Valley. Don Andres Pico, with Ramon Carrillo, had routed the U.S. Army of the West and continued to harass the survivors. It would be the last success of the Californios in the San Diego region, and the night marked a turning point in San Diego's future. The Bandinis and Carrillos would go their separate ways, leaving San Diego to the ever increasing influx of American troops. Soon four war sloops would be anchored in the harbor, while 600 U.S. soldiers and sailors drilled in the old plaza. U.S. troops would occupy Presidio Hill, and the abandoned church of San Diego de Acala would become a stable for their horses.

With the end of the war and with the United States flag flying permanently above the plaza, San Diego fell back into the isolation of its first days as the only colony. Gone were the brigs of the hide and tallow trade. Gone were the pastoral days of old California. Not until the harbor again became a naval base, not till the railroad brought commerce would San Diego be reborn.

Sights

Of the new town of San Diego, now the city of San Diego, I can say that I was the founder . . . At that time I predicted that San Diego would become a great commercial seaport from its fine geographical position and from the fact that it was the only good harbor south of San Francisco.

WILLIAM HEATH DAVIS, 1850

New San Diego has grown into the second largest city in California. Its protected harbor has continued to attract ships and sailors, including the headquarters for the 11th Naval District. And the beaches have become even more appealing since the hide depot days at La Playa, making tourism one of San Diego's most profitable industries. The "new town" first focused its building activity around the harbor, then with the stimulation of the railroad at the end of the century it started to sprawl south to the Rancho de la Nacion (the former presidio grazing lands, now called National City) as well as north around False Bay (now Mission Bay) to La Jolla, and across the pastures once overseen by Franciscan friars. Despite so much modernity to overwhelm the first Californian settlement, San Diego has been able to preserve many of its historic sites. And with the border so near, it has never lost the Mexican influence in food, crafts, architecture, and language.

A 52-mile scenic drive loops between the harbor, Shelter Island, Point Loma, Old Town, and Mount Soledad. This road is marked by seagull signs and provides a pleasant route for visiting many of the following sights.

Historic San Diego

★★★ Old Town □ As U.S. San Diego grew up around the bay and beach, the old town remained basically intact, if somewhat left behind. With the passage of years, some of the old adobes were abandoned, others fell into disrepair, and Bandini's adobe was even transformed into Albert Seeley's Cosmopolitan Hotel. Today, attention again centers on Old Town Plaza (Mason and San Diego streets), now the heart of the **Old Town State Historic Park.** Here the ococilla and lavendar, the chaparral of the early days line pedestrian streets and many of the old buildings have been reconstructed into restaurants, bakeries and other establishments appropriate to early California. And a few have been made into museums.

One of the finest restorations is the ★★★ **Casa de Estudillo** (San Diego and Mason; fee) furnished in period decor and with a lovely veranda-surrounded garden. While typical of the homes of the wealthiest San Diegans, this adobe also boasts a cupola from which the family could watch events on the plaza without getting mussed. Inside you can visit the family chapel that once served the entire town, the *sala* ornately decorated with items purchased through the China trade, as well as the kitchen and servants' workrooms. Next door, the **Casa de Bandini** (2660 Calhoun at Mason) may have been transformed by its Anglo-style second floor and present restaurant status, but its graceful balconies are still reminiscent of the days when the elegant Don Juan entertained all of California, and even conquering commodores, with nights of waltzing.

Don Juan Bandini . . . gave us the most graceful dancing that I had ever seen. He was dressed in white pantaloons, neatly made, a short jacket of dark silk, gaily figured, white stockings and thin morocco slippers upon his very small feet.

DANA, 1835

It's worth the short walk down Mason to see the contrast with the finer homes provided by the ★ **Machado-Stewart Adobe** (Congress at the foot of Mason). This early adobe (1820s), simple and unwhitewashed, with its frugal vegetable garden, represents the more modest but respectable existence of most of San Diego's early residents. On his return to San Diego decades after his first voyage, Dana learned that his former shipmate Jack Stewart lived here with his wife, Rosa Machado, and remarked "I was glad to hear that he was sober and doing well."

A number of early American establishments can be found in the state park, among them the **Mason Street School** and the ★ **Seeley Stable** (Calhoun, between Mason and Twiggs; fee) with its exhibits on early stage coach travel and 18-minute video show on the history of Old

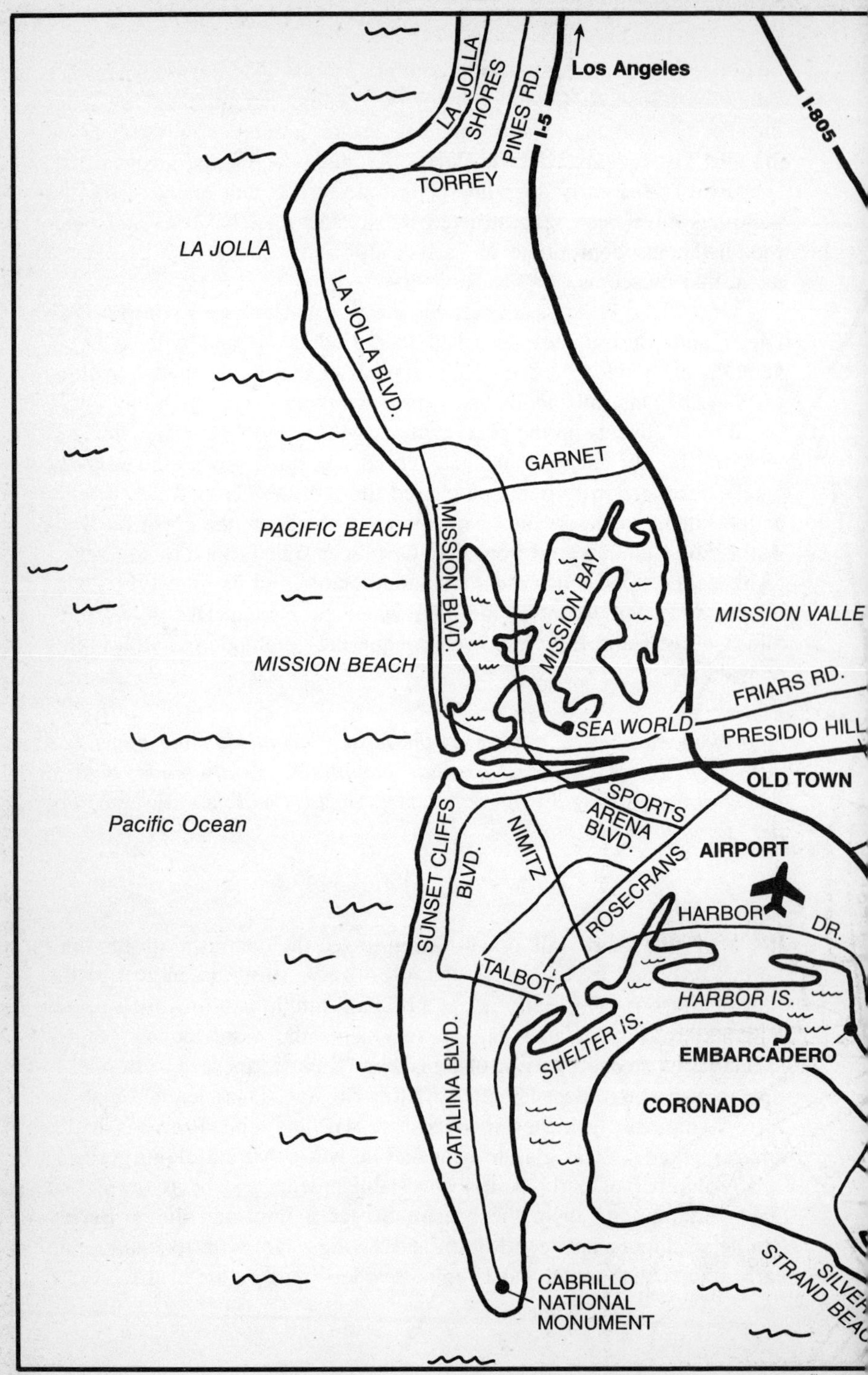

Los Angeles
I-805
LA JOLLA SHORES
TORREY PINES RD.
I-5
LA JOLLA
LA JOLLA BLVD.
GARNET
PACIFIC BEACH
MISSION BLVD.
MISSION BAY
MISSION VALLE
MISSION BEACH
FRIARS RD.
SEA WORLD
PRESIDIO HILL
OLD TOWN
SPORTS ARENA BLVD.
Pacific Ocean
SUNSET CLIFFS BLVD.
NIMITZ
AIRPORT
ROSECRANS
HARBOR DR.
TALBOT
HARBOR IS.
SHELTER IS.
EMBARCADERO
CATALINA BLVD.
CORONADO
CABRILLO NATIONAL MONUMENT
SILVER STRAND BEAC

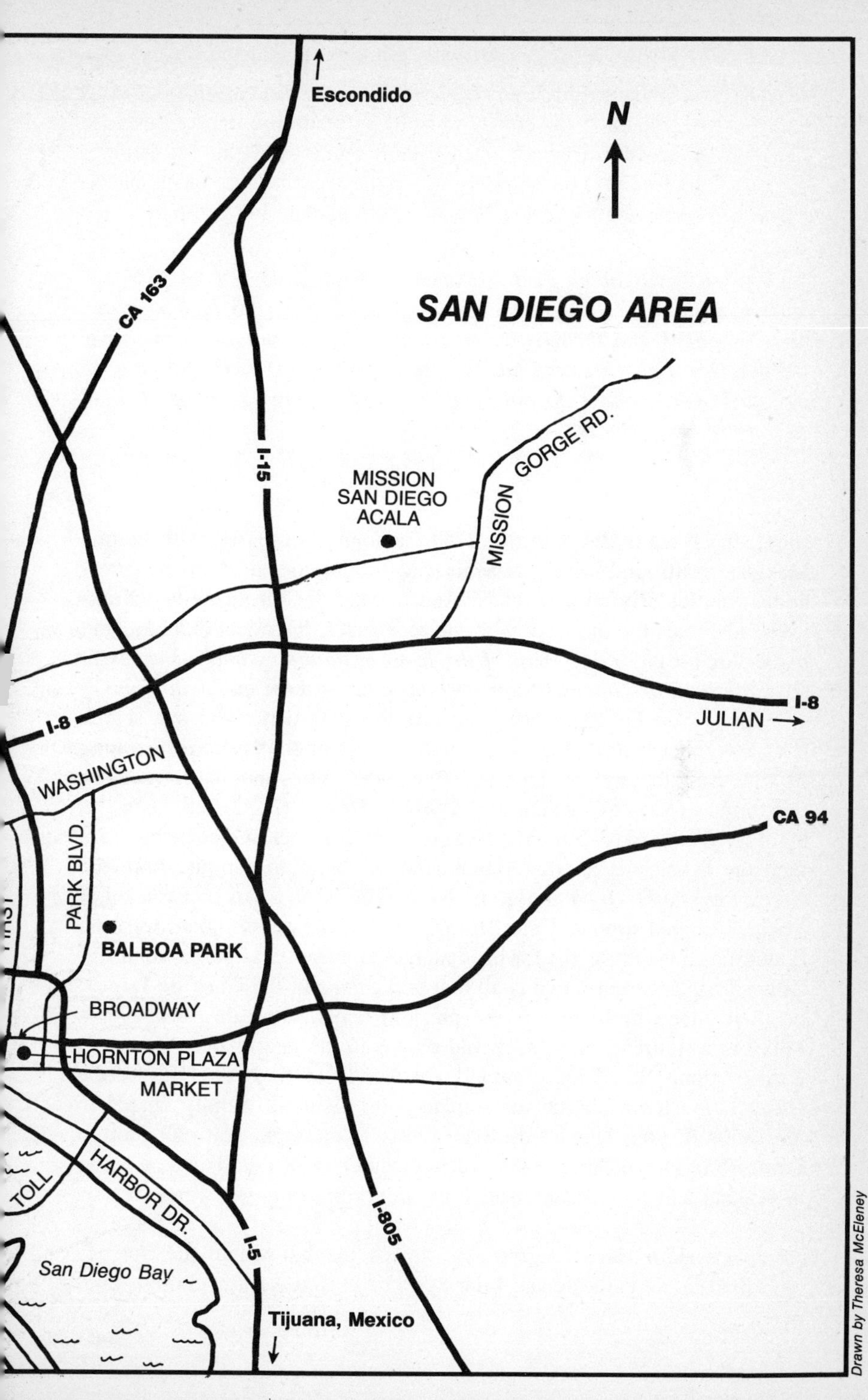

Drawn by Theresa McEleney

Town (every hour on the hour). Across from the plaza, on San Diego Avenue, you can shop for crafts, visit the **information center** (#2645; 237–6770), or take a free guided tour leaving from the Machado y Silvas Adobe (#2741) daily at 2 p.m. On the opposite side of the plaza, where the last governor of the Mexican period spent his youth,

> *. . . when I was about twelve years old, more or less, Don Jose Antonio Carrillo . . . taught me to write. Senor Carrillo had me draw lines on paper and then he would write from one margin to the other ''Senor Don Felix Maria Callejas'' so I could copy it. He never gave me other words and I do not know how many reams of paper I filled with those same words.*
>
> PIO PICO, 1813

stands the **Bazaar del Mundo** (2754 Calhoun; 296–3161))with its fine Mexican crafts and with mariachis and folklorico dances many afternoons, particularly on weekends. And in May the **Fiesta de la Primavera** celebrates the old days with music, dances, historical exhibits, and barbecues (461–3661). *Most of the historic buildings and museums in the state park are open 10 a.m.–5 p.m. daily, except major holidays.*

Along San Diego Avenue, outside the state park, you can search for a few other historic sights among the souvenir shops and restaurants. If you want to pay the fee, visit the oldest brick house in southern California (1856–57) called the **Whaley House** (2482 San Diego at Hartley; Wednesday–Sunday, 10 a.m.–4:30 p.m.; closed at lunch). Behind the Whaley is another Bandini house. Now an antique shop, the Greek Revival **Derby-Pendleton House** (Harley St.) was constructed in Maine, shipped around Cape Horn in 1851, and reassembled by Juan Bandini as a wedding gift for his daughter and Captain Charles Johnson. Down Twiggs Street remains all that still stands of the **Casa de Lopez,** the first adobe built outside the presidio walls. Now the facade of a Mexican restaurant, only a few old photos in the interior recall its past. Further along San Diego, turn down Conde to find the **Old Adobe Chapel,** the town church that replaced the Estudillo family chapel in the 1850s. If your legs need more exercise, you might go to **El Campo Santo** (San Diego Ave. at Arista), the cemetery of Old Town, now no more than a tiny park surrounded by an adobe wall. Few markers survive.

Presidio Park □ From the top of the hill where the Spanish built their crude palisade and Friar Serra dedicated the first church, freeways now obscure the view out over Mission Bay, Old Town, and Point Loma. And, unfortunately, all that remains of the old presidio once described by Alfred Robinson are archaeological trenches.

. . . we called upon the General . . . His house was located in the centre of a large square of buildings occupied by his officers, and so elevated as to overlook them all, and command a view of the sea. On the right hand was a small Gothic chapel, with its cemetery, and immediately in front, close to the principal entrance, was the guard-room, where the soldiers were amusing themselves; some seated on the ground playing cards and smoking, while others were dancing to the music of the guitar; the whole was surrounded by a high wall, originally intended as defence against the Indians.

1829

Although the early buildings are gone, even the fort later built by Stockton, you can visit the handsome Spanish revival style building that houses the **Serra Museum** (open Tues.–Sat., 9 a.m.–4:45 p.m., Sun. noon–4:45 p.m.; closed major holidays. Fee. 297–3258). Here you can see a few exhibits on the early history of San Diego as well as a model of the presidio. There's picnicking in the pleasant surrounding park. *From Old Town follow Hartney off San Diego Ave., turn left onto Juan, and wind your way up Presidio Hill.*

★ **Mission San Diego De Acala** □ The first of the California missions has gone through many transformations, first as a mere hut on Presidio Hill, then as the pole-and-reed complex burned down in the 1776 Diegueno rebellion. Finally, in 1813, the permanent adobe mission was completed, graced by a three-story terraced bell tower. The San Diego mission was never among the wealthiest; the surrounding arid lands defeated grandiose agricultural projects, but at least sustained the groves that produced some of early California's best olive oil. By 1827 the mission had already begun its long road toward decay and eventual destruction.

The quite fine appearance of this establishment loses much on nearing it; because the buildings, though well arranged, are low and badly kept up. A disgusting slovenliness prevails in the padres' dwelling . . . Nevertheless, their [the padres'] welcome was as kind as their house was dirty.

A. DUHAUT-CILLY

With secularization in 1834 and occupation by American troops at the conquest, the mission was pillaged, then crumbled. Today the church has been restored to its original starkness, a proper reminder of its difficult beginnings. Handpainted beams and altar adorn the church; the remains of the martyred Friar Jayme rest in the sanctuary. A small museum with vestments and Indian baskets and excavations of mission ruins can be seen. A mission **fiesta** commemorates the founding for three days on the weekend nearest July 16. *Open 9 a.m.–5 p.m. except Christmas. Fee. Mass on Sundays. Self-guided tape tours available. Take I-8 east, from the foot of Presidio Hill or from I-5, and continue about 5m to the Mission Gorge Rd., turn left under highway, then left at light onto Twain Rd., and follow signs for a mile or so.*

The Harbor

It is the harbor that attracted the first Spanish explorers, led to San Diego's colonization, and provided a safe port to American ships from 19th-century trading brigs to the most advanced submarines of the U.S. Navy. The harbor today remains a fascinating spot from the bustle of the navy yards, to the tuna fleet and cruise ships on the Embarcadero, to the sportsfishing and yachts on Point Loma. Along the **Embarcadero** (N. Harbor Dr. near Broadway) you can stroll to the Maritime Museum (1306 N. Harbor Dr.) with its fleet of 3 ships to visit, including the three-masted bark ★ *Star of India* dating from 1863 and now outfitted with Maritime exhibits (9 a.m.–8 p.m.; fee; 234–9153). Or you can consider a **Harbor Excursion,** a one- or two-hour cruise around the bay or a dinner and dancing version (234–4111) or just a brief ferry ride to Coronado Island (N. Harbor Dr. at Broadway Pier; fees).

The high promontory separating Mission Bay from the harbor is called **Point Loma.** In the canyons here smugglers hid, hoping to trade their goods for furs and hides. Where now are beautiful homes surrounding the Southwestern Yacht Club (off Rosecrans just above Talbot and overlooking Shelter Island), Yankee brigs deposited their loads of hides and horns at what then was called La Playa. And just north of La Playa stood the old customs house first administered by Juan Bandini until he was caught being less than scrupulous. At the tip of Point Loma is the ★★ **Cabrillo National Monument,** a stupdendous spot for viewing the harbor, the coast, and for whale watching (mid-Dec. to mid-Feb.). A statue of Juan Rodriquez Cabrillo, discoverer of the bay, faces his landing spot at Ballast Point where, nearly three centuries later, Captain Shaler confronted Spanish cannons. Reports of Cabrillo's 1542 expedition first described the safety of the harbor.

. . . they discovered a port, closed and very good . . . while they were in this port a heavy storm occurred, but since the port is good they did not feel it at all. It was a violent storm . . . the first storm which they have experienced.

CABRILLO EXPEDITION, 1542

The visitor center includes exhibits on Spanish exploration as well as a model of Cabrillo's flagship. Also here is an 1854 lighthouse furnished just as it was when abandoned in 1891 and an excellent 2-mile nature trail down to the tidal pools. Toward the end of every September Cabrillo's landing is reenacted during the **Cabrillo Festival,** which also includes folk dancing, a historical seminar, and other events. Write Box 6366, San Diego 92106. *The monument is open daily 9 a.m.–5:15 p.m. in winter, till sunset in summer; free; 293–5450, but try to plan your visit when there is no morning fog to obscure the views. To reach Point Lomas follow I-5 to Rosecrans Avenue, the old Spanish route along the Point, then turn on Canon Drive and follow the scenic drive out to the monument.* If you return from Point Lomas along Harbor Drive, you will see the marker for the **Spanish Landing,** where the members of the Portola expedition reunited (near the Sheraton East across from the Shelter Island—neither of which existed in 1769).

Other Sights

Balboa Park □ No description of the sights of San Diego can omit Balboa Park, a great complex of recreational and cultural activities, including the world-famous **San Diego Zoo** (mid-June–Labor Day, 8:30 a.m.–6 p.m.; November–February till 4 p.m.; otherwise till 5 p.m.; fee; 234–3153). In the park the desert has been transformed into groomed lawns and lagoons and local California mission architecture into the ornate, Churrigueresque Mexican style, all to provide an appropriate setting for the many fine arts galleries, museums of natural history, botany, and space, a planetarium, sports stadium, Shakespeare theater, and much more. In particular, seek out the **Museum of Man** for its superb exhibits on American Indian civilizations (daily 10 a.m.–4:30 p.m.; closed major holidays; fee; 239–2001). Covering more than 1000 acres, *the park is in the downtown area, with its main entrance at Sixth and Laurel.* Cross Cabrillo Bridge to the Plaza de Panama and you'll find maps and information there at the **House of Hospitality** (239–0512) as well as **Museum of the City of San Diego History** (planned opening date 1988) in the nearby Casa de Balboa.

Sea World □ Another popular San Diego attraction, Sea World features many marine exhibits along with shows of performing seals, whales, dolphins, and even otters. Perhaps the most exciting exhibit of all is Penquin Experience in the Antarctic exhibit area. *Open 9 a.m.–dusk, summers till 10 p.m.; fee; 226–3839. Located on Mission Bay at 1720 South Shores Rd.*

Beaches □ San Diego attracts summer vacationers who enjoy its many beaches and plentiful opportunity for watersports, particularly the windsurfing and water skiing on **Mission Bay.** One of the lovelist beaches can be found at **Torrey Pines State Park** just north of La Jolla and surrounded by 1100 acres of high cliffs, nature walks, and wildlife. **La Jolla Cove,** fronted by manicured lawns and La Jolla elegance, is the best spot for diving. **Mission Beach,** including its northern extension, Pacific Beach, is where the action is—broad expanses of beach lined with a boardwalk full of roller skaters, surfers, and hangers-on. And **Silver Strand State Beach** is a fine, long beach located on Coronado Island where a visit requires paying the bridge or ferry fee for crossing to the island.

Downtown □ Long ignored for the outdoor pleasures provided by its setting, the center of San Diego is experiencing a revival led by **Horton Plaza** (Broadway between First and Fourth) a jazzy shopping and entertainment center that is worth seeing just for some of the whimsy and color of its architectural details. Surrounding Horton Plaza is the **Gaslamp District,** where each year brings more renovated Victorian buildings offering handsome settings for restaurants and shops.

Excursions

Asistencia Santa Ysabel □ So vast were the lands of the Mission San Diego that they extended not only west to the harbor but east past El Cajon to the area of the present town of Julian.

In a place called Santa Isabel, toward the sierra, they count a goodly number of souls, about two hundred, and there are prospects of more conversions.

Friar Vincente de Sarria, 1818
(Engelhardt)

In addition to the many potential neophytes in Santa Ysabel, the land there was fertile and produced much needed wheat, barley, corn, and beans. The missionaries from San Diego de Acala regularly visited the site, celebrating mass on a portable altar. By 1822 they had established a formal branch of the San Diego mission, with a permanent chapel, a granary, and cemetery. The chapel wasted away with secularization, but was replaced by a new one in 1924. Today religious services are provided to the surrounding Diegueno reservations. The old Indian cemetery can be visited as well as a very small museum. Picnic tables are available, and for desserts and bread (16 varieties, including jalapeno and mission grain) try the Dudley Bakery near the highway junction of CA 79. *Open 9 a.m.–dusk; donation; 765–0810. The church is located about 60 m east of San Diego on CA 78, just north of the junction with CA 79 and near the town of Julian.*

The asistencia itself hardly warrants the approximately 120-m and 3-hour round trip from San Diego. But if you want to enjoy a half day of the country quiet of the interior mountains and valleys where farms, ranches, and orchards still predominate, then the following loop tour might be for you. Go east on I-8, then follow CA 79 north through the living museum of plants and wildlife in **Cujamaca State Park** (800–952–5580) and continue to the tiny western town of ***Julian*** with its gold rush period buildings and roadside stands selling apple butter in the fall. Just 7 m beyond Julian is the junction for turning right to Santa Ysabel. After spending a few minutes at the church, return to the junction and go west past the Dudley Bakery and continue on CA 78 toward Escondido. The many orchards along here make for pleasant driving, and just 7m east of Escondido you pass the **San Pasqual State Historic Monument** marking the spot where Andres Pico defeated the exhausted troops of Stephen Kearney during one of the many Californio squirmishes after the U.S. conquest. From Escondido you can pick up I-15 south to CA 163 into San Diego.

Anza Borrega Desert State Park □ Another reason for exploring some of the interior valleys near Santa Ysabel is the Anza Borrega Desert, just beyond the Santa Ysabel church on CA 78 north (see above). The park commemorates Captain Juan Bautista de Anza, the trail blazer who led San Francisco's (see that chapter) colonists across this desert in 1776, the first expedition that would later be followed by adventurous fur trappers and gold-crazed forty-niners. Today over 600,000 acres of this desert wilderness is preserved and offers camping, picnicking, bridle trails, and flowering cactus in the early spring. *Visitor center and motels in the oasis of Borrega Springs. Fees. 619–767–5311.*

Tijuana □ In the days when San Diego belonged to Mexico, the Rancho Ti Juan to the south of Old Town Plaza was the property of the family of Comandante Arguello. Today, a border must be crossed

(16 m south of downtown) in order to visit the city of Tijuana (tee-WHAH-nah), but this procedure is so easy that thousands cross into Mexico to enjoy a day of shopping (along Avenida Revolucion between 2nd and 9th Sts.) combined with watching Jai Alai, horse races, or bullfights (on Sundays in the summer). For U.S. citizens, no passport or tourist card is necessary for such a brief visit. And even the hassle of car insurance can be avoided by parking your car at the border on the U.S. side or by taking the San Diego Trolley from the Santa Fe Depot (Kettner at C St.) to the border (40 minutes). In either case, you can take a brief cab ride into Tijuana center. Organized tours to Tijuana are plentiful.

Accommodations

There are three historically special hotels in the San Diego area. Certainly first among them must be the world-renowned **Hotel del Coronado,** the chosen lodgings of 11 presidents, the Duke of Windsor, and countless celebrities. The original Victorian complex retains its turrets and cupolas, its mahogany pillared lobby with palm court and gilded elevator cage, its rambling verandas with wicker rockers. Here the nearly 400 rooms have been constantly renovated while retaining their old-fashioned ambience. Newer rooms have been added; those 100 in the poolside wing blend comfortably with the old section. Some weekends the architectural tours, weddings, and conventions all combine to make for too much bustle, but even then the miles of beach and sea have a soothing presence. Numerous restaurants, including the old Crown Room with its extraordinary wooden dome, lounges, and shops. Two pools, health spa, and tennis. Parking. ***Very expensive.*** Located across the Coronado Bridge at Silver Strand Beach on Coronado Island. (Write 1500 Orange Ave., Coronado 92118; 522–8000.)

While those involved in affairs of state seem drawn to "the Del," as it's locally called, the likes of Tennessee Williams and Greta Garbo made **Hotel La Valencia** in La Jolla their hideaway. This small and very pink Spanish revival style hotel sits on the bluff overlooking La Jolla Cove, while also fronting the fashionable main street of town. The 1920s interior is full of character, from quirky painted ceilings to a tiny paneled elevator, from handsome Spanish furnishings to gracious verandas and fine sea views. Though the 100 units vary, most have sea views, some suites have kitchenettes, and all are airy, light, and comfortable. Lovely rooftop restaurant and popular outdoor cafe, handsome lounge areas. Pool, tennis, Jacuzzi, and sauna. Parking. ***Very expensive.*** (Write 1132 Prospect St., La Jolla 92037; 454–0771.)

The third historic hotel has hosted both stars and presidents at its in-town location, but has not had the good fortune to operate continuously since its founding in 1910. Nonetheless the 1985 reincarnation of the **U.S. Grant Hotel** is as opulent as past ones with its lobby of majestic marble columns, Chinese porcelains, and glistening chandeliers. Although the 283 rooms have been gutted and modernized, they are handsomely furnished in period decor, each different from the next. Attractive restaurants, particularly the Grant Grill, and piano bar. Limousine service to sports club and health spa. Parking. ***Very expensive.*** Located across from Hornton Plaza in downtown San Diego. (Write 326 Broadway, CA 92101; 232–3121, 800–542–6082 in CA, 800–854–2608 within the U.S.)

Other hotels offer great convenience to the sights. There are two Holiday Inns near the Embarcadero, the **Holiday Inn Harbor View** is located near the nexus of roads that take you everywhere in San Diego, and many of its 200 units have views of the harbor and the Star of India. The rooms have been pleasantly refurbished—some are large junior suites—and they cost a bit less than the other Holiday Inn nearby. Helpful service. Rooftop restaurant and lounge. Laundromat. Tiny pool and spa. Parking. ***Expensive.*** (Write at 1617 First Ave., CA 92101; 239–6171, 800–465–4329 within the U.S.) Just two blocks up Harney Street from Old Town is the Victorian **Heritage Park Bed and Breakfast,** with 9 rooms decorated in period antiques and sharing bath facilities. ***Expensive.*** (Write at 2470 Heritage Park Row, CA 92110; 295–7088.)

To experience San Diego the resort town, you have many choices; only some are included here. There are two **Sheraton Harbor Island** hotels with a combined total of 1000 rooms and many sports activities (800–325–3535; ***very expensive***). Around the recreational facilities of Mission Bay you can choose from the **Hyatt Islandia** (1441 Quivira Rd., CA 92108; 224–1234; 800–228–9000; ***very expensive***), the family oriented **Vacation Village Resort** (1404 W. Vacation Rd., CA 92109; 274–4630, 800–542–6275 U.S.; ***very expensive,*** but weekly and monthly rates also available); and the less costly **Bahia Resort Hotel,** wedged between Mission Bay and Mission Beach (998 W. Mission Bay Dr., CA 92109; 488–0551, 800–542–6010 CA, 800–821–3619 within the U.S.; ***expensive***). There also are a variety of other chains to investigate, including **Best Western** and **TraveLodge.**

Motel row is inland a bit, in Mission Valley near the intersection of I-8 and CA 163. Here you can find Motel 6, Ramada Inn, TraveLodge and other less expensive accommodations. Closer into town, on Pacific Highway near the Embarcadero there are other motels, a 7 + 1 Motel and TraveLodge among them. For more extensive information on inns, write to **San Diego Bed & Breakfast Register,** Box 22948, CA 92122; 560–7322.

Restaurants

Seafood is plentiful here and its skillful preparation in local restaurants makes for many enjoyable meals. In fact, my favorite restaurant in San Diego is the **Pacifica Grill** (1202 Kettner Blvd.; lunch weekdays, dinner nightly; reserve at 696–9226; ***moderately expensive***), with its imaginative California-style preparation of seafood. Although the menu changes often, you might be lucky and find listed the lemony light and wonderful seafood sausage for an appetizer, ravioli with smoked fish and a delicate parmesan sauce for pasta, or Hawaiian ahi (tuna) prepared in shitake mushroom and ginger butter and a subtle halibut with oriental butter for entrees. Fish can always be mesquite grilled or blackened; entrees are served with a pleasing array of vegetables. The service is good, and the atmosphere in this sleek, modern downtown complex (near the Santa Fe Depot) is tranquil and comfortably chic. The Grill's sister restaurant, **Cafe Pacifica** in Old Town (2414 San Diego Ave.; lunch weekdays, dinner nightly; reservations at 291–6666; ***moderately expensive***) is good, too, though not quite as good, I think. Casual, yet sophisticated in ambience, and with a more limited menu (changes daily), you can enjoy offerings like a very fresh sashimi, maki maki with pesto, and an excellent ahi with shitaki mushroom sauce. More traditional in its offerings, **Anthony's Star of the Sea Room** (1360 N. Harbor Dr.; dinner only, closed holidays; reservations at 232–7408; tie and jacket required; ***moderately expensive-expensive***) has a fine spot overlooking the harbor and elegant surroundings in which to eat baked salmon en croute, coquille Veronique, and abalone gourmet. While the Star of the Sea Room is the flagship, other Anthony's branches nonetheless offer fresh if more basically prepared seafood at more moderate prices. Just next door is **Anthony's Fish Grotto** (lunch and dinner daily; no reservations; ***moderate***) and next store to that is **Anthony's Fishcette** (lunch and late snacks; ***inexpensive-moderate***) a raw bar and fried appetizer, serve-yourself spot with tables on a deck overlooking the harbor. For a trendier, more swinging restaurant check out the Pacific Beach boardwalk restaurants, such as **World Famous** (701 Thomas Ave.; lunch and dinner daily; no reservations, 483–6630; ***moderate***) where a decent piece of swordfish comes accompanied with soup and salad.

After seafood, it's Mexican cuisine that prevails, particularly when you can consume it in Old Town. One of the loveliest places to eat enchiladas suizas, arroz con camarones (rice with shrimp), or even a beautiful chicken and fruit salad is in the garden patio of the historic **Casa de Bandini** (Old Town Plaza; lunch and dinner daily; reservations; 296–3267; ***inexpensive-moderate***) where mariachis stroll (Wed.–Sun.). The favorite place for *carnitas,* shredded pork served with freshly made tortillas, avocado, tomatoes, and salsa for making your own delicious tacos is the **Old Town Mexican Cafe** (2489 San Diego Ave.; lunch and dinner daily—popular and crowded at night; no reservations; 297–4330; ***inexpensive-moderate***). And the best place for a machaca burrito lies just outside Old Town at the take-out stand called **El Indio** (3695 India St.; lunch and dinner daily; 299–0333; ***inexpensive***) where you may have to wait in long lines before getting to lunch on one of the nearby benches. (To find El Indio, follow Washington St. where it skirts Old Town, then turn onto India).

If it's meat you want, there are many places to try. One of the most elegant certainly is the **Grant Grill** (U.S. Grant Hotel, 326 Broadway; lunch weekdays, dinner Mon.–Sat.; reservations; 239–6806; ***expensive***), decorated to seem like a private club with leather chairs and mahogany panelling, the offerings here include appetizers of snails and sweetbreads along with rack of lamb, prime rib, and duckling from the rotisserie. Less formal, but still attractive is the nearby **Golden Lion Tavern** (Fourth Ave. at F; lunch and dinner daily; reservations; 233–1131; ***moderate***), offering steak sandwiches and salad in a refurbished 1907 tavern crowned with a stained glass ceiling and dominated by an old wooden bar. Even more casual is **Hamburguesa** (Bazaar del Mundo in Old Town; lunch and dinner; 295–0584; ***inexpensive***) with a variety of hamburgers along with some Mexican fare. And for fast food atmosphere, the hefty steer-burgers found around town in the branches of **Boll Weevil,** one of which is located in La Jolla (1100 Prospect; ***inexpensive***).

Some restaurants are San Diego institutions. The **Crown Room** (Hotel del Coronado, 1500 Orange Ave.; 435–6611; ***moderately expensive***) is the absolute favorite for Sunday brunch. **Old Trieste** (3225 Morena Blvd.; reserve at 276–1841; lunch Tues.–Fri., dinner Tues.–Sat.; jacket required; ***expensive***) offers dining on excellent Northern Italian cuisine in grand old booths at its location near Old Town, while the somewhat crotchety waiters at ***Lubach's*** (2101 N. Harbor Dr.; reserve at 232–5129; lunch weekdays, dinner Mon.–Sat.; closed holidays; ***expensive***) are part of the expected ambience coming with the continental food. Also well established is the very contemporary food and ambience of **Gustav Anders** (2182 Avenida de la Playa, La Jolla Shores; reserve at 459–4499; lunch and dinner daily; ***expensive***) with its caviar bar, cassoulet, lamb with dill, and excellent seafood.

Suggestions

Directory □ The zip code varies within the city, but the area code is 619 except for toll-free 800 numbers. ★ For helpful information write **San Diego Convention & Visitors Bureau,** 1200 Third Avenue, Suite 824, Department 700, CA 92101 or call 232–3101. ★ A 24-hour current event recording can be heard at 239–9696.

Getting Around □ If, unlike most Californians, you want to try getting around by local buses, then contact **San Diego Transit** (238–0100) for their schedule. ★ Car rentals are plentiful, and there are numerous taxi agencies. ★ For tours, they range from the bus tours of **Gray Line** (1670 Kettner Blvd., CA 92102; 231–9922), the fringed trolly tours of San Diego neighborhoods and sights offered by **Molly Corporation** (739 Fifth Ave., Suite 20, CA 92101; 233–9177), the museum and historical tours of **San Diego Angels Mini Tours** (Box 5992, CA 92105; 264–3570), to the personalized tours of **Tours Unlimited** (4095 Bonita Rd., Suite 223, Bonita 92002; 475–2049).

Arrival □ The international **airport** is merely a few miles from downtown, right across from Harbor Island. Here there are numerous car rental agencies, including **National Car Rental** (800–CAR–RENT) as well as other international agencies, limousine and taxi service. The Santa Fe Depot (1050 Kettner Blvd.) houses **Amtrak** with its train service up the coast (800–648–3850) and nearby are **Continental** (201 W. Broadway; 232–2001) and **Trailways** (120 W. Broadway; 239–9171).

Weather Tips □ Although summers bring the most tourists, the temperate climate of San Diego is year round, with a sweater often necessary on a summer evening, a swim suit for pools in the winter. ★ In the winter there is occasional rain. ★ Average temperature in January 63° F high, 47° F low. ★ Average temperature in July 73° F high, 63° F low.

ALONG THE CAMINO REAL: THE PADRES

. . . I am not afraid to assert that human motives will not suffice for such a ministry and that only the enthusiasms of religion, with the rewards it promises, can repay the sacrifices, the boredom, and the risks of this kind of life.

COMTE DE LAPEROUSE 1786

The pioneer missionaries faced starvation, overcame Indian attacks, and struggled with the reluctance of Spanish officialdom to colonize yet another province. Against all odds, these friars befriended and converted the native Californians and began the missions that eventually would sustain the colony. Padre Juan Crespi, respected by his fellow pupils in Mallorca for being a mystic, was also the great missionary-explorer of California. Chaplain for the Portola expedition, he was the first friar to cross into California and the only one to explore the coast up to Monterey and beyond to the discovery of San Francisco Bay. With yet more feats before him, he set sail on an expedition exploring the Northwest Coast and Alaska. His colleague, Fray Junipero Serra, laid the foundations for the Spanish province of Alta California, establishing nine missions along the coast to convert, pacify, and control the new region. Not only was his first mission at San Diego burnt and destroyed, but as late as the founding of the seventh at San Juan Capistrano, Serra faced the "danger of being killed by pagans." Yet threats of martyrdom disturbed him less than the loneliness of the frontier.

Truly this state of solitude shall be for me the greatest of my hardships, but God in His infinite mercy will see me through.

FRIAR JUNIPERO SERRA, 1770
(Geiger)

The more introspective Padre Fermin Lasuen later established nine missions himself, five in just one year. At the age of 65 he continued to saddle-up his horse and ride the Camino Real, visiting the eighteen missions under his charge that stretched from San Diego to San Francisco Bay.

Once the missions were established, most friars lived a very settled life. Although they no longer faced personal danger (several, however, may very well have been poisoned by their neophytes), all confronted an amazing number of obstacles to the success of their missions. To instruct the Indian converts in the basic beliefs of Catholicism, the friars needed to learn at least one, if not more, of the hundreds of native languages spoken in California, languages that sounded to the Spanish ear of Friar Font as ''rough and most difficult to pronounce because it has so many crackling sounds.'' And where language simply failed, more inspirational techniques had to be contrived.

The pictures requested are for the purpose of stimulating devotion among the converts. Although they need not be works of fine art, nevertheless . . . I trust that . . . they are neither crude nor ridiculous.

FRIAR JOSE SENAN, 1806

However difficult the conversion process might have been, the friars were at least promoting the faith they had so assiduously studied in their Spanish homeland. It's unclear how these studies prepared them for other mission responsibilities.

In the mission of San Luis Rey de Francia the Fernandino Father is like king. He has his pages, alcaldes, majordomos, musicians, soldiers, gardens, ranchos, livestock, horses by the thousand, cows, bulls by the thousand, oxen, mules, asses, 12,000 lambs, 200 goats, etc.

PABLO TAC *(born 1822, a neophyte at San Luis Rey)*

With or without preparation, the two friars at each mission found themselves responsible for the planting of fields, vineyards and orchards, for the raising of livestock, and the weaving of cloth. And in order to create their self-supporting, ''kingly'' estates out of the wilderness, they had to train their converts who had never before farmed the land, or even ridden a horse or sheared a lamb. Out of necessity, the padres were doctors, untrained but nonetheless they ''themselves prescribed medicines." They were merchants, trading their surpluses where they could in order to purchase the altars for churches and the nails for construction of corrals.

Also shipped from this Mission were four chests containing 160 otter pelts . . . Although mention is made of choice otter pelts, I should like to point out that all those in the shipment are good to excellent in quality.

FRAIR SENAN, 1806

And when their administrative labors ended, some relaxed by attempting to perfect the church choir, like Padre Duran at San Jose, and a few engrossed themselves in scholarship, such as Fray Geronimo Boscana who became California's first Franciscan anthropologist with his *Chinigchinich,* an account of the myths and traditions of the Indians at San Juan Capistrano. Others toyed with more practical matters, like Friar Ripoll of Santa Barbara who designed a grist mill. All generously entertained the passing traveler, receiving in exchange for a hearty meal and a fresh mount, the news of the country and some companionship.

The most enduring achievements of the padres have been the mission churches, from the frank simplicity of adobe chapels to the grandeur of San Luis Rey and San Juan Capistrano. Sometimes soldiers helped in the construction of the missions, occasionally a carpenter or mason was available, or a clever jack-of-all-trades from one of the visiting brigs. More often the friars were left to their own devices, as at San Luis Obispo where fire had caused enormous damage to thatched-roof buildings.

. . . the Fathers decided to put on a roof of tile which one of them was ingenious enough to make, although none of them had ever learned . . . how to do it.

FRAY FRANCISCO PALOU (1787)

Frustrations created the red roof-tiles of California, earthquakes led to thick walls and buttresses. Missionary zeal alone produced the elegant neo-classic facade at San Luis Rey, the finely crafted cupolas and arches at San Juan Capistrano, and the picturesque belltowers and well-proportioned masses so characteristic of all the missions. Certainly what was said about one church applies to all:

The construction of this edifice would have been nothing to excite surprise, had it been built by Europeans; but if one consider that it is the work of poor Indians, guided by an ecclesiastic . . . then one cannot tire in admiration of this religious, the talent he has shown, and the care he must have taken for such a building.

A. DUHAUT-CILLY, 1827

While today only the mission walls stand in tribute to the padres' accomplishments, in the past their success was measured by the devotion of neophytes. The 138 Franciscans who served in old California must have differed as much as the adornments of their churches, but Padre Laseun, unlike some, assures us that whatever their personalities none "could be called . . . cruel." Nor could many have been of the caliber of Fray Antonio Peyri, missionary of San Luis Rey for over thirty years. From the founding of San Luis Rey, Fray Antonio built and inspired the growth of the largest mission in California, with nearly 60,000 head of cattle, sheep, mules, pigs, and other livestock, as well as with numerous ranches such as the great one at Las Flores and the *asistencia,* or branch mission, at San Antonio de Pala. Padre Peyri became legendary not just for the size of his herds, however, or for the magnificence of the church of San Luis, but also for his benevolence. His kindness won the loyalty of many neophytes, and nearly 3000 converted Indians lived at San Luis Rey, a good thousand more neophytes than at any other mission.

Truly, his mission was that, of all California, where these poor people were the best treated. Not only were they well fed and clothed; but still more, he gave them some money on feast days. Every Saturday he distributed soap among the women. On this occasion, all passed before him, and while two men took out of enormous baskets and gave to each one her share, the padre spoke to each in turn. He knew them all: he praised one, mildly reproached another; to this one a joke befitting the occasion, to that a fatherly reproof: all went away satisfied or touched.

DUHAUT-CILLY, 1827

At the age of 63, Friar Peyri, unable to witness the destruction of the missions under secularization, decided "with tears of regret" to retire to the tranquility of a monastery in his native Spain. Yet Peyri was not finished with good deeds. Sailing with him from the San Diego port were two "very talented" young neophytes, Pablo Tac and Agapito Amamix, destined for the College of Propaganda in Rome. After traveling to Mexico, the native Californians continued their voyage to New York and Paris before landing in Barcelona with Fray Antonio, who had paid all their expenses out of his meager pension.

I had the good fortune of being able to place them . . . in Rome . . . where they are very contented and which I doubt not they will leave bright men.

FRIAR ANTONIO PEYRI, 1834

Fate was not to be so kind to the promising youths. Agapito became ill and died at the age of 17; Pablo lived a few years longer, studying philosophy and preparing his reminiscences of life at the mission, the only such document written by a neophyte. But Pablo, too, fell ill and "with remarkable tranquility and cheerfulness of mind" died of consumption at the age of 20. The good padre, finding no peace in the Spain of that time, reported his sorrow at having left "my California." He wished to return "but the doctors forbid me on account of my ill health and advanced age."

The Indians who had always retained for this saintly man [Peyri] a respect bordering on adoration, saw him depart [in 1832] with despair . . . after our arrival at [Rancho] Las Flores, the Indians advanced to meet me . . .

"Captain, we understand that you have just come from Spain. Have you seen the king?"

"Yes."

"And Father Antonio?"

"No; but I know that he is at Barcelona."

"We have heard," added the other leader "that he is dead." My first interrogator turned toward his colleague with a look of consternation.

"No senor, this Father cannot die," he replied.

EUGENE DUFLOT DE MOFRAS, 1840

Sights

In the days when Castilian roses and oak groves covered the hills between San Diego and the Pueblo of Los Angeles, the Camino Real pushed north from the first colony, passing the Rancho Santa Fe and skirting modern day resorts like Del Mar and Encinitas. The old road remained somewhat inland all the way to the mission of San Luis Rey, then it hugged the coast and passed through what is now the town of San Clemente, before arriving at Mission San Juan Capistrano.

To reach San Luis Rey de Francia the shore should be followed, when the tide is low, as far as Mission San Juan Capistrano. The usual route, however, lies one or two leagues inland.

DUFLOT DE MOFRAS, 1840

Highway engineers have pretty much followed Duflot de Mofras' advice and have built I-5 parallel to the Camino Real, yet much closer to the sea. But I-5 heads inland at San Juan Capistrano, and passes Disneyland at Anaheim before arriving at Los Angeles, much as the old King's Highway wandered through the Santa Ana Valley and ranch lands before arriving at Mission San Gabriel.

Today, the Spanish missions of San Luis Rey and San Juan Capistrano, two of the most beautiful in the entire chain, successfully compete for attention with the make-believe of Disneyland. And while you drive past historic locations, like Dana Point or Camp Pendleton (the former Rancho Las Flores), you can enjoy the sights more typical of Southern California. On one leg of your trip, you can struggle with traffic along the coast south of L.A. to see the surfing scene at Huntington Beach, the oil rigs lined up north of opulent Newport, the art colony of Laguna Beach, and beach after beach—some the tiny coves of Orange County fame, and others now guarded by military bases or nuclear power plants such as the one at San Onofre. Seldom does a region offer so much travel through time, from the historical beginnings of Alta California to the present nuclear age, and beyond to Disney's Tomorrowland.

★★★ **San Luis Rey Mission** □ Even if the affable Friar Peyri no longer greets visitors, this once great mission remains worthy of a stopover. You can sense the vastness of this, the largest of all missions, just by glancing at the extent of the quadrangle, once surrounded by storehouses and workshops, by the friary and church. The facade alone had an arcade of 32 columns, the entire building covered about six acres. To one side stood the largest of all Indian mission villages, to the other (on the picnic grounds) were the barracks, now in ruins, that housed the unusually large mission guard that included an officer and 11 soldiers. Padre Antonio Peyri planned this finely proportioned complex and constructed it to endure by devising a kind of concrete, reinforced with bits of tiles and stone.

In the morning he [Peyri] said Mass, and then he planned how he would baptize them, where he would put his house, the church, and as there were five thousand souls . . how he would sustain them . . . They could understand him somewhat when he . . . ordered them to carry stone from the sea . . . for the foundations, to make bricks, roof tiles, to cut beams, reeds and what was necessary. They did it with the masters who were helping them, and within a few years they finished working.

PABLO TAC (1835)

The church, graced with a terraced belltower and beautifully crowned with a dome, best shows Peyri's skills as an architect. In the spacious interior the friar allowed "his talent for decoration to shine" with an elaborate, neoclassical altar that has been called California's best. The mortuary chapel (north side) is unusually lovely and octagonally shaped. Renovated and still providing religious services, the 1811 church has endured just as Peyri planned.

Architecturally, San Luis Rey de Francia is the most beautiful, the most symmetrical, and the most substantial mission in California.

DUFLOT DE MOFRAS, 1840

The mission now functions as a seminary, and along with the church many of its old buildings have been restored. The reconstructed friary and workshops have been combined into a very fine museum that also includes excellent colonial period paintings and statuary imported from Mexico. The monastery gardens, containing the first pepper tree in California, have also been revived, while across the road ruins of the laundry and sunken gardens can be seen.

The garden is extensive . . . The pears, apples, peaches, quinces, pomengrantes, watermelons, and melons are for neophytes, the others that remain [figs and vegetables] for the missionary. None of the neophytes can go to the garden or enter to gather fruit. But if he wants some he asks the missionary who immediately will give him what he wants.

TAC (1837)

In the middle of July, the mission celebrates its **annual fiesta** with dancing and other entertainment, and in December a lovely Yuletide ceremony can be enjoyed. *Located 35m north of San Diego, just 5m inland from Oceanside on CA 76 at 4050 Mission Ave. Open daily, except holidays, 10 a.m.–4 p.m.; Sun. 12–4 p.m.; church closed to tourists during mass; fee; map of site and tours of church; 619–757–3651.*

★ **San Antonio De Pala** □ Further inland on CA 76 you come to an *asistencia* of the Mission San Luis Rey that was founded with a chapel in 1816. Earlier Friar Lasuen, while searching for an appropriate site for the mission itself, had considered this valley "encircled on all sides by very rugged mountain ridges" but decided against its small size. Also, its location was too distant from the Camino Real, and the padre had not enjoyed his journey to Pala.

I completed it in six days, traveling over roads that are safe to travel only once in a lifetime.

FRIAR FERMIN LASUEN, 1797

The chapel and asistencia buildings were renovated in this century as part of the Pala Indian Reservation, the largest Indian settlement in California. Today, in a very tranquil and lovely valley, the ancient church bells again call Indians to mass in the chapel, now adorned by frescoes painted by the Palas. There is a small museum with church relics and Indian artifacts, a museum shop with local products and crafts, and an Indian cemetery. This is a pleasant spot for picnicking and sometimes there's Indian fry bread for sale in the village. The **Corpus Christi Festival** (end of May or early June) begins with a morning outdoor mass before continuing with processions, dances, and a barbecue. *Open 10 a.m.–3 p.m. except Mon. and major holidays; fee; 714–742–3317. The chapel is located 20m east of San Luis Rey Mission on CA 76 (also called Mission/Pala Rd.), then left onto CA 16 for 1.5m. Note that there is an approach route directly from San Diego via the Escondido freeway (45m).*

Rancho Santa Margarita Y Las Flores □ In the days when Mission San Luis Rey counted 26,000 head of cattle and nearly the same number of sheep, some of the herds grazed on these ranch lands, now part of **Camp Pendleton Marine Corps Base.** After secularization, Pio Pico merged the two great ranches of Santa Margarita and Las Flores into one of 250,000 acres, an estate with 35 miles of coastline, 3 mountain ranges, and numerous ponds and streams. Though drill stations and barbed wire have replaced vaquero's adobes and corrals, the commander's private residence, called "The Ranch House," recalls some of the past if you want to take a tour along Vandegrift Street, the road leading off the main entrance to the base. After 8 m, you pass an "intersection," and on your left stands what was formerly the 20-room Santa Margarita adobe of the Englishman "Juan" Forster, who bought the ranch from Pico, his brother-in-law. *To visit the base enter the main gate on I-5 between San Clemente and Oceanside and sign in; 619–725–5566.*

★★★ **San Juan Capistrano** □ A tourist's favorite, this romantic *mission* has inspired songs and movies alike. While the spring return of the swallows to nest in the ruined church walls has inspired much of the interest surrounding the mission, San Juan Capistrano itself warrants the attention. In 1796 when the padres of the mission decided to build a great stone church, they searched for a master mason who might be trusted to build the beautiful church they envisioned. They couldn't find even "a moderately-able mechanic." Finally, a mason from faraway in Mexico was enticed to California, only to be killed too soon in a construction accident. The friars found themselves the architects, the neophytes the builders. Carting stone from six miles away and "at the cost of supplication and labors," they built an exceptional church with seven domes, a belltower 120 feet high, and with well-crafted neoclassical pilasters and adornments.

. . . *it must have been more perfect than any other of its kind.*

Alfred Robinson, 1829

Then the great earthquake of 1812 took away what had been so arduously constructed. The disaster struck at sunrise mass when few were in the church, but of the 46 neophytes present only six escaped.

In a moment it completely destroyed the new church built of masonry. It required more than nine years to construct it, but it lasted no more than six years and three months . . . The tower tottered twice. At the second shock it fell on the portal and bore this down, causing the concrete roof to cave in . . .

Friars Francisco Suner and
Josef Barona, 1812

Overwhelmed by the calamity, the padres never rebuilt the stone church, nor did they construct a new one. Instead they retreated to the adobe mission chapel founded by Serra in 1777.

Today, the ruined state of the great stone church couldn't be more picturesque, its monumental arch rising from bougainvillea and surrounded by gardens. The Serra chapel, perhaps the oldest building preserved in California, and definitely the only church remaining where Serra actually said mass, has been refurbished with an old reredo brought from Spain in 1906, the ornate likes of which never were found in pastoral California. Other sides of the quadrangle have been enclosed: a renovated friary containing a museum with vestments and religious art is on one side; a reconstructed workshop wing finishes the third side; and a new convent totally encloses the patio. *Open 7:30 a.m.–5 p.m. daily; fee; tour maps and self-guided tapes; 714–493–1424.* As for the swallows, they return from South America in the spring, including on St. Joseph's Day, March 19, when the **Fiesta de las Golondrinas** is celebrated with parades and dances. They depart for Argentina in the fall, including on St. John's Day, October 23, when you can participate in the **Adios a las Golondrinas.**

The *town* that grew up around the old mission after secularization offers a number of historic adobes to view, including the **Blas Aguilar Adobe** (31806 El Camino Real), part of which may date back to 1794 when the stewards of the mission resided here. Behind the old Santa Fe train station you find the 1843 **Rios Adobe** (Los Rios St. at Verdugo) granted to a local justice of the peace, and now the oldest single dwelling in California continuously occupied by the same family. This adobe originally stood on a ranch of merely seven acres, while the **Rancho Boca de la Playa Adobe** (now a sprawling shopping center on El Camino Capistrano), controlled 6600 acres of coastal land from Doheney and Capistrano beaches to San Clemente. Of course its owner, Emigdio Vega, was not merely a justice of the peace but a *juez del campo,* organizer of rodeos, as well. Other adobes (and Victorian buildings, including the wonderful train depot) can be seen while browsing in shops just south of the mission. Across from the mission El Peon has a map of the old adobes on its front wall. Here on Sundays, at 1 p.m., you can join a walking tour of the town (fee).

San Juan Capistrano lies near the junction of I-5 and the Pacific Coast Highway, 4 miles inland from Dana Point, 26m north of Oceanside, and about 65m south of L.A.

Dana Point Harbor □ This cove today accommodates over 2000 pleasure boats in its carefully landscaped Mariner's Village Park. Over a century ago different kinds of sailors anchored here, some to trade with San Juan Capistrano Mission and others to pillage it, like the pirates under Bouchard in 1818 who "destroyed much wine and spirits" during their stay. But it is for a friendlier visitor that the point is named, commemorating Bostonian Richard Henry Dana's 1835 description of hide trading from the great heights of Dana Point where "we pitched the hides, throwing them, and they swayed and eddied about, plunging and rising in the air, like a kite when it has broken its string . . . and as fast as they came to ground, the men below picked them up." Dana's description of this now bustling cove makes you realize the great distance in time that has been traveled these last 150 years.

San Juan is the only romantic spot on the coast. The country here for several miles is high table-land, running boldly to the shore, and breaking off in a steep cliff, at the foot of which the waters of the Pacific are constantly dashing . . . we strolled about, picking up shells, and following the sea where it tumbled in, roaring and spouting, among the crevices of the great rocks . . . there was a grandeur in everything around, a silence and solitariness which affected every part! Not a human being but ourselves for miles, and no sound heard but the pulsations of the great Pacific.

DANA 1835

If you're interested in the harbor, write to *Dana Wharf Sportfishing,* (34675 Golden Lantern St., CA 92629; 714–496–5794 for boat rentals or a whale-watching cruise, late December through March. A quiet view of the point can be enjoyed from the Ritz Carlton Hotel at Laguna Niguel (see *Accommodations* below). *Dana Point is just off I-5, 4m west of San Juan Capistrano and about midway between L.A. and San Diego.*

Other Historic Sites □ When Portola trekked through this region, one of his corporals must have taken a particular liking to the Santa Ana Valley for by 1810 Jose Antonio Yorba held one of the first land grants in California, the Rancho Santiago de Santa Ana, covering nearly 50,000 acres where today stand the cities of Santa Ana, Olive, Orange, and Costa Mesa. Bernardo Yorba, one of his sons, added yet more acreage and grazed his herds from Riverdale to Newport Beach, while another heir became the epitome of the Spanish don.

Upon his head he wore a black silk handkerchief, the four corners of which hung down his neck behind an embroidered shirt, a cravat of white jaconet tastefully tied, a blue damask vest, short clothes of crimson velvet, a bright greencloth jacket with large silver buttons, and shoes of embroidered deer skin, comprised his dress. I was afterwards in-

formed . . . that on some occasions, such as a particular feast day or festival his entire display often exceeded in value a thousand dollars.

ROBINSON, 1829

Jose Sepulveda owned the great San Joaquin hacienda next to the Yorbas, and other dons claimed the region until an Irish immigrant, James Irvine, gradually bought up his share of them to make the Irvine Ranch that covered twenty percent of Orange County. Although cattle still graze on parts of the Irvine Ranch that have not yet been bulldozed into developments, and though from the freeways you can glimpse groves of Valencia orange trees here and there, most of the great range and agricultural lands of Orange County have given birth to modern cities, such as Mission Viejo and the town of Irvine, just within recent decades. To find the past, you should definitely stop at the mission revival-style building of the ★ **Charles W. Bowers Museum** (2002 N. Main St., Santa Ana) with a fine History Room exhibiting paintings, jewelery, and other items from the estates of the Sepulvedas and Yorbas, with chests and saddles from the great ranching days. Also in this museum is an exquisite collection of California baskets in the Native America Arts Room. Open *Tues.–Sat. 10 a.m.–5 p.m.; Sun. noon–5 p.m.; closed major holidays; donation; good museum shop; 714–972–1900. To reach the museum, follow signs off I-5.*

Disneyland □ Even the great Padre Antonio Peyri couldn't have contrived the concrete fantasies of Disneyland. While belonging to no epoque but our own, this favorite of all attractions must at least be listed. Any visit here requires just about a full day to meet Mickey Mouse, to travel about the 76 acres by spaceship or buggy, and to visit the seven main areas: Fantasyland with its Sleeping Beauty Castle; Main Street, USA; New Orleans Square, including a pirates' cruise; Frontierland with its old riverboat; Bear Country with its country-western musical review; and, of course, Tomorrowland with its exhibits on space. *Open in summer, 9 a.m. to midnight daily except one hour later on Sat. night; rest of year Wed.–Fri. 10 a.m.–6 p.m., weekdays till 7 p.m.; various price packages for admissions, rides, and exhibits. For more detailed information write Disneyland, 1313 Harbor Blvd., Anaheim, CA 92803 or call 714–999–4000. Disneyland is located off I-5, also known as the Santa Ana Freeway, in Anaheim, just 35m south of L.A. and 30m north of San Juan Capistrano.*

Suggestions

Getting There □ From either San Diego or L.A., you can follow I-5 approximately along the route of the Camino Real. If you are making a round trip from L.A., then you can return via the Pacific Coast Highway (CA 1) to Long Beach (see Index) and then into L.A. A round trip from San Diego can be diversified via the mission branch at San Antonio de Pala and I-15. ★ The two main sights in this section, namely the missions, basically lie midway between the two major cities which are about 125m apart. ★ Trains also approximate much of the Camino Real and Greyhound and Trailways buses run between the two cities via San Juan Capistrano and Oceanside, near San Luis Rey. ★ Gray Line offers tours from L.A. to some of the sights, particularly daytrips to Disneyland (213–481–2121). ★ Orange County has its airport in Santa Ana, with commuter and some national airlines serving it.

Practical Tips □ Summer is the big season, but this warm region certainly can be enjoyed from fall to spring. ★ If you're near Laguna Beach in July make sure you check out the **Pageant of the Masters,** where famous paintings are re-created by tableaux of costumed residents. (For tickets up to 8 months in advance, write Festival of the Arts, Box 1659, Laguna Beach 92682; 714–494–1147).

Restaurants

After visiting San Luis Rey, you might want to continue south on the coast to enjoy the surfside location and good seafood at **Jake's Del Mar** (1600 Coastal Blvd. in Del Mar; Sunday brunch, Tues.–Fri. lunch, dinner nightly; 755–2002; ***moderately expensive***). For a casual meal in the center of Laguna Beach, there's the **Tavern by the Sea,** right on the Pacific Coast Highway, and with delicious linguini with clams and garlic bread, and with a few sea views from the oyster bar (open dinner only; no reservations; ***inexpensive to moderate***). In San Juan Capistrano, you can dine on Mexican dishes and salads in the historic adobe that once belonged to Miguel Yorba at **El Adobe Dining** (31891 Camino Capistrano; open daily lunch and dinner; 714–493–1163; ***inexpensive-moderate***). Despite the fact that the lobby area of this restaurant once was the town jail (1812), the service is most pleasant. There're clusters of restaurants along CA 76 between Oceanside and San Luis

Rey, and at Dana Point. There is picnicking at San Luis Rey Mission and at the many state beaches along the Pacific Coast Highway.

Accommodations

Although L.A. or San Diego can be used as a base for sightseeing in this section, you might want to arrange your tour while you're traveling from one to the other. A full visit to Disneyland requires an overnight in the region, if not in L.A.; and the resort towns beckon to those who like to travel in a leisurely way. For Disneyland visitors, Anaheim offers all the chain motels as well as the **Disneyland Hotel,** a family resort that's the official hotel of the ''Magic Kingdom,'' and connected to it by the monorail. With over a 1000 rooms, 10 tennis courts, and 3 pools, the hotel also offers numerous restaurants and lounges. ***Expensive*** to ***very expensive.*** Write 1150 W. Cerritos Ave., Anaheim 92802; 714–635–8600 or 800–854–6165.

Along the coast, there are some moderate chains at Dana Point, including a Best Western, but the landmark hotel is **The Ritz-Carlton** near Laguna Beach, an opulent, modern hotel on a cliff overlooking Dana Point and two miles of beautiful beach and surf. The lobby and corridors are sumptuously decorated with Italian marble, thick carpets, and Chippendale furnishings, but breaking the formality are the large windows framing the sea. The formality extends to the evening when men must wear jackets and ties in the lobby and most restaurants. The 396 units are very large and well-furnished, with balconies (half with sea views) and extravagant marble bathrooms. Three restaurants, lounges, shops, and library. Two pools, Jacuzzi, and beach; fees for 18-hole golf course, tennis courts, fitness center with aerobics program, weights and massage. Valet parking. ***Very expensive.*** To reach hotel from I-5, turn west onto Crown Valley Parkway, then south on the Pacific Coast Highway to Shoreline Drive (right). Located between Dana Point and Laguna Beach. Write 33533 Shoreline Dr., Laguna Niguel 92677; 714–240–2000, 800–44–BEACH CA, 800–241–3333 elsewhere in the U.S.

THE RANCHEROS OF LOS ANGELES

Your commissioners could not but be amazed seeing the disorder and the manner how the streets run . . . whose aspect offend the sense of the beautiful which should prevail in the city.

Los Angeles Commission, 1836
(*Guinn*)

In 1781 when Governor Felipe de Neve founded the farming community of the Pueblo de la Reina de los Angeles (Town of the Queen of the Angels), he followed the most detailed royal regulations concerning good city planning. First, he designated the central plaza with its corners oriented to the cardinal points so as to diminish the force of the north winds. He delineated the streets radiating straight from the plaza before indicating the location of the church and other public buildings. Then he parceled out the surrounding land into neat house lots measuring 55 by 110 feet. The farm lots were carefully plotted into 550-foot squares near the River Porciuncula, away from town to leave room for future growth. As the pueblo grew from its reed-hut beginnings to more substantial abodes, house additions blocked intersections and straight roads deviated into meandering lanes. Originally shaped by careful planning, the pueblo of Los Angeles early promised the sprawl and independence for which it would later be internationally renowned.

It's hard to know what went wrong. Maybe the 1815 flooding of the river caused some of the town's disorder. Or perhaps it started with the first colonists themselves. Neve had hoped for 24 experienced farmers, skilled in the making of tools and dams and

. . . *without any known defect or vice which would make him undesirable in a town to be established in the midst of numerous heathen.*

Felipe de Neve, 1779

But recruiting such impeccably qualified individuals proved difficult. Not many Mexican citizens could be tempted to make a six-month journey only to live in a province so isolated and so close to starvation, not even when they were promised monthly salaries, clothing and tools, and grants of land, seed, and livestock. Only eleven families colonized the pueblo. Within the first year three were exiled for laziness. Although Governor Neve assigned officers to the pueblo to "bestir the settlers," many believed the new settlement doomed.

The main fault, in my opinion, lies in the indifference of the colonists and their disinclination toward hard work; they prefer to hold in a hand a deck of cards rather than a hoe or plow.

FRIAR JOSE SENAN, 1796

Unbelievably, the settlers produced enough wheat and corn to supply the presidios and make Neve's experimental colony a success. Showing the temperament that would become the hallmark of the California don, the settlers satisfied their obligations without even laying down their cards.

The Indians cultivate the fields, do the planting, and harvest the crops: in short, they do almost everything that is done.

SENAN, 1796

With such a shaky start, few could foresee the pueblo's future as the most populous and wealthiest settlement in Alta California. But progress came gradually if not instantaneously. The pueblo, with the help of soldiers and their families retiring from the presidios, grew from its original 46 settlers to 315, then doubled that by 1820. Self-government was finally permitted by the governor. The first *alcalde,* or mayor, of Los Angeles was Jose Vanegas, a Christianized Indian from Mexico and one of the first settlers. By 1818, a few substantial adobes had already been built, such as those of Francisco Avila, alcalde at one time, and Jose Antonio Carrillo who, along with his brother-in-law Pio Pico, would be "constantly mixed up in some intrigue" regarding Southern California politics. Despite the growth, pueblo life in the early years must have been a bit dull. No pirates or smugglers attacked the inland town, no foreign visitor yet ventured across the 25 miles separating the coast at San Pedro from the pueblo, a short distance that even later travelers found difficult.

. . . came to anchor at 11 [at San Pedro]. Started for a Rancho about 3 miles off to obtain horses for the Pueblo. At 12 arrived hot as damnation . . . After about an hour's ride through fields of mustard bushes, briars, and across gulches and quagmires, arrived. Got a noble horse and started again going like lightning and coming very near getting my head broke by branches of trees which I found confounded annoying . . . At last we came on to a good and tolerably hard road and at 2 p.m. arrived [at the Pueblo] . . .

FAXON DEAN ATHERTON, 1836

The time came when the pueblo required a proper church, one that would be a monument "for all time" as well as suitable to the religious devotion of the gente de razon.

On my arrival in Los Angeles my attention was called by the prayer at dawn—which I afterwards learned to be the general custom of all the Californians—to give thanks to God in a loud voice at the break of day. One voice rose above the others and to it the others responded in the prayer.

JOSE ARNAZ, 1840

The pueblo already had a small chapel, one so dilapidated the mission friars from San Gabriel refused to conduct mass in it. At first the settlers uncharacteristically responded to their need for a church, quickly laying the foundation. Then, seemingly having exhausted themselves, they did nothing more, causing one of the local padres to worry that the church wouldn't be finished "by the year of Doom." Seven years later the church was completed, but by dint of mission labor and mission alms. The gente de razon contributed in their own way, buying up, and presumably consuming, the barrels of brandy and white wine donated by the missions to the building fund. In 1822 the church on the plaza was dedicated, accompanied by the ringing of a pair of bells given by Alcalde Avila as payment of a fine for smuggling at Malibu cove. A few years later, Captain Henry Fisk added a third bell, a penance for his elopement with Josefa Carrillo.

Angelenos were soon to find ranching much to their liking. The Crown required little of the ranchero other than that he build a stone or adobe house on his land and stock it with animals.

Manuel Perez Nieto, soldier of the Royal Presidio of San Diego, before Your Worship with the greatest and due honour, appears and says; . . . I have my herd of horses as well as of bovine stock . . . I request Your Worship's charity that you be pleased to assign me a place situated at three leagues distance from the Mission of San Gabriel . . .

MANUEL NIETO, 1784
(*Caughey*)

The fortunate Nieto, retiring from the presidio, was given one of the first land grants in California, a grant that would eventually spread over nearly 200,000 acres. And little was expected of him for this grant, only that he not interfere with the mission and

that he must have some one to watch it, and [he must] go and sleep at the aforementioned Pueblo [of Los Angeles].

GOVERNOR PEDRO FAGES, 1784
(*Caughey*)

A ranchero could, and did, live in his townhouse most of the year, retiring to his ranch in order to oversee his Indian vaqueros during the spring *rodeo,* or roundup, and the fall *matanza,* or slaughter.

The vaqueros, *mounted on splendid horses . . . performed by far the most important part of the labor. When the mayordomo pointed out the animal to be seized, instantly a lasso whirled through the air, and fell with dexterous precision upon the horns of the ill-fated beast . . .*

ALFRED ROBINSON (1846)

Unfortunately only too few could achieve the lifestyle of a ranchero under Spain. The Crown permitted hardly any grants, no more than 25 in all of California, though the Angelenos managed to receive most of them. Under Mexico they would receive many more.

With the free trade of the Mexican period, the little pueblo found itself at the major crossroads of trade. New overland routes forged through Utah and Nevada avoided the warring Apaches, and opened trails that always seemed to end with the hospitality of an Angeleno, be it Friar Sanchez at San Gabriel greeting the fur trapper Jedediah Smith, or San Bernardino rancheros welcoming New Mexican Antonio Armijo with food and wine. And though the harbor at San Pedro afforded little protection during storms, ships still anchored there attracted by the vast cattle ranges managed by missionaries—San Gabriel and San Fernando Rey themselves boasted of 25,000 head of cattle—and the increasing number of private ranchos.

I was riding through the rich valley of Los Angeles . . . The plains were covered with its moving wealth, some of which was being converted into currency, hides, tallow, to pay for the necessities imported . . .

William Heath Davis, 1847

As caravans from Santa Fe arrived along the Old Spanish Trail to trade their brightly colored blankets for California mules and horses, and as brigs anchored at San Pedro, their supercargos braving the wretched road to the pueblo in order to exchange silks and slippers for cattle hides and tallow, the ranchers found their lives transformed. From living in the thatched-hut on land granted him in 1810, an ordinary soldier like Antonio Lugo

frank in his manners, in character rather jocose, his language a little free

Jose Arnaz, 1840

could find his vast herds suddenly valuable and himself among the wealthiest of California's elite.

. . . I met the principal ranchero of all California, *named Don Antonio Maria Lugo. In farm property he was the richest owner, for it was said he was the possessor of 20,000 head of cattle and a proportionate number of horses and mules . . .*

Arnaz, 1840

Although Don Antonio would continue to live frugally, his preferred attire a prized multi-colored serape from Saltillo, his son Vincente would build a two-story townhouse and sport gold-embroidered shoes and silver-spangled, velvet jackets. Vincente's horse would be no less richly adorned. The age of the *hacendado,* or land baron, had arrived.

Merchants and trappers alike came to trade. They enjoyed the people and climate, and many settled. They opened shops on the plaza, built warehouses at San Pedro and, with time, they married into California families and became hacendados themselves, a situation that didn't always please their compatriots.

No Protestant has any political rights, nor can hold property . . . Consequently Americans and English, who intend to reside here, become Papists—the current phrase among them being "A man must leave his conscience at Cape Horn."

RICHARD HENRY DANA, 1835

The Yankee Abel Stearns married the 14-year-old daughter of Juan Bandini, and eventually became the richest man in California with many businesses, as well as more than 200,000 acres of land just in and around Los Angeles. Others found their opportunities excellent: the Americans "Juan" Temple and B. D. Wilson, who became Don Benito; the Frenchman Jean Louis Vignes who at least didn't have to change his religion; and the Scotsman Hugo Reid who married Victoria Bartolomea Comicrabit, "a native daughter of this country" raised at San Gabriel Mission. Even those with the most wanderlust, such as the trapper William Wolfskill who forged part of the Old Spanish Trail, added their number to the tiny town of the angels. And all, whatever their origin, "fell heart and soul in with the customs" of the California don.

Town life reflected the growing wealth of the citizens. Houses grew more spacious, that of Abel Stearns being of such great size it was dubbed "The Palace." Religious festivals became more elaborate, as on Corpus Christi Day when a procession led by the padre and accompanied by the choir left the church and began a two-hour march around the plaza, stopping to pray at the magnificent altars temporarily erected by the dons in front of their homes. And on Christmas morning, when every family attended *la misa del gallo,* or rooster's mass at 4 a.m., one man remembered

the large number of beautiful and richly caparisoned horses that were tied to the railing surrounding the old plaza, the rays of the cold, rising Christmas sun reflected back from silver ornaments on headstall and saddle.

ARTURO BANDINI, 1840s

The plaza was also the center of Sunday afternoon pleasures such as a bull-and-bear fight, or better yet, a bullfight, the bull bare-horned and the toreador mounted on his trusted horse. But the bull never was killed, just teased for awhile, then released so the sons of hacendados could show off their agility in the far more dangerous *colear el toro*.

The chief delight of the rancheros was in twisting the bull's tail, as he came out of the plaza . . . a large number of men on horseback rushed after the bull to see which should be the first to seize him by the tail and throw him down at full speed, holding the tail by the knee . . . if the horse made a misstep and stumbled, it fell with its rider, costing the lives of some . . .

ARNAZ, 1840

The Californios were as devoted to their fandangos and balls as they were to bullfights and horses. The opportunity to wear thousand-dollar silks imported from China, and stylish French gowns could never be turned down, especially when it meant dropping everything for eight days of festivities, such as in the celebration of Pio Pico's wedding at the Carrillo adobe. An elegant state dinner for the governor at Don Abel's "palace" concluded with dancing till dawn at his in-laws, just across the street. But before the ball could begin, rain turned the unpaved street into mud, threatening satin slippers and lace mantillas alike. Undaunted, Stearns called for his covered carriage, the only one in town, to shuttle his venerable guests over the width of the street.

In the early days of the pueblo, everyone attended the fandangos, rich and poor, both haughty senoritas and less virtuous ones. But as the town flourished, there was an attempt among the "decent and honorable" to establish their own select circle.

In fact, on the 16th of September, 1840, there were two public balls held, one in the plaza under an arbor, which was attended by the greater part of the populace. The other, given at the house of Abel Stearns, was attended by the most prominent members of the population, who came by invitation.

ARNAZ, 1840

Such elitism offended many. Don Abel's house was stormed, but the populace found the door protected by an armed guard. The resultant broken windows deterred the new aristocracy not at all, and Don Abel's house became the undisturbed center of high society for many years. Not until the American period would the gentry be disrupted again in their festivities, and then by a group of gamblers who, believing that "on national occasions one American was as good as another," crashed the George Washington ball with cannon and a battering ram. They had, however, underestimated the dons.

. . . one game little fellow, who was one of the exclusives, was dancing directly in front of the burst-in door, and had a battery of Colts buckled to him, either of which was nearly as large as himself. This patriotic exclusive stepped directly to the door and plugged the first gentleman who attempted to enter. Then another, and another . . .

HORACE BELL, 1853

Prosperous Los Angeles was the largest settlement in the territory, and with a population of 1500 it found itself larger than even the capital at Monterey. With so much wealth and so many gente de razon concentrated in the pueblo, Angelenos naturally considered themselves, not the northerners in Monterey, as the true *Californios*.

. . . Los Angeles was the older and more populous town, while Monterey and the other presidios were nothing more than military posts.

PIO PICO, 1828

Years of sectional strife between southern and northern California followed, years that included battles in which maybe a horse would be wounded, a mule killed. In 1835 Carrillo managed to convince Mexico City to designate Los Angeles the provincial capital. Monterey officials naturally were reluctant to move to the southern heartland, and for many years avoided doing so because the Angelenos, despite their growing civic pride, couldn't bring themselves to donate property for the *palacio del gobierno*—though one gentleman did offer his hall at a discount. Not until an 1845 battle made southern partisan Pio Pico governor did Los Angeles assume its new role, and then for just one year.

The time has arrived when the city of Los Angeles begins to figure in the political world, as it now finds itself the capital . . . although it is but a small town, it should proceed to show its beauty, its splendor and its magnificence in such a manner that when the traveler visits us he may say, "I have seen the City of the Angels . . . it is a Mexican paradise." It is not so under the present conditions, for the majority of its buildings present a gloomy, a melancholy aspect . . .

REGIDOR LEONARDO COTA, 1845
(*Guinn*)

Even as capital city, Los Angeles persisted in its old ways with its peculiar brand of disorder embarrassing Governor Pico. It seems that too many buildings required brightening by whitewash; others littered the main streets, whether half-collapsed or half-built it was hard to say, but either way they detracted from the town's "splendor." The new capital, Pico said, needed a beautification plan.

Events surely precluded any urban renewal. Within a year, the governor learned that U.S. troops were approaching the pueblo from the south. Forming an unusual, if not unique alliance with the northerners, Pico gathered his troops "here in the public plaza" and put them under the command of General Jose Castro. Unfortunately Castro deserted to Mexico and Pico found little desire for battle among his officials.

The deputies . . . observed that the majority of our forces were civilians—rural people—and to expose them to the dangers of war was to place their families in tribulation . . . I insisted upon the necessity of doing something . . . The assembly resolved that I should leave the country . . . so that there would be no one in authority to negotiate with the enemy.

PICO, 1846

So it was that Commodore Stockton, landing at San Pedro, and Major Fremont, arriving by land, joined forces at the very empty capital city of Los Angeles and raised the American flag over the plaza without firing a shot.

. . . our entry having more the effect of a parade of home guards than of an enemy taking possession of a conquered town.

JOHN C. FREMONT, 1846
(*Guinn*)

Deceived by the ease of victory, the commodore withdrew from town, leaving fifty troops under the command of Lt. Archibald Gillespi.

No more unsuitable individual than Gillespi could have been left in charge of the pueblo of the hacendados. The land barons may have wisely followed a passive course against the superior forces of their conquerors, but they could tolerate no more than two weeks of martial law under the lieutenant. So when the puritanical Gillespi stopped all public gatherings, even of two dons strolling down Main Street, there certainly were mumblings of complaint. When he closed down the taverns, few were pleased; when home entertaining also was banned, revolution was not far away. To cap it all, Lt. Gillespi ordered the arrest of all who galloped their horses through the streets. Added to such insults was the tyranny of sudden arrest on whatever suspicion and surprise searches of townhouses. The Angelenos revolted, and soon all of southern California joined them. Not until 1847, after numerous skirmishes and a major battle won by Pico's brother Andres, would the United States again fly its flag over the plaza.

Soon after the U.S. conquest, one observer claimed the pueblo's appearance had improved if not its morals. Disbanded American troops "settled" here. Gold found nearby in the San Fernando Valley attracted many strangers from the Sonoran border. Then, the San Francisco gold rush led forty-niners traveling the overland trails right through town. The plaza became the center of gambling halls and saloons. Streets planned by Felipe de Neve became warrens for thieves and murderers, gamblers and prospectors.

During the years of '52 and '53, it was a common and usual query at the bar or breakfast table, "well, how many were killed last night?" then "who was it?" and "who killed him?" The year '53 showed an average mortality from fights and assassinations of over one per day in Los Angeles . . .

HORACE BELL, 1853

Understandably, these new visitors received no invitations to enjoy the generous hospitality of the Californios, and the former *palacio del gobierno,* so briefly occupied by Pico, more profitably became La Bella Union Hotel. The old townhouses more often than not stood empty, as the dons retreated to their ranches.

The gold rush may have ruined the tranquility of the pueblo, but it also prolonged the pastoral lifestyle of the Californios. A steer whose hide once brought two dollars could sell for beef at the mining camps for fifty to seventy dollars. Already comfortable, the dons now lived their most idyllic existence.

Back to the hacienda . . . where the oranges leaned over the dark fountain pool. Then into the patio, where fragrant coffee from Mexico, tortillas and tamales de gallina were served steaming hot from the big fireplace in the kitchen. Though we danced until morning, there was not a sleepy eye in the house. When daylight came we went to our rooms or took siesta in hammocks under the verandas and were ready for almuerzo [lunch] when the bell rang.''

JOSE RAMON PICO, 1840s

The pueblo would await the decades for its renaissance, but it would be reborn. The age of the dons, finally destroyed by drought and taxes in the 1860s, was never to return.

Sights

From a capital city of 1500 gente de razon surrounded by about 40 Mexican ranches and considerably more head of cattle, the county of Los Angeles now covers 459 square miles with its population of 13 million. Where rugged trails once led from the plaza to the missions of San Fernando Rey and San Gabriel, to the harbor at San Pedro and the ranches of what is now Long Beach, eight-lane freeways now tie together the 140 communities that sprawl between the San Gabriel Mountains and the Pacific Ocean. The benign though smog-ridden climate here continues to attract peoples from around the world to the beaches at Santa Monica and funky Venice, to neighborhoods like Little Tokyo, and to the sets of Hollywood studios. Despite the enormity of the changes, Los Angeles retains the largest Spanish-speaking population in California and, in fact, in the United States. The culture of the Mexican-Americans enlivens the Grand Central Public Market just as it has revived the old plaza area of El Pueblo. The ranches have been subdivided into oblivion, but period adobes remain, such as Pio Pico's in Whittier, Hugo Reid's in San Gabriel, Juan Temple's in Long Beach. And the magnificent old missions have been restored. In this giant ''city of the future'' the past still can be discovered—in the central city, in excursions to Long Beach and to the valleys of San Gabriel and San Fernando.

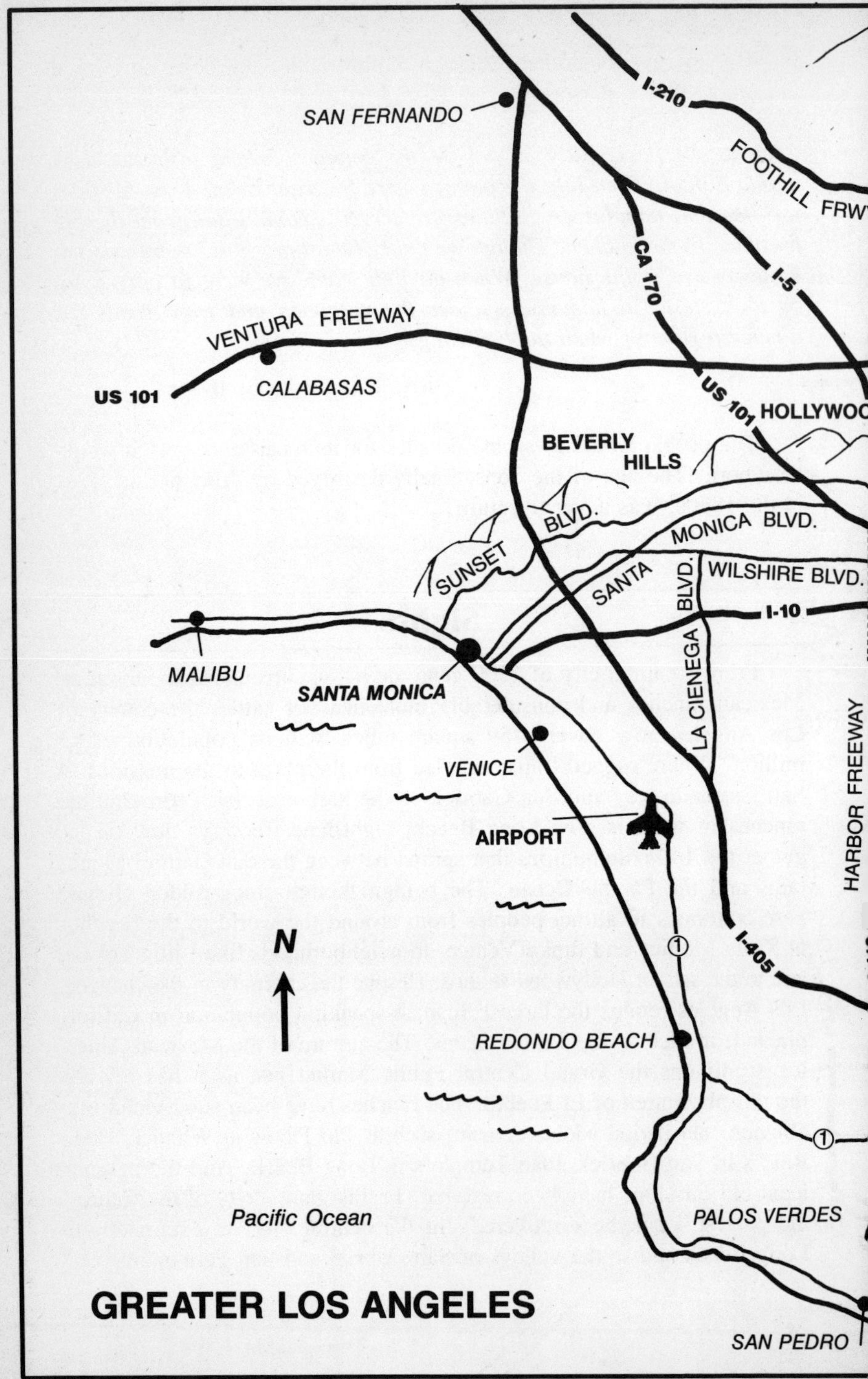

GREATER LOS ANGELES

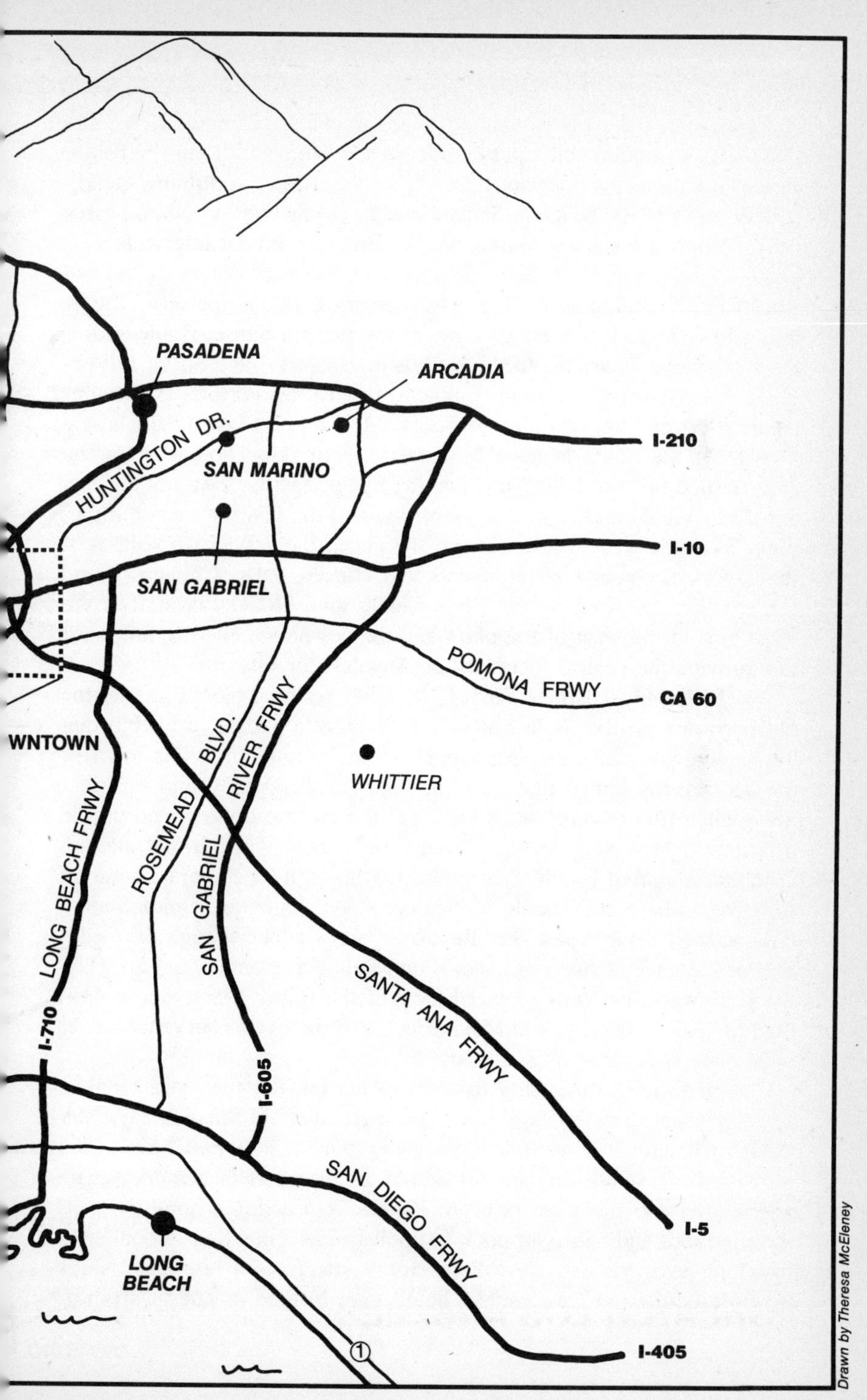
PASADENA
ARCADIA
HUNTINGTON DR.
SAN MARINO
I-210
I-10
SAN GABRIEL
POMONA FRWY
CA 60
WNTOWN
WHITTIER
LONG BEACH FRWY
ROSEMEAD BLVD.
SAN GABRIEL RIVER FRWY
SANTA ANA FRWY
I-710
I-605
SAN DIEGO FRWY
I-5
LONG BEACH
1
I-405
Drawn by Theresa McEleney

Central L.A.

Although the plaza remains the geographical center of L.A., the fame of the modern city lies to the west where you'll find Wilshire Boulevard threading its way through high-rises and continuing nearly twenty miles to the beach at Santa Monica. On the way Wilshire passes near the famed Farmer's Market and La Brea Tar Pits; it intersects with another boulevard, Santa Monica, that leads north to Beverly Hills and Rodeo Drive, and south to futuristic Century City and the ABC Entertainment Center. It is west you travel, whether on Sunset Boulevard or the Hollywood Freeway, to the studios of Universal and NBC, following a route crossed in another time warp by the Portola expedition. Again it's west that you pick up scenic Mulholland Drive to ride along a ridge of the Santa Monica Mountains overlooking homes of movie stars nestled in ''the Hills'' and passing by spectacular views of the San Fernando Valley and L.A. No doubt, most of the favorite tourist attractions lie to the west. But back near the plaza, the downtown section of modern skyscrapers boasts theaters and concert halls, Chinatown and Little Tokyo, as well as the Civic Center and ARCO Plaza. It is the large area to the west of the plaza and the downtown encroaching on it that provide the central focus of Los Angeles, the city.

★ **El Pueblo Historic Park** □ The few restored blocks around the old plaza are all that is left of Felipe de Neve's pueblo, a pueblo that has undergone many transformations since its founding. The town of the hacendados turned first into Sonoratown, then partly into a Chinatown where the townhouse of the elegant Vincente Lugo ended up the property of Hop Sing Thong. Around 1870 there was the first attempt at renewal, started by Pio Pico himself, who built an elaborate hotel on the corner where the Carrillo adobe once stood. Later yet, Union Station (Alameda St.) wiped out Don Benito Wilson's adobe though the building for his general store still stands on Main near Commercial St. Then the Hollywood Freeway replaced most of the Baker Block where Abel Stearns' palace once graced Main Street, and the Civic Center took over what once were pueblo farm lands.

As if to reflect the early disorder of the pueblo, the plaza today is circular rather than the royally mandated rectangle of Spanish days. Although Chinatown is just one block away, the 1822 **Plaza Church** (535 N. Main) still stands on the west side of the plaza, its facade once again adobe after too many years of Anglo bricks. Carrillo's home with its red-tiled roof and ballroom floor ''as polished as a bowling saloon'' was lost long ago, yet the 1869 **Pico House** stands as a reminder of the luxury this finest of Los Angeles hotels once offered its guests, from its tropical courtyard, velvet carpets and lace curtains, to the latest in water-closets. (Not open to the public.) Just off the plaza, around the corner on Main, is Los Angeles' first playhouse, the **Merced Theater.** When built in 1870, the first floor contained William Abbot's undertaking business, the third his family home, and ingloriously wedged in between was the theater. On the east side of the plaza only a little garden, backed by a roaring freeway, marks the site of Vincente Lugo's home, so the don may be best remembered attired in his finest, perhaps down to the typical Californio's boots described by Duhaut-Cilly as "made tight in the middle of the calf by a cord braided of gold and silk, the work of their lady-love."

The liveliest and most famous street of El Pueblo is **Olvera Street,** off the north side of the plaza. The Mexican market atmosphere of the street attracts most visitors who enjoy the many booths selling curios from across the border and the old houses now filled with craft shops and restaurants. Olvera is always lively on Sunday afternoons when Mexican-Americans visit there after mass in the Plaza Church and everyone comes to El Pueblo for the afternoon bandstand concerts. The street is even more gay on Mexican **holidays** (try May 5 or Sept. 15) and before Christmas when Mary and Joseph's search for an inn is reenacted in *posadas* that end with the traditional breaking of pinatas (Dec. 16–24).

The oldest house in L.A. stands on Olvera Street. ★★ **Avila Adobe** (14 Olvera), built by the son of one of the pueblo's founders in about 1818, has been restored with wonderful furnishings from the 1840s, some antiques from the Sepulveda Ranch at Palos Verdes, and some simple reproductions. From the ornate decor provided by the goods of the China trade to the simplicity of the outdoor courtyard, the adobe provides the most attractive and interesting historic monument in El Pueblo. Tues.–Fri. 10 a.m.–3 p.m.; weekends 10 a.m.–4:25 p.m.; free; fee for guided tours. Just beyond the adobe, on the other side of Olvera is the **Visitors Center,** housed in the 1887 Casa Sepulveda and offering an orientation film twice daily. Weekdays 10 a.m.–3 p.m.; Sat. 10 a.m.–4:30 p.m.) *El Pueblo de Los Angeles Historic Park* is located where the Hollywood, Harbor, and Pasadena freeways converge, four blocks north of First St. at Main. Look for exits to Olvera Street or El Pueblo.

Other Downtown Sights □ Some of the architecture of downtown L.A. might interest you, and you can get a sense of its diversity by walking a few blocks north of El Pueblo on Main. Near First Street you come to the massive government complex called the **Civic Center**.

On a clear day you can orient yourself to L.A. by visiting the 27th floor observation deck in **City Hall** (200 N. Spring St.; 10 a.m.–4:30 p.m. daily except holidays). Several blocks to the west is the famous **Music Center** (First and Grant) where the Academy Awards take place. And at Third and Broadway is the heart of the Mexican community, the **Grand Central Public Market** (317 S. Broadway) with its seemingly endless stalls of food, clothing, and housewares (Mon.–Sat. 9 a.m.–6 p.m.). Just on the corner next to the market stands one of the first great movie palaces, the **Million Dollar Theater** (307 S. Broadway). And across the street is the plain exterior of the 1893 **Bradbury Building** (304 Broadway) whose atrium and wrought-iron elevator cages are beyond belief. Another turn-of-the-century beauty stands nearby, enclosing a magnificent marble and stained glass lobby (**Banco Popular Building**, 345 S. Spring). In fact L.A.'s art deco extravaganzas and early movie palaces dot the streets of downtown all the way past graceful Pershing Square to 11th Street where perhaps the most outrageous of them all, the **Mayan Theater** (Hill near Olympic), can be seen. If you want to see more, try one of the special tours of downtown L.A. conducted by the Los Angeles Conservancy on Saturday mornings (fee; 849 S. Broadway, Suite M-22, CA 90014; 623–2489).

Highland Park □ A few miles north of El Pueblo in the Highland Park section and clustering around Figueroa Street, are several interesting sights. Most famous is the ★★ **Southwest Museum** (234 Museum Dr.) with its superb collection of Indian art from both the Southwest and California, with both ancient and contemporary works. The "People of California" exhibit contains not only many beautiful objects, but it provides an excellent introduction to the lifestyle of California Indians before the Spanish conquest. *Open 11 a.m.–5 p.m. Tues.–Sat., 1–5 p.m. Sun.; closed major holidays; fee; 221–2163.* A few blocks away is a branch of the museum called ★★ **Casa de Adobe** (4605 N. Figueroa). Although the building is only a replica of an 1850s ranch, the furnishings are not only authentic but exceptional, and include antiques from L.A.'s oldest families as well as fine religious paintings from the Caballeria Collection. *Open 1–5 p.m. except Mon. and major holidays; free.* Just off the Pasadena Freeway is **El Alisal** (200 E. Ave. 43), the handcrafted home of the historian Charles Lummis who established the Southwest Museum and who, through his magazine *Land of Sunshine,* did so much to generate interest in pre-Anglo California. Appropriately his picturesque home now is headquarters for the Historical Society of Southern California. *Wed.–Sun. 1–4 p.m.; closed* *holidays; free; 222–0546. To reach this section of Highland Park take the Avenue 43 exit off the Pasadena Freeway and follow signs to the museum.*

Exposition Park □ About 3 miles south of downtown are the many museums and exhibit halls of this park, now surrounded by the University of Southern California campus. Here the ★ **Natural History Museum** (900 Exposition Blvd.) offers its exhibit "California and the Southwest 1540–1940" with dioramas and displays of life in the early colony. *Open 10 a.m.–5 p.m. Tues.–Sun.; closed major holidays; fee; 744–3411. Exposition Park is located off the Harbor Freeway at the Exposition Blvd. exit.*

Other Museums □ More museums can be found to the west, and far west of the coast about 20 miles away, is the most famous and wealthiest of them all, the **J. Paul Getty Museum** (17985 Pacific Coast Highway) set in Malibu and surrounded by fine park land and formal gardens. Here a sumptuous replica of a villa at Herculaneum has been constructed with marble—marble floors, walls, and sometimes even translucent marble windows—to house stunning displays of Greek and Roman art. Until a new building is finished for the ever growing European collection, the second floor of the villa contains some fine paintings by Gentile de Fabriano and Van der Weyden, Raphael and Rembrandt, Degas and Cezanne, as well as changing exhibits of rare manuscripts, drawings, and photography. (*Open Tues.–Sun. 10 a.m.–5 p.m.; closed major holidays; admission and parking free,* but to discourage parking in the surrounding residential area, the Getty permits no entrance to pedestrians so bus travelers should get a pass from the drivers, and those arriving by car require a *parking reservation* that should be requested one to two weeks in advance by writing the museum at Box 2112, Santa Monica, CA 90406 or calling 458–2003; cassette tours and free introductory tours every 15 minutes; museum shop, and good food in the Garden Tea Room.) *Reaching the Getty Museum is a pleasure: after following the Santa Monica Freeway west and out of the city, drive north on the Pacific Coast Highway past the sea and broad expanse of the Santa Monica beach to Malibu.*

Far away in spirit from the Getty is the **Rancho La Brea Tar Pits** (Hancock Park at Wilshire Blvd.) in the mid-Wilshire District. Here the Gabrileno Indians came to get tar to waterproof their baskets and to secure arrowpoints to shafts. Later, Angelenos came to haul away the sticky substance to roof their adobes. In 1792 a scientist on an official reconnaissance of California reported on the pits.

I have observed a different kind of spring, rare in nature, of petroleum, pitch, and other volcanic substances . . . To the west of said town [Los Angeles] there is a large lake of pitch, with many pools in which bubbles or blisters are constantly forming and exploding . . .

JOSE LONGINOS

Longinos collected a number of fossils from the inky pit and speculated that animals had gotten mired there some time in the past, and then after who knew how many years, their bones reemerged through the bubbles "as if petrified." Now scientists know that the skeletons of mammoths and saber-tooth tigers discovered here date back to the ice age of over 30,000 years ago. Excavations continue in the asphalt deposits where life-size replicas of extinct animals have replaced their fossils. *Tours of the grounds begin at the observation deck Thurs.–Sun. at 1; the observation deck is open weekends 10 a.m.–5 p.m. except holidays, but it can be viewed from the outside and even along Wilshire Blvd.; free; 936–2230.* Sharing Hancock Park with the tar pits is the **George C. Page Museum of Brea Discoveries** (5801 Wilshire Blvd.), which offers exhibits of the reconstructed fossils as well as a prehistoric video show (15 minutes). *Open Tues.–Sun. 10 a.m.–5 p.m. except major holidays; fee; 936–2230.* Next door is the **Los Angeles County Museum of Art** (5905 Wilshire Blvd.) with its collections of Asian art and silver, with paintings by Lawrence, Gainsborough, and other Europeans, by Homer and other Americans. *Tues.–Fri. 10 a.m.–4:30 p.m.; weekends till 5:30 p.m.; closed major holidays; fee; 857–6111.*

Hollywood □ Long before bronze placques commemorated movie stars on Hollywood Boulevard, comedy and drama were already a tradition at what was known as Rancho Cahuenga. Here, across from where Universal Studios now sprawls, Kearny and Fremont signed the 1847 peace treaty with the rebel Californios. And here, a few years before, Pio Pico commanded troops in one of the north-south sectional squirmishes so typical of those times. In mid-battle, Pico noticed that General Castro had stopped firing on the enemy. Not knowing that the two opposing generals had an officers' agreement as to who would win, Pico angrily went in search of Castro and discovered his general in a role best suited for Chico Marx.

. . . [I] bumped into Castro who appeared to be hiding behind a small hill near the culverin. He was wrapped in a serape, and instead of his hat, he has another made of straw such as is made by the Indians . . .

PIO PICO, 1835

Today both the dramatic and absurdist traditions live on in L.A., even if the heart of Hollywood has become a bit seedy. Still you can enjoy the land of the stars by shopping (or watching *them* shop) along Rodeo Drive in **Beverly Hills,** or by taking tours of Hollywood and Beverly Hills (contact the **Hollywood Visitors Center,** 6801 Hollywood Blvd.; 466–1389). Better yet settle for a studio tour, particularly a full-day tour complete with King Kong destroying a helicopter at **Universal Studios** (Hollywood Fwy. at Lankershim Blvd. exit in Universal City; in winter 10 a.m.–3:30 p.m. daily; 9:30 a.m.–3:30 p.m. weekends; 9 a.m.–5 p.m. in summer; closed major holidays; fees; 818–508–9600). But the stars aren't just in the studios or Beverly Hills, they are all over L.A. on location and **Hollywood on Location** (8644 Wilshire Blvd., Beverly Hills; 659–9165; fee) guides you to them with listings and maps issued each weekday.

Accommodations

Four older hotels have made their mark lodging royalty and Hollywood tycoons. The only one downtown is an architectural landmark of the twenties, the elegant **Biltmore Hotel,** overlooking Pershing Square and located in the chic shopping district of downtown L.A. The ornate lobby has murals painted on the ceilings and other fine details, including a majestic staircase. The 700 units are decorated in soft colors, and recently refurbished. Restaurants and lounges. Pool and fine health club including Jacuzzi and weights. Valet parking. ***Very expensive.*** Write 515 S. Olive St., CA 90013; 624–1011, 800–252–0175 CA, or 800–421–0156 elsewhere in the U.S. Even more elegant, perhaps, and perfectly located is the **Beverly Wilshire Hotel** at the foot of fashionable Rodeo Drive. The poshly quiet lobby with crystal chandeliers and thick carpeting provides a fine setting for lounges, restaurants, boutiques. The 450 units are decorated with French-style furnishings; some are suites with 24-foot-high ceilings. Lovely pool, saunas, Jacuzzi, and weight room. Valet parking. ***Very expensive.*** Write 9500 Wilshire Blvd., Beverly Hills, 90212; 275–4282, 800–282–4804 in CA; 800–421–4354 elsewhere in the U.S. Also in Beverly Hills and a long-time favorite of the stars are the 12 very well landscaped acres of the **Beverly Hills Hotel**. Famous for its somewhat funky pink and green lobby, its driveway lined with limousines, and its Polo Lounge, meeting place for the stars, this hotel offers 325 units that include bungalow retreats for the famous. Restaurants and lounge. Lovely pool and cabana area. Tennis.

Valet parking. ***Very expensive.*** Write 9641 Sunset Blvd., Beverly Hills 90210; 276–2251. Robert Redford's preference, however, is for the **Hotel Bel-Air,** more like a country inn than town hotel. Overlooking acres of gardens, a stream, and lovely duck pond, the less than 100 units here vary considerably, but all are comfortably furnished and many have fireplaces and patios or balconies. Restaurants, one on the patio; lounge. Pool. Valet parking. ***Very expensive.*** Write 701 Stone Canyon Rd., Bel Air 90077; 472–1211.

Other favorite accommodations include the very modern complexes of shopping and entertainment anchored by hotel towers. The ultramodern **Century Plaza Hotel** in Century City is probably the most famous of these complexes. Located across from the ABC Entertainment Center and at the edge of Beverly Hills, the 867 units here are well furnished and complete with many amenities including balconies, refrigerators, and 3 phones. Restaurants and lounges. Pool and arrangements for tennis, golf, and health spas. Valet parking. ***Very expensive***. Write 2025 Avenue of the Stars, L.A. 90067; 277–2000, 800–228–3000. Nearby is the **Beverly Hilton,** low slung rather than towering and more traditional than sleek. The more than 600 units have refrigerators and are decorated in pastels. Restaurants and lounges. Pool and health spa. Valet parking. ***Very expensive.*** Write 9876 Wilshire Blvd., Beverly Hills, CA 90210; 274–7777, 800–445–8667 elsewhere in the U.S. Downtown there's the mirrored tower **Westin Bonaventure** enclosing a dramatic, open atrium lobby and shops. The 1000 rooms here primarily cater to convention groups. Restaurants and lounges. Pool and arrangements for other activities. Valet parking. ***Expensive-very expensive.*** Write 404 S. Figueroa, L.A. 90071; 624–1000, 800–228–3000 within the U.S. Closer to the Music Center and Old Town is the **New Otani Hotel** with its lobby graced with contemporary art, its Japanese roof gardens with waterfalls and pools. The 450 rooms include some Japanese suites with huge tubs, and a futon area. Restaurants, lounges, shops. Jacuzzi and arrangements for golf and tennis. Parking. ***Expensive-very expensive.*** Write 120 S. Los Angeles St., L.A. 90012; 629–2100, 800–252–0197 CA, 800–421–8795 within the U.S.

Not part of imposing complexes but nonetheless very good are the two following hotels. The **Beverly Plaza Hotel,** a small, modern, and ıdsomely decorated hotel, has a terrifically convenient location. Just w steps from the fashionable Beverly Center shopping complex and in walking distance of some of West Hollywood's trendiest restau- the hotel offers 100 attractive, more than ample rooms, a restau- nd a lounge with entertainment, a small fitness center and a Jacuzzi.

Free valet parking and free limousine service within 5 m of hotel. ***Expensive,*** but only moderately so. Located just off La Cienega at 8384 W. Third St., L.A. 90048; 658–6600; 800–334–6835 CA, 800–624–6835 within the U.S. More expensive, but also more of a resort hotel is the venerable **Ambassador Hotel,** once frequented by Charlie Chaplin. Located in the mid-Wilshire district, the hotel may have aged a bit, but its 500 rooms remain quite decent, its 23 acres of gardens are as beautiful as ever, and its sports facilities are extensive. Restaurant, coffeeshop, and lounge. Pool, tennis, weight room, putting green, and jogging track. Near golf. Valet parking. ***Expensive.*** Write 3400 Wilshire Blvd., L.A. 90010; 387–7011, 800–252–0385 CA, 800–421–0182 elsewhere in the U.S.

There are many **motel rows,** most notably near the interchange of the Santa Monica and San Diego freeways, and in the area of the Hollywood Freeway toward the Hollywood Bowl. But Holiday Inns dot the area, as do Best Westerns, and a TraveLodge is near Century City. For B & B options, contact **Bed & Breakfast of Los Angeles** (32074 Waterside Lane, Westlake Village, CA 91361, 818–889–8870) or **California Houseguests International** (18533 Burbank Blvd., #190, Tarzana, CA 91356, 818–344–7878).

Restaurants

California cuisine has influenced cooking throughout the United States, sending chefs off in search of the freshest baby vegetables and buffalo mozzarella, Hawaiian ahi, or tuna, and Chesapeake Bay crabs, and resulting in nouvelle French, Italian, Chinese, and what can only be called "Californian" delicacies such as snail-filled ravioli, warm duck salads, pizza topped with smoked lamb, roasted peppers, and eggplant. L.A. restaurants often have been trend setters, with **Spago** (8795 Hollywood Blvd., entrance at 1114 Horn, in West Hollywood; dinner daily; reserve at 652–4025; ***expensive***) top among them. The originator of California pizza, Spago continues to experiment, and offers the best of California cuisine—Chinese-style duck with shitake mushrooms, grilled liver with red-onion marmalade, pasta with smoked salmon and California caviar, and rich chocolate desserts. The ambience here has been a trend setter, too, casual and noisy, a bit quirky but exciting.

Joining Spago in West Hollywood, a lively and artsy community wedged between Beverly Hills and Hollywood, are more contemporary restaurants than one visit to L.A. could possibly include. Just along the main drag of Melrose Avenue, interspersed with the art galleries and antique shops, you can find just about every cuisine and ambience. Especially popular is the stylish **Tommy Tang's** (7473 Melrose, daily lunch and dinner; 651–1810; ***moderate***) for Thai food; **Teddy's** (at 8406 Melrose, breakfast-dinner; 651–2852; ***moderate-moderately expensive***) for catfish and hushpuppies; and **Trumps** (8764 Melrose, lunch, tea and dinner; reserve at 855–1480; ***expensive***), an innovator in American nouvelle, with seasonal offerings such as fried cornmeal cakes with chicken and clams, fried plantain and caviar, lobster and finnan haddie stew served in an ultramodern and colorful setting of poured concrete and contemporary California works of art. Also along Melrose is **Chianti Cucina** (7383 Melrose; dinner daily, lunch Mon.–Sat.; reserve at 653–8333; ***moderate-moderately expensive***), the bustling and casual hi tech "kitchen" for the very good, but formal northern Italian Chianti restaurant next door. The menu changes constantly, but the reasonably priced offerings can include angel hair with a satisfying sauce of eggplant and goat cheese, or duck filled tortellini with red pepper and cream sauce, along with good seafood, and a veal with basil—exceptionally good food for the price.

West Hollywood has other famous streets and restaurants, and as the trendy area continues to attract newcomers, the stylish shopping and entertainment complex of the Beverly Center (La Cienega and Beverly Blvd.) will anchor even more restaurants than it already does. Nearby is **385 North** (385 B, La Cienega; dinner daily, lunch Tues.–Fri.; reserve at 657–3850; ***moderately expensive***), a restaurant serving California cuisine at modest prices and in a very contemporary setting softened by pastel furnishings. Some of the offerings have Chinese accents like the mussels and clams with crispy noodles and black bean sauce, but I particularly enjoyed the mixed salad of string beans and sun dried tomatoes and a succulent mesquite smoked duck with cassis and ginger. The bar here is a good place for snacks (the tuna sashimi served with cucumber, onions and jalapeno is a fine choice) or for a late night dessert. In the opposite direction from the Beverly Center you can sample Chinese nouvelle at **Monkees** (170 N. La Cienega; lunch and dinner; 652–4187; ***expensive***), a sedate and elegant Chinese restaurant, handsomely decorated with lanterns and enamel screens, and serving what I ınd to be pricey offerings of salmon in cream sauce and red caviar, ıgeness crab in ginger, and other seafood specialties. More modestly ːd and more casual are some of the restaurants right at the Beverly ːr, like the hip **Hard Rock Cafe** (8614 Beverly Blvd.; lunch and ˉ daily; 276–7605) for good sandwiches and hamburgers, or the very popular **California Pizza Kitchen** (121 N. La Cienega; daily lunch and dinner; no reservations, but take-out; 854–6555, ***moderate***) where you can enjoy all sorts of freshly prepared pizzas from the simple but good ones topped with fresh tomato, basil, and garlic to the more elaborate duck sausage, sun dried tomatoes, and roasted garlic option.

Heading from West Hollywood toward the mid-Wilshire District, you can find more traditional offerings including the Mexican food at **El Coyote** (7312 Beverly Blvd., dinner daily; no reservations; ***inexpensive-moderate***) and the very famous **Farmer's Market** (convenient to La Brea Tar Pits and the L.A. County Museum of Art at Fairfax and W. Third; 9 a.m.–7 p.m. except Sun. 10 a.m.–6 p.m.; ***inexpensive-moderate***) where you can shop among the stalls for fresh fruit and take-out for your picnic, or take your tray and choose among the many stalls offering everything from fresh seafood salads to bakery delicacies and pot roast to eat at market side tables. A favorite place for breakfast and lunch.

Downtown L.A. has its restaurants and trendmakers, too, and **Rex II Ristorante** (617 S. Olive St.; lunch weekdays, dinner Mon.–Sat.; reserve at 799–0977; more toward very expensive than ***expensive***) certainly is among them with its red beet fettucini in butter and basil and sea bass ravioli, its salmon in green sauce and veal with hazelnuts. The atmosphere is elegant, in a restored building with art deco touches, Lalique fixtures, and a mural depicting the encounter between the old and new worlds. The restaurants in El Pueblo are earthier and less costly, that of **Las Golondrinas** (W. 17 Olvera St.; open lunch through dinner daily; 628–4349; ***inexpensive-moderate***) offers an attractive sidewalk cafe as well as dining in the 1850 Pelanconi House, the first brick house in L.A. While listening to the occasional strolling musicians you can try huge tostada salads, more traditional chile colorado or carnitas, or even hamburgers. If Mexican food doesn't interest you, then head a few blocks north on Main Street to Chinatown and try the seafood at the less formal and often preferred branch of **Monkees** (679 N. Spring; lunch and dinner daily; no reservations; ***moderate)*** where the service and ambience are basic, but the preparation of the scallops, Dungeness crab, and even squid are very good indeed. Or try the less hectic **Plum Tree Inn** (937 N. Hill St.; lunch and dinner daily; reserve at 613–1819; ***moderate***) and enjoy the Hunan lamb.

Beverly Hills is an area with many fine restaurants, among them the prestigious **L'Ermitage** (730 N. La Cienega Blvd.; dinner Mon.–Sat.; reservations required; 652–5840; toward the very expensive end of **expensive**), elegant and serene, and serving impeccable French cuisine including such specialties as saddle of lamb with herbs and green onions, Maine lobster with sweet pepper, as well as daily specials. **Prego** (362 N. Camden; open daily for lunch and dinner, except Sun. for dinner only; reserve at 277–7346; ***moderate-moderately expensive***) is more casual, with hi-tech decor and trattoria style Italian dining. The offerings range from cold shrimp in lime and mint vinaigrette with feta cheese, and pasta shells with artichoke and pancetta to California pizzas and grilled meats and chickens. **Mr. Chow LA** (344 N. Camden Dr.; lunch and dinner daily; reservations required, 278–9911; ***expensive***) is an elegant Chinese restaurant, all black and white chic and with beautifully prepared dishes such as chili chicken. For more casual dining while visiting Beverly Hills, you might step off Rodeo Drive to the **Cafe Roma** (350 N. Canon; lunch and dinner Mon.–Sat., dinner only Sun.; 274–7834; ***moderate-moderately expensive***) to sip a cappuccino, to try a delicious calzone or even a more formal meal, but definitely to enjoy the very Hollywood scene that often can be observed in the late afternoon. Also stroll through **DDL Foodshow** (244 N. Beverly Dr., breakfast-dinner Mon.–Sat.; 859–7741; ***moderate-expensive***), Dino DeLaurenti's extravagant food emporium with bakery, and cheese shops, with all sorts of prepared foods to take out, and with an Italian bistro upstairs looking over it all.

Excursions

Harbor Region

While the Harbor and Long Beach freeways take you most directly to the sights of this section, you might consider a scenic detour across the 15 miles of cliffs of the Palos Verdes Drive South, between Palos Verdes Estates and San Pedro. A slightly shortened, but more convenient itinerary would begin at **Marineland** in Palos Verdes, stopping off if you want for the aquatic shows and natural sea lion habitat, as well as a snorkeling tank that you share with thousands of fish (open 10 a.m.–sunset; closed most Mon. and Tues. in winter; fee; 541–5663; located by following the Harbor Freeway to the San Diego Freeway, I-405, then exit Hawthorne Blvd. south to the sea). Once you've picked up Palos Verdes Drive South at Marineland, continue east past the dramatic **Wayfarer's Chapel** (5755 Palo Verdes Dr. South) designed by Frank Lloyd Wright's son, and then just enjoy the winding drive above the rocky coast until you come to San Pedro, or continue on to the sights at Long Beach. **Note:** if you're spending only a day in this area, plan on visiting Long Beach in the afternoon when the old ranches are open, and when you can enjoy the local restaurants.

San Pedro □ Combined with the facilities at Long Beach, the San Pedro harbor is the largest artificially made port in the world, with some of the most modern technology to be found. Industrial San Pedro hardly calls to mind the old steamboat days when the Sepulvedas, owners of Rancho Palos Verdes that extended to here from the nearby peninsula, arranged for passengers to be rowed out to their ships from Sepulveda's Landing. Only in its bustle of activity does San Pedro resemble the days of hide-and-tallow trade.

Boats were plying to and fro—launches laded with the variety of our cargo . . . On shore all was confusion. Cattle and carts laden with hides and tallow, "gente de razon," and Indians busily employed in the delivery of their produce . . . groups of individuals seated around little bonfires . . . and horsemen racing over the plain in every direction.

ALFRED ROBINSON (1846)

Today Sepulveda's Landing is **Ports O'Call** (Berths 76 and 77 off Harbor Blvd.), a mock New England seaport with shops and restaurants, and facilities for tours of the harbor (open 11 a.m.–9 p.m.; closed Christmas; for cruises call 548–1085). Next door is the ★ **Los Angeles Maritime Museum** (Berth 84, Harbor Blvd. at the foot of 6th St.), well worth a visit for its models of tall ships and exhibits on the history of the harbor. (Tues.–Fri. 9:30 a.m.–4:30 p.m.; weekends 10 a.m.–5 p.m.; closed holidays; free; 548–7618.) If you want to see more of the harbor, visit the aquarium at the **Cabrillo Marine Museum** (3720 Stephen White Dr.; Tues.–Fri. noon to 5 p.m.; closed major holidays; free; 548–7562. Located off Pacific St., near where it intersects with 22nd St.) or take a 2-hour ferry trip to **Catalina Island,** discovered by Cabrillo in 1542 and now a favorite recreation spot with beaches, golf courses, and horseback riding. (Check out the Catalina Terminal under the west end of the Vincent Thomas Bridge, or reserve in advance one of the Catalina Cruises; 775–6111.)

San Pedro is reached from L.A. at the end of the Harbor Freeway (I-110), about 25m from downtown. From Long Beach it is 10 m via US 47 across the Vincent Thomas Toll Bridge. To reach Palos Verdes and Marineland (10m) follow 25th St. out of San Pedro.

Long Beach □ The up and coming city of Long Beach can be visited for its five miles of clean oceanfront beach, and for the calm waters of Alamitos Bay, the perfect spot for sailing and windsurfing. It can be enjoyed for serene drives along Ocean Boulevard past the **Long Beach Museum of Art** (2300 E. Ocean Blvd.; Wed.–Sun. noon–5 p.m.; closed major holidays; 439–2119) with its changing exhibits of very contemporary West Coast art, or for a short stroll along the pedestrian *Promenade* linking a reviving downtown with its perfect Bonnie and Clyde bank (First National Bank dating from 1906: 101 Pine Ave.) to the art deco buildings and slick glass ones on E. Ocean Blvd., and beyond to the modern entertainment and convention center. (For tours and maps contact the Convention and Visitors Council, 180 E. Ocean Blvd., Suite 150 CA 90802; 436–3645). Many visit for the **Long Beach Marathon,** a people's event in early May (1825 Redondo Ave., CA 90804); 494–26MI) and for the April **Grand Prix,** which is actually driven on city streets and along scenic Shoreline Drive (110 W. Ocean Blvd., CA 90802; 437–0341). Even more, visit for the luxury liner **Queen Mary** permanently anchored in the harbor, and open for touring of its exquisite art deco interior (Pier J off Shoreline Dr., 10 a.m.–5 p.m.; fee; 435–4747. The tour can include Howard Hughes' flying boat, the *Spruce Goose*.)

Long Beach can be visited also for the two exceptional ranch adobes preserved here. When Manuel Nieto received one of the first land grants in 1784, his ranch encompassed land from the San Gabriel Mountains to the Pacific here at Long Beach. Later, his decendants divided the land into five ranches, and even later their *Californio* friends married foreigners like Abel Stearns and Juan Temple who eventually came to purchase Rancho Los Alamitos and Rancho Los Cerritos.

The native Californios were about the happiest and most contented people I ever saw, as also were the early foreigners who settled among them and inter-married with them, adopted their habits and customs, and became, as it were, a part of them.

WILLIAM HEATH DAVIS, 1840s

A bit more time would pass and the lands would go into the hands of the sheep-ranching Bixby family who fortunately preserved the old adobes. About 5 m north of downtown Long Beach you can visit ★★ **Rancho Los Cerritos** (4600 Virginia Rd., just north of the junction of the San Diego and Long Beach freeways). Built in 1844 by Juan Temple, this handsome two-story adobe, with its broad balcony, fine patio and garden has changed considerably over the years, and now is furnished to the Victorian period. However, the solid adobe wings of the quadrangle are far more reminiscent of Mexican ranching days, with a blacksmith shop and bedroom furnished to the 1850s. Toward the end of the year the public is invited to celebrate a Victorian Christmas at the adobe's open house (open Wed.–Sun. 1–5 p.m.; closed holidays; free guided tours; 424–9423. Exit the San Diego Freeway north at Long Beach Blvd. then turn left onto San Antonio Dr. before picking up signs to Virginia Dr.). The ★★ **Rancho Los Alamitos** (6400 Bixby Hill Rd., just 5m east of downtown near the junction of San Diego and San Gabriel Freeways) is a delightful place, surrounded by magnificent gardens, many with plants over 100 years old. The original adobe here was built around 1806 by the Nietos, and later was added to and modified by Abel Stearns, and then the Bixbys. As you enter the living room of the Bixbys' house today you pass through the four-foot-deep adobe walls of the Nieto adobe, the oldest ranch house in southern California. The house now contains the belongings of the Bixbys' just as they were left when the ranch stopped functioning. Guided tours take you through the old ranch house adobe and to the barns, blacksmith shop, and other more modern buildings of the ranch. An open house and Victorian Christmas is celebrated each year. (Open Wed.–Sun. 1–5 p.m.; closed holidays; free guided tours; 431–2511. Exit the San Diego Freeway at Palo Verde Ave. to reach the ranch.)

After touring you might feel the need to eat and relax. One place to begin is at Alamitos Bay on a soothing gondola ride through the canals of the elegant residential area of Naples, while nibbling cheese and salami and enjoying whatever drink you want to bring. (**The Gondola Getaway,** 5437 E. Ocean; 433–9595.) Or consider a Chinese chicken salad for lunch in a converted 1938 Texaco station at the **Filling Station** (762 Pacific Ave., lunch and dinner daily; 437–3324, ***moderate***) or a really good hamburger at the sports bar and restaurant **Legends** (5236 E. 2nd St., lunch and dinner daily, brunch on weekends; 433–5743; ***moderate***), located in the trendy neighborhood of Belmont Shores near Alamitos Bay. For more formal dining consider the **Atrium** (180 E. Ocean Blvd.; lunch and dinner daily; 491–0677; ***moderately expensive-expensive***), a sleek, contemporary restaurant conveniently located near the Promenade and offering imaginatively prepared seafood. Although the menu changes daily, perhaps you'll have the good fortune to taste their smooth and tangy chilled avocado soup, their scallop appetizer with diced red pepper and ginger, or the perfectly cooked halibut with angel hair pasta. But if more continental fare tempts you, dine aboard the *Queen Mary* with views of the city and harbor from **The**

Chelsea (Queen Mary, Pier J; open lunch and dinner; 435–3511; ***moderately expensive***). Although seafood dishes such as tuna with a sauce of cream and peppercorns are the specialty here, the prime rib of beef is very good.

Some people nostalgically dream of a trans-Atlantic voyage with sea gulls outside their port hole, promenades along teakwood decks, dancing in the quintessential Art Deco lounge, and sleeping in handsomely paneled staterooms with their crafted fittings perfectly snug and watertight. The **Hotel Queen Mary** satisfies these romantic fantasies by offering 390 staterooms, four restaurants, lounges including the original Observation Deck, shops, promenades, and a jogging track. Valet parking on pier. ***Expensive.*** Write Box 8, CA 90801; 435–3511, 800–421–3732 within CA, 800–352–7883 elsewhere within the U.S. If you want to stay in Long Beach, but prefer to be on land the **Breakers Hotel** offers its own kind of nostalgia. This Spanish revival style hotel was built in 1926 as the deluxe beachfront property of the then booming resort of Long Beach. Today the hotel has been restored to its former elegance, and most of its 242 rooms have harbor views even if land fill has forced the surf elsewhere. Skyroom restaurant and walnut-paneled lobby lounge. Parking. ***Expensive.*** Contact at its Promenade area location at 210 E. Ocean Blvd.; CA 90802; 432–8781, 800–255–5053 US, 800–221–8941 CA.

Long Beach lies 25m south of L.A. via the Long Beach Freeway (CA 7) or via the Harbor Freeway (I-110) south to the San Diego Freeway (I-405) east.

San Gabriel Valley

Centuries ago this lush valley northeast of downtown was called "a place of beautiful proportion." Back then it belonged to Mission San Gabriel, with its vast ranches at San Bernardino and Santa Anita. Today, the church of the Archangel San Gabriel still administers to the spiritual needs of the valley's residents, and numerous botanical gardens recall the fertility of the mission's cultivated fields. The Reid ranch adobe reminds us of the period after secularization when mission lands fell into the hands of *hacendados,* and the sights of Pasadena with its "Millionaires Row" bring us all the way to the beginning of the 20th century, when Anglo architects like Charles and Henry Greene created the California Craftsman-style. A loop through this region should probably be planned, with Pasadena and San Marino visited toward the end, since the museums there open only in the afternoons. **Note:** limited visiting hours at many of the sights listed. Pasadena is also a good place to be when you're ready to have lunch or dinner, although the arboretum has picnic grounds. Only the Pico Mansion is a bit out of the way here; whether you can include it on a one-day excursion depends on how fast you travel.

★★ **Mission San Gabriel** □ A decade before the pueblo of Los Angeles was founded, Franciscan friars were searching for a site near what they called the "River of Earthquakes," in order to establish the fourth mission in Father Junipero Serra's chain. Before they could even construct the crudest ramada

. . . a great multitude of gentiles [heathens] came up all armed and under the direction of two captains who, with blood-curdling yells, tried to hinder the proceedings. As the fathers feared that a battle was imminent . . . one of them produced a canvas on which was painted the image of Our Lady of Sorrows and held it up in view of the barbarians . . . all, subdued by the vision of the beautiful image, threw down their bows and arrows . . .

PADRE FRANCISCO PALOU, 1791

By the time the pueblo was founded, San Gabriel was building its first stone and adobe church, but at a new location closer to their increasingly productive fields. The neophytes numbered well over 1000, and the canvas of Our Lady of Sorrows was kept near at hand. Although the old river, now known as the Santa Ana, had been left behind, the mission cattle were still branded with the mark for *temblor,* or earthquake. And by the turn of the 18th century, Mission San Gabriel was flourishing, well on its way to becoming the wealthiest of the missions. Not the least of its achievements were its vineyards, the first in all of California, and the largest of their time.

From the latter [grapes] they make yearly from four to six hundred barrels of wine, and two hundred of brandy; the sale of which produce an income of more than twelve thousand dollars.

ALFRED ROBINSON (1846)

Today the church of San Gabriel provides an exceptional example of mission architecture, with strongly buttressed walls, and a particularly handsome belfry that is asymmetrical. Its domed baptistery and altarpiece are original, its sacristy solid and worn with age. Although you can see the canvas of Our Lady of Sorrows in the sanctuary, and you can look into the old winery, it is the museum here that makes a visit so special, filled as it is with rare books—some dating back to the 15th-century—with vestments and furniture, and with unique examples of Indian artistry depicting the Stations of the Cross. The **annual festival** occurs on Labor Day weekend. *Open daily 9:30 a.m.–4:15 p.m.; closed major holidays; fee; 818–282–5191; self-guided tour map. The mission is located about 12m from downtown, off the San Bernardino Freeway (I-10) east. Exit at either Atlantic Blvd. in Alhambra (then north 1m to Mission Rd., turn right and continue 3m), or at Rosemead Blvd. north (turn left onto Mission Rd., continue 2m).*

★ **Hugo Reid Adobe** □ Soon after the Scotsman Reid set up his shop in the pueblo of Los Angeles in 1834, he fell in love with and married Victoria Comicrabit, daughter of a Grabileno chief and ex-neophyte of San Gabriel Mission. Senora Reid was one of the very few Indians ever to receive the land due them after the break-up of the missions through secularization. While much of the now reconstructed adobe was built by Reid in 1839, the land was part of his wife's inheritance of the Rancho Santa Anita. The intercultural Reid family became the inspiration for the romantic novel *Ramona,* and the beauty created at Santa Anita must have inspired its current surroundings of the **Los Angeles State and County Arboretum**. For as one visitor long ago described the ranch, it was one of the "fairy spots." Another said:

It was then the most picturesque spot of Southern California, with mountains, valleys, springs, and running silvery streams. You would observe in riding over the rancho its having more than its pro rata *of towering and over-spreading live oak trees,* manzanita, *laurel, and other forest in comparison with other* ranchos.

William Heath Davis, 1840s
(*Reid*)

Even if a visit today to the Reid Adobe, furnished to the period with ranching era displays including a silver tooled saddle once belonging to Pio Pico, does not satisfy you entirely, the trip here is worth it just for the grounds of the arboretum. Peacocks roam through the 127 acres, waterfalls and streams water prehistoric and semi-tropical gardens from around the world. *Open 9 a.m.–5 p.m. except Christmas; fee; self-guided tour maps and tram tours; 818–446–8251; special picnic area. Located 9m from downtown at 301 N. Baldwin Ave. near Santa Anita Park just south of Foothill Freeway (I-210), or 8m north of San Gabriel*

Mission, left up Rosemead Blvd., right onto Huntington, then north onto Baldwin.

The "Ramona" story inspired by the Reids is reenacted each April in the town of Hemet, near Riverside, where since 1923 a dramatization of the novel has been performed. (Write Ramona Pageant, Box 755, Hemet 92343; 714–658–3111.)

San Marino □ This small town wedged between Arcadia and Pasadena contains the spectacular collections and gardens of the ★★ **Huntington Library, Art Collections, and Botanical Gardens.** Although you can visit the Huntington Gallery here with its collection of British art, including Gainsborough's portrait "Blue Boy," and you can see paintings by Benjamin West and Gilbert Stuart in the Virginia Steel Scott Gallery of American Art, it is to the main library that you should go for the changing exhibits on *Early California,* and displays from the Huntington's collection of rare books that includes a 15th-century Chaucer manuscript, the Gutenberg Bible, and a 16th-century Ptolemaic world sphere. Then you can stroll among the 130 acres of formal gardens or relax in the Garden Restaurant. *Open Tues.–Sun. 1–4:30 p.m.; closed holidays; reservations required for Sun.; 818–405–2100; tour weekdays at 1 p.m.; museum shop. From the Foothill Freeway (I-120) take the Allen exit, then follow signs for the Huntington.*

If you're going onto Pasadena, you might want to take a pleasant drive en route to **El Molino Viejo** (1120 Old Mill Rd., off Oak Knoll) the old grist mill constructed by neophytes for the San Gabriel Mission. Today the mill has period furnishings and changing art exhibits. (Open Tues.–Sun. 1–4 p.m.; closed holidays; free; 818–449–5450.) To reach the mill from the Huntington, take the Oxford Rd. exit from the museum, turn right, and then after 2 stoplights turn right onto Monterey St. After ½m or so, turn right onto Old Mill. To reach Pasadena continue past the old Huntington Sheraton Hotel.

Pasadena □ Primarily a residential community, Pasadena is renowned for its sunny climate, its Rose Bowl Parade on New Year's Day, and its turn-of-the-century architecture. Although most of the mansions along Millionaires Row have been converted to condos, you can still enjoy a drive along Orange Grove Blvd., and even visit the Italianate **Wrigley Mansion** (at number 391), now headquarters of the Tournament of Roses Association. (Open Wed. 2–4 p.m. Feb.–Sept.; gardens open daily; free; 818–449–4100.) Another style of architecture can be seen at the **Gamble House** (4 Westmoreland Place on Orange Grove Blvd., just a few blocks north of the Wrigley Mansion), a masterpiece of Craftsman style. The interior, still furnished with the original designs of Greene & Greene, is open to the public (10 a.m.–3 p.m. Tuesday, Thursday, and some Sundays; fee; 818–793–3334). Downtown you can follow Colorado Blvd. to see the many examples of Spanish revival and Art Deco buildings now being renovated in the "Old Town" section. (For tour maps, and even an occasional architectural walking tour, write Pasadena Heritage, 80 W. Dayton St., Pasadena 91105; 818–793–0671.) And if the architecture doesn't interest you, visit the **Norton Simon Museum** (411 W. Colorado Blvd., at Orange Grove) that not only has a very strong collection of modern sculpture, particularly works by Maillol and Henry Moore, and Impressionist paintings, including works by Monet and Degas, but also masterpieces by Memling and Cranach, and works by Goya and Rembrandt. (Open Thurs.–Sun. noon–6 p.m.; closed major holidays; fee; 818–449–6840; museum shop.)

Pasadena is a good place to dine while exploring this region. Two contemporary French restaurants to try are **La Couronne** (142 S. Lake Ave.; lunch and dinner daily; 818–793–3151; ***moderately expensive-expensive***) where the fixed-price luncheon is considerably more moderate than dinner, and **Stoney Point** (1460 W. Colorado Blvd.; lunch weekdays, brunch Sun., dinner daily; 818–792–6115; ***moderately expensive-expensive***) with such innovations as snails in a ramekin with chorizo and leeks as well as more traditional dishes. For more casual dining, go into town on Colorado and turn onto Raymond St. where in the vicinity of Old Town and the Spanish revival building called Castle Green, you can choose between the elegant luncheon salads (poulet piquante or duck) of the **Cafe Jacoulet** (91 N. Raymond; open lunch Mon.–Sat., dinner Tues.–Sat.; 818–796–2233; ***moderate***) and the sandwiches, omlettes and unusual salads served in the patio of **Birdie's** (17 S. Raymond; open breakfast till 4 p.m. daily; 818–449–5884; ***inexpensive***).

If you really would like to spend some time touring Pasadena, then perhaps the historic landmark **Crown Bed and Breakfast Inn** would appeal to you, since it is a fine example of the Craftsman style. The five rooms here all have brass beds and sitting areas; all share bathrooms. ***Moderate***. (Write 530 South Marengo Ave., CA 91101; 818–792–4031.)

Pasadena is just about 7m from downtown via the Pasadena Freeway (I-110). By taking the Oak Knoll exit, you can follow signs to Colorado Street where it is easy to reach downtown restaurants and the Norton Simon Museum. To continue on to San Marino or Arcadia, pick up the Foothill Freeway (I-210) just a hop and a jump from where I-110 ends.

Pico Mansion □ Although the Picos managed to become owners of numerous ranches totaling more than 530,000 acres, it was to the Rancho Paso de Bartolo that Pio retired in 1852. Pio Pico typified the values of the southern California don. His hospitality was unflagging, his manner of conducting business straightforward and simple. After the U.S. peace treaty with Mexico in 1848, Pico turned himself into the authorities:

. . . we had several disagreements concerning the type of passport he [Col. Stevenson] was granting me. I was of the opinion that I did not need any . . . I said that all he had a right to demand of me was my word of honor.

PIO PICO (1877)

Pico lived to the age of 93, having enjoyed life in California under Spain, Mexico, and the United States. Despite his worldliness, he never adjusted to the American way of conducting business. As a result, like so many other hacendados, he was swindled of all his land and left destitute during the years just before his death. Even the courts refused to rectify the injustice.

. . . a decree will not be vacated merely because it was obtained by forged documents or perjured testimony.

CALIFORNIA SUPREME COURT, 1890
(*Pico*)

The mansion where Pico lived and entertained was mostly destroyed by flooding of the San Gabriel River. However, the 13 rooms of the **Pio Pico State Historic Park** are again undergoing restoration and the state is making an attempt to locate period furnishings, some belonging to Pico himself, to make the house into a monument of the last half of the 19th century. How interesting you find the displays may depend on the progress made in the restoration. *Usually open 1–4 p.m. Wed.–Sun., closed major holidays, but check first; fee; 695–1217; picnic area. Once located on the Camino Real, the Pico Mansion now is right at the Whittier Blvd. exit of the San Gabriel Freeway (I-605) in Whittier. From downtown take US 101 to the Pomona Freeway (CA 60) east, then I-605 south, for a total distance of about 15m.*

San Fernando Valley

On the far side of the Santa Monica hills is ''the valley,'' as it's known, a sprawl of bedroom communities and shopping malls with their ''valley girls'' where once great herds of cattle roamed and vaqueros rode their mustangs hard.

. . . It was the rule of all the ranchos that with the luzero *(morning star) every man had to be in saddle and on the go until eleven o'clock, when he returned for breakfast.*

HORACE BELL, 1852

Today a trip along the freeways to the north and west of L.A. can carry you back in time to a remaining ranch house and to a few of the yet undeveloped spots, such as San Fernando Mission and even Placeritas where gold attracted the first rush into California. There're picnicking facilities along the way and dining spots in Calabasas.

★★ **San Fernando Rey Mission** □ The Franciscans had determined long before the 1797 founding of the mission that one was desperately needed for the numerous and, yet, still heathen Indians living in the valley.

. . . the whole pagandom between the mission [in Ventura] and that of San Gabriel . . . is fond of the Pueblo of Los Angeles . . . Here we see nothing but pagans passing, clad in shoes, with sombreros and blankets, serving as muleteers to the settlers and rancheros . . .

FRIAR VICENTE SANTA MARIA,
1795 (*Caughey*)

Soon enough a site would be selected and the good friars would be relieved to see the Indian muleteers converted to Christianity and mission work. But San Fernando always found itself in competition for land with the surrounding ranches, such as Rancho Simi and its 113,000 acres owned at one time by Pio Pico. Later its vast San Francisco Ranch would be granted to the del Valle family, whose handsome Camulos ranch house and chapel (near Piru; not open to the public) would become the setting for the novel *Ramona*. And in 1845 Governor Pico leased the mission to his brother Andres for just $1100 a year despite an earlier estimate that the mission was worth more than $130,000.

I put up the missions for sale, succeeding in getting rid of some of them for such an insignificant amount that it makes one ashamed to mention it. But I was determined to end the mission system at all cost, so that the properties could be bought by private individuals.

PIO PICO, 1845

Although much of the mission fell into ruin, many of the structures have been reconstructed (too heavily, I think) to show once again Indian painted door- and church-decorations, ornate wrought-iron work, and a trompe l'oeil choir loft balustrade. The long, arcaded convento has been rescued from its status as a hog farm (1896) and made into an exhibition space for religious art. Many of the workshops and storerooms, such as the winecellars and smokehouse, have been re-created. In front of the church the manicured courtyard decorated with a Moorish fountain was part of an elaborate water system. Across the road from the mission you find **Brand Park,** planted with flowers and shrubs from all 21 missions. *Mission open Mon.–Sat. 9 a.m.–5 p.m., Sun. 10 a.m.–5 p.m.; last admission at 4:15; guided tours Sat. afternoons; closed major holidays; fee; 818–361–0186. Located at 15151 San Fernando Mission Blvd. near the town of San Fernando and near the junction of Golden State (I-5) and San Diego (I-405) freeways, and easily reached from both Pasadena and downtown L.A. From L.A. travel about 25m along the Ventura Freeway (US 101) to the Hollywood Freeway (CA 170) north then exit onto CA 118 west and exit at Sepulveda Blvd., turn right.* As you continue right onto Brand Ave. immediately on your right is the **Andres Pico Adobe** (10940 Sepulveda Blvd.), just a few blocks from the mission and one of the older houses in the region with its origin as a simple mission building in 1834. While Andres preferred to live in the mission convento, his adopted son lived here and added a second story to make it more fit for a hacendado. The adobe is now headquarters for the San Fernando Valley Historical Society (open Wednesday–Sunday 1–4 p.m.; free; 818–365–7810).

Placerita Canyon Park □ In 1842 the first California gold rush began because Francisco Lopez, tired of his search for stray horses on the Rancho San Francisco, decided to rest under a shady tree.

. . . Lopez, with his sheath-knife, dug up some wild onions, and in the dirt discovered a piece of gold, and searching further, found some more. He brought these to town [L.A.], and showed them to his friends, who at once declared there must be a placer of gold. This news being circulated, numbers . . . commenced prospecting . . .

ABEL STEARNS, 1842
(*Caughey*)

In the first two years up to $100,000 of gold was prospected, and still the hopeful arrived, many from Sonora, Mexico. Rumor spread that the padres had secretly been panning gold from what was virtually their backyard, and soon scavengers hunted for the "padres' treasure," digging under the altar of the San Fernando Rey church. The rush continued until gold was discovered further to the north in 1849. By then, California belonged to the U.S. and the pueblo of L.A. had become Sonoratown. Today you can picnic in this small park next to the "Oak of the Golden Dream." *Located just beyond the mission, the park entrance is 5m east of Newhall on CA 14.*

★ **Leonis Adobe** □ The heydey of Miguel Leonis, the Basque smuggler turned sheep rancher and good California citizen, belongs to the 1860s and 70s. But the original adobe that he and his Indian wife, Espiritu Chujilla, turned into an exceptionally handsome two-story home actually dates from 1844. The house is well furnished to the Leonis period including a copper and walnut-paneled bathtub. To enter the Leonis rancho today, you pass through the **Plummer House** (1870), originally part of Rancho La Brea in L.A., which has special exhibits on costume and lifestyles in the Anglo ranching era. *Open Wed.–Sun. 1–4 p.m.; donations; 818–712–0734. 23537 Calabasas Rd., Calabasas. Located about 20 minutes from L.A., exit the Ventura Freeway (US 101 west) at Mulholland Dr.-Valley Circle. Take a sharp right off the freeway, then curve left to Valley Circle Blvd., go over the freeway overpass, then make a right onto Calabasas Rd.*

The tiny town of Calabasas is a pleasant place to visit, proud as it is of its old western traditions and offering arts and crafts as well as comfortable dining. A number of restaurants cluster about the Leonis Adobe, the most popular seeming to be the **Sagebrush Cantina** next door with its outdoor dining, salads and Mexican food ***(moderate)***, and Sunday champagne brunch (***moderately expensive***). Although closed some Sundays, **Sandy's Gourmet** across the street also has an outdoor patio for breakfast and lunch and takeout foods (***moderate***).

Suggestions

Directory □ The zip code varies throughout the region but the 213 area code is constant except when otherwise specified or for 800-toll free numbers. ★ The *Greater Los Angeles Visitors and Convention Bureau* can be visited at ARCO Plaza downtown, 505 S. Flower St.,

Level B, L.A. 90071; 239–0200. ★ 24-hour tapes on air quality (800–242–4022), road conditions (626–7231) and community services (800–242–4612).

Getting Around □ Although L.A.'s car culture has reached the level of freeway flirtations, the bus service throughout the area and to many sights is good. **RTD buses** offers a free brochure on how to use public transportation for self-guided tours of the region (write RTD, L.A. 90081; 626–4455). ★ Taxis can be called by phone and are also located at stands in front of major hotels; they don't cruise the streets for business. ★ Car rentals, even Rolls-Royce limousines, are available. ★ Tour companies are plentiful for both within the region and outside, from **Gray Line Tours** (481–2121 or hotels) to **LA Custom Tours** (454–5730) specializing in art, garden, and history tours.

Driving the **freeways** is essential if you're traveling by car, and with a little preparation, it usually is the fastest and easiest way to get across this sprawling urban area. Familiarize yourself with the freeways, their destinations and numbers by writing to your automobile club, or to the Visitors Bureau for a copy of their maps and visitors guide (cost about $2.50). ★ Note that the Santa Monica Freeway is the best route from downtown through all the neighborhoods to the west and on to the beaches, the area where you most likely will be dining and staying. ★ Try to avoid the freeways during rush hours (weekdays 7–9:30 a.m. and 3:30–7 p.m.), but if you can't, consult your map for alternative routes if a freeway seems jammed up (like Wilshire Blvd. and Santa Monica Blvd. as alternatives for the Santa Monica Freeway). ★ Exits from the freeways are marked well in advance so you should have little difficulty positioning yourself in the correct lane at the right time.

Arriving □ The L.A. International **Airport** (LAX) located near Inglewood is the third largest passenger airport in the world. Providing service for the greater Los Angeles area is the **Airport Bus** (800–962–1976 CA, 800–962–1975 elsewhere in the U.S.), but **RTD** also provides service into L.A. neighborhoods. Information on ground transportation services is posted in the baggage areas along with direct telephone connections and taxi rates, and bus tickets are available on the sidewalks in front of the terminals. Car rental agencies are plentiful, from **Hertz** (646–4861) and **National** (670–4950) to **Rent-a-Wreck** (478–0676). ★ Other airports serve the region with major airline service: Long Beach, Burbank-Pasadena, Orange County in Santa Ana. ★ **Amtrak** operates out of the Union Station near El Pueblo (800 N. Alameda St.; 800–USA–RAIL). ★ The **Trailway** terminal is also in Union Station (742–1251) and **Greyhound** is at 6th and Los Angeles (620–1200).

Weather □ Summers may be preferred for the beach, but the weather year round is balmy with very low humidity—the little rain that falls occurs mostly from November–March. ★ January average high 65° F, low 46° F. ★ July average high 81° F, low 60° F. ★ The weather creates an outdoor culture that results in casual, even trendy elegance for formal occasions rather than the usual attire worn outside southern California, but men may feel most comfortable at the finer restaurants with a tie and jacket.

LAND OF THE CHUMASH: THE SANTA BARBARA REGION

The Indians adored three sacred "bodies"—earth, air, and water. The sun was their chief god. They adored the sun.

FERNANDO LIBRADO,
a Chumash born in 1804

Set against the rugged backdrop of the Santa Ynez mountains, a great expanse of beach skirts the Pacific from Ventura to Santa Barbara, and on to the pass at Gaviota before reaching its turbulent end at Point Conception. In this land of mountains, sea, and sun lived the Chumash. The sea yielded its bounty in food as well as otter skins for blankets and chiefs' capes, clamshells for tweezers, abalone for mother-of-pearl ornaments, and whale bone for tools. The mountains provided acorns and seeds, mule deer and bear as well as the wood for canoes and carved bowls. The swamps and lagoons nurtured the grasses for coiling and twining into baskets. The earth oozed the asphaltum for caulking boats and fastening arrows to their shafts. For over half a millennium the Chumash thrived in this bountiful land under their beneficent sun.

. . . an old man told him that we are all brothers, and our mother is one: this mother earth. He has always believed what the old people told him when he was a boy—that the world is good.

FERNANDO LIBRADO

Then one October, in the Chumash month of he who "taught people the use of the canoe," Spanish ships anchored in the channel. Eager to welcome the foreigners, the Chumash stroked their plank canoes out to the ships and greeted Captain Juan Rodriguez Cabrillo and the other members of his 1542 expedition. Here the explorers were to spend most of their six months along the California coast, finding shelter on the islands and food generously given by the Chumash. And here Juan Cabrillo would die from a fall on San Miguel Island. Sixty years later the Chumash eagerly greeted Vizcaino's ships, much in the same fashion as they had those of Cabrillo.

. . . a canoe came out to us with two Indian fishermen . . . rowing so swiftly that they seemed to fly. They came alongside without saying a word to us and went twice around us with so great speed that it seemed impossible; this finished, they came aft, bowing their heads in the way of courtesy.

SEBASTIAN VIZCAINO, 1602

Over a century would pass before the Chumash again encountered the Spaniards, but Cabrillo and Vizcaino would be just the first of many whom the Chumash favorably impressed.

This channel of Santa Barbara is very well settled, with towns composed of large huts roofed with thatch and with a very great number of peaceable and friendly Indians . . . There may well be ten thousand souls along the channel from the first town of Assumpta [Ventura] to the Punta de la Concepcion.

FRIAR JUAN CRESPI, 1769

One of the larger Chumash towns may have had as many as 1500 people living in it. Like the other villages along the coast, it had numerous houses "large like those of New Spain," conical in shape and furnished with platform beds raised four feet from the floor and covered with mats for both the comfort and privacy of the up to seventy individuals residing there. Interspersed among the houses were several subterranean sweathouses, entered each day by men and women alike before they immersed themselves in the cool waters of the nearby pool. (Some Spaniards, like Jose Longinos, found this Chumash "fondness for soaping themselves at all hours" particularly "repugnant to our way of life.") To the side of the villages were cemeteries with whale bone grave markers. In the center were two enclosed plazas, one for their game of stick ball played much like soccer, the other for ceremonies.

Within these enclosures they have many timbers set up like thick masts. On these poles they have many paintings, and we thought that they worshipped them, because when they dance, they go dancing around in the enclosure.

CABRILLO EXPEDITION, 1542

As for the Chumash themselves, the Spaniards couldn't have been more enthusiastic. Some might have preferred that the Chumash men cover themselves with more than mere body paint and an occasional fur cape against the cold, or that the women would extend their antelope skirts to the level of their shell necklaces. Yet Vizcaino thought one chief "was so intelligent that he appeared to be not a barbarian but a person of great understanding." And others found the Chumash so distinctive from the more nomadic Californians that they believed the civilizing Chinese must have landed along the channel in the ancient past. Chumash dexterity could be seen in their baskets woven with the "utmost delicacy," their cleverness in cooking with soapstone bowls that lasted for years, even generations. Their ingenuity was never more apparent than in their canoes

so well constructed and built that since Noah's Ark a finer and lighter vessel with timbers better made has not been seen.

VIZCAINO, 1602

Not only skillful, the Chumash were hard working, providing for themselves as well as the visiting Spaniards piles of roasted fish and bowls of seeds and nuts ground into *atole*. And their goodwill toward the Spaniards knew no bounds. Joyful at having guests, they entertained them, often the night long, with their wooden flutes, cane whistles, and rattles of deer hooves and sea shells.

In the afternoon the chief men came from each town, one after the other, adorned according to their usage, painted and loaded with plummage and some hollow reeds in their hands, to the movement and noise of which they kept time with their songs and the cadence of the dance, in such good time and in such unison that it produced real harmony.

CRESPI, 1769

Soon the channel's bounty and Chumash hospitality would attract permanent settlements of Spaniards. Adobe houses would replace Chumash huts, Franciscan churches their enclosures, and violins and flutes their rattles and whistles. So great was the Chumash population around the channel that Father Serra envisioned three missions there. In 1782 he dedicated the first, San Buenaventura, then planned for another at La Purisima and started negotiations for one with Yanonali, chief of the Santa Barbara villages. Eventually a fourth would be founded at Santa Ines, but Serra would live to see only the first mission at Ventura materialize. His ambitious plan was stalled by Governor Neve until the province could be more securely protected by a new presidio at Santa Barbara. Only once the fort was established would the other missions be founded. It is easy to understand the governor's caution. Even with the Santa Barbara presidio there were only 150 Spaniards in the channel region while the Chumash numbered in the thousands.

You will see to it that they are treated with the greatest gentleness and sweetness lest this foundation be repugnant to them. You will carefully avoid giving them the least occasion for pain.

FELIPE DE NEVE, 1783 (*Geiger*)

Whatever delays Neve's policy created, it seemed to work in keeping the peace. Ten years later Vancouver found the Spaniards and Chumash living and working harmoniously together. The presidio and mission at Santa Barbara were far enough along to be impressive. From a grove of trees near the seashore, the presidio with its white walls and bright red roof tiles excelled all others "in neatness, cleanliness, and other . . . essential comforts." And the mission was already functioning as a botanist with Vancouver reported:

The Granaries Storehouses Workhouses & dwellings together with a large Church enclosd very snugly a square space, within which the various mechanical occupations for the support of the Settlement were separately carried on.

ARCHIBALD MENZIES, 1793

Although Chief Yanonali had yet to accept Christianity, his people enjoyed the payment received from the presidio commander for their work.

. . . if I have enough beads to hand out to them as gifts, I feel that I shall be able to finish the presidio in short time.

LT. JOSE F. ORTEGA, 1782 (*Geiger*)

Other Chumash had converted, about 500 of them, still living in their conical huts but neatly "clothed and maintained by the Fathers."

Decades of building prefected the Santa Barbara presidio and completed La Purisima mission. The early years brought enough success to build the fourth mission at Santa Ines, and to construct a Moorish fountain with a nearby laundry for the now adobe village of 1700 mission converts at Santa Barbara. The church at San Buenaventura was rebuilt after a fire and the new gilding on its altars was just about dry. Then came the earthquake of 1812. The earth trembled causing the mission bells "to swing till they gave forth their chimes," the earth split open "emitting water and black sand." The quake was terrible. Then another struck, and another, again and again.

. . . the terrible earthquakes . . . their violence as well as their continuance have been extraordinary. They began on December 8, 1812, and continued until last February with great violence. Since then they have been considerable, although they did not occur with such force and frequency.

FRAY JOSE SENAN,
APRIL, 1813 (*Engelhardt*)

The quakes left much of the presidio in disrepair and most of its residents "suffering from fear." They destroyed the Santa Barbara church and turned La Purisima into a total ruin. Santa Ines was unfit for mass while San Buenaventura was temporarily abandoned because

. . . the ocean, owing to the shocks, was running so high we feared its waters would flood the mission.

SENAN (*Engelhardt*)

At the very moment the region most needed tools and building supplies from Spain it received none—not chisels or carpenter's tools. The war of independence in Mexico cut off the annual supply ship once and for all. And the blockade in Canton, due to the 1812 War, discouraged the foreign ships that once smuggled their wares along the coast. The blockade discouraged most ships, that is, but not the *Mercury* of Captain Eayrs known around Santa Barbara as "Jorge," or George.

I left China in the year 1808, with the small amt of cargo and about five thousand Dolls, my first Business was Hunting Furs. This Business

I entered into with the Russian Governor & continued several years, in which time I was in the Winter season as far South as California for supplies and the purpose of taking Seal Skins.

George Washington Eayrs, 1814

Don Jorge found it quite worth his while to anchor at small coves like that off the Rancho El Refugio, the family ranch of former presidio commander Ortega. Here the Boston captain would gladly trade, unofficially of course, the tools and clothes needed by the priests and settlers in exchange for grain, beef, and specially those otter skins obtained by the Chumash in their canoes. Or if business called elsewhere, arrangements could always be made as long as a customs house was not nearby.

Friend Don Jorge: It is necessary that early in the morning a boat be landed to enable me to embark and purchase that of which I have spoken to you. So, as soon as a fire on shore is seen, despatch the boat, since thus I must manage in order to act with safety.

Friar Pedro Maria de Zarate
(*Eayres*)

While the Californians didn't have ships, Peruvians in the service of his majesty did. So one day when Eayrs was carefully avoiding the landbound officials, he was captured by the South American frigate *Flora* and charged with smuggling.

My dealings have not been clandestine, but with the full and tacit consent of the governors. Let Fray Marcos Amistoy at Santa Barbara be questioned in verbo sacedotis, tacto pectore *[on his sworn word] concerning these transactions.*

Eayrs

No matter that he had been friend to friar and officer alike. No matter that he had ''clothed many naked'' and relieved their distress. Eayrs was imprisoned for two years pending an investigation. His Indian wife ''whom he esteemed equal the same as if lawfully married to him'' and his 25-day-old daughter were held at the Santa Barbara mission. As for his ship:

Senor Noe, Captain and owner of the frigate Flora, *has taken prisoner the notorious smuggler known as Jorge . . . Noe is now sailing the* Mercurio, *the vessel he captured . . .*

FRIAR SENAN, 1813

The *Mercury* was out of the smuggling business, but other vessels soon replaced it, keeping the Ortega ranch at El Refugio flourishing.

. . . Asked what the vessel was doing there, my father replied that he would like some beef for the ship's use. He engaged in some conversation . . . and invited Senor Ortega on board the ship . . . On leaving the vessel he was presented with a number of choice and elegant articles . . .

WILLIAM HEATH DAVIS, 1816

Knowing that smugglers favored El Refugio, authorities set a trap for them that led to the capture of two American ships and the imprisonment of 21 Yankees in the Santa Barbara jail. Captain Davis, however, escaped arrest. Perhaps the jail was overcrowded or perhaps his sumptuous entertainment of Comandante Martinez influenced events, but the American captain was able to anchor safely at El Refugio numerous times. And each time he made a great profit in gold and silver as well as otter skins. In return the Spaniards received more than enough to cover their nakedness.

. . . silks, satins, crepe shawls, fancy silk handkerchiefs, satin shoes, sewing silk of all colors, and other elegant finery.

DAVIS

So famous was El Refugio that the pirate Hippolyte Bouchard, en route from Argentina, the Philippines, and the burning of Monterey, determined to loot it. While the forewarned Santa Barbarans evacuated to Santa Ines and the friars buried their mission furniture and fled to the cold mountains with their most cherished church ornaments, Bouchard landed at the Ortega ranch.

. . . we made a village, called the Ranch . . . The men remained all night, and next morning the place was plundered.

PETER CORNEY, 1818

While the pirates plundered, some Spaniards under the command of Sgt. Carrillo in the nearby canyon, waited to ambush them.

About noon a lieutenant and two seamen having strayed a short distance . . . a party of horsemen rushed on them, threw the la's-aws [lassos] over their heads and dragged them up a neighboring hill.

CORNEY

Enraged, Bouchard torched all the ranch buildings before setting off. So great was the destruction and plundering that El Refugio never regained its wealth.

As the years passed, some soldiers seemed to have forgotten the early warnings of Governor Neve on how to get along with the Chumash. His advice to avoid causing them pain had led to over forty years of peace. Despite the epidemics which decimated their number, the Chumash had become good Christian farmers and vaqueros. They built missions and forts and they enthusiastically volunteered to fight Bouchard, eager to defend their "king, their country, and their religion." But in 1822 soldiers beat some neophytes at San Buenaventura so abusively that Father Senan feared an uprising, only "God delivered us . . . but the threat of a recurrence some other day is most alarming." The tensions between the gente de razon and the Chumash continued to mount.

Now you see this is the sort of justice they show us. We have advised him [Comandante de la Guerra] many times of the damage that the soldiers cause every year to our gardens; cutting down our wooden fences, treating us badly, robbing us of our watermelons and other fruits which we have planted, often beating the old men and women who care for them . . . but we got nowhere . . . we are called imposters and are told that we never tell the truth.

SANTA BARBARA CHUMASH, 1824
Related by Friar Ripoll (*Geiger*)

In February 1824 Valentin Cota unjustly, but nonetheless mercilessly flogged a neophyte at Santa Ines. He might as well have lit the torches the retaliating Chumash then used to burn the mission. The uprising spread like a brush fire to La Purisima where the Chumash took control of the mission from their armed guard and barricaded themselves against a military assault. At Santa Barbara the neophytes armed themselves, then fearing military reprisals, fled to the hills. Their worst fears were realized as soldiers killed innocent Chumash and trashed the mission.

The soldiers robbed with such a lack of shame that when the captain heard of it, he placed himself at a corner of the presidio and took some of the loot from them.

RIPOLL (*Geiger*)

Troops from Monterey joined those of Captain de la Guerra. Santa Ines and La Purisima were retaken and punishments meted out. But Santa Barbara was retaken only because no neophytes were there to resist. Soldiers pursued them into the interior where they fought, but little was gained since not one neophyte returned to the mission.

What are we to do at the mission since the soldiers have robbed all our belongings, seeds, etc.? We shall maintain ourselves with what God will provide for us in the open country.

SANTA BARBARA CHUMASH, 1824
(*Geiger*)

Not until the end of June, when amnesty was offered and a trusted priest reassured them, did the Chumash return to Santa Barbara. Even then not all returned—or ever would. After four turbulent months, the 1824 uprising was over.

Despite the earthquakes and uprisings, life along the channel was far from harsh for the gente de razon. Few ever died from violence and most lived a life of leisure. So good was their lifestyle that only a bit of prosperity was needed for Santa Barbara to flourish as a center of southern California gentility. Mexican free trade policy provided just the right stimulus.

Among the Mexicans there is no working class . . . and every rich man looks like a grandee, and every poor scamp like a brokendown gentleman.

RICHARD HENRY DANA, 1835

Brigs that once had landed in the dark of night at El Refugio now unfurled their sails in the harbor and anchored by sighting the glistening white and magnificent mission church. And the presidio walls once required against pirates gave way to the elegant homes of former officers like the Carrillos and the de la Guerras. The grandest of homes were sumptuously decorated with furnishings imported from China, Mexico, and New England. The town thrived and soon 200 adobes scattered "without order" around the presidio and

. . . it was no uncommon thing to find laces and satins in the houses of the most needy.

ALFRED ROBINSON (1846)

The presidio plaza became a center of entertainment, for Easter bullfights or Sunday ballgames played by the Chumash "Presidio" and "Mission" teams. Only the wealthiest could join in the waltzing at Don Jose de la Guerra's home, yet all participated in the pageantry of a wedding procession. While mission and presidio cannons traded salutations, a band would lead the newlyweds from the mission church to the festivities, and all the town would follow mounted on their gaily decorated horses. When Angustias de la Guerra married Manuel Jimeno the 20 Chumash musicians in attendance were specially dressed

. . . in a uniform of red jackets trimmed with yellow cord, white pantaloons made after the Turkish fashion and red caps of the Polish order.

ALFRED ROBINSON, 1833

If the entertainment in town became tiresome, the wealthy dons and their families could retreat to their ranches or plan a *merienda,* or picnic, at the Laguna Blanca. Filling a covered wagon with *tamales* and turkeys, roasted beef and mutton, the picnickers would ride into the country for a day of recreation.

A large white table-cloth was spread on the grass, upon which are tastefully arranged our different dishes . . . and around this we accommodated ourselves, some reclining, others seated upon the ground. At the conclusion of the dinner the boys amused us with a "toro" or bull . . . but he soon managed to escape, and made his way to the centre of the pond, where he remained quite secure from their torments. Being foiled in this amusement they commenced racing their horses, and gave us a good specimen of their superior skill in riding . . . others of the party scattered about in little groups, where the music of the guitar and singing seemed more attractive.

ROBINSON

Open trade brought not only prosperity, but a great diversity of peoples. Joseph Chapman, captured in the 1819 Bouchard raid, became one of the first United States residents when he married Guadalupe Ortega. But others, mostly from the hide and tallow ships, soon followed. Both the Englishman William Hartnell and the American Alfred Robinson married into the de la Guerra family and French, Portuguese and Chileans found the easy lifestyle much to their liking. The sea otter trade brought others—Hawaii Islanders, Aleuts, and even American beaver trappers like George Nidever who were the first to shoot otter while standing straight up in a rocking canoe.

. . . a number of trappers and hunters came into Southern California and settled down in various towns . . . the whole country was much excited over their hunter clothes, their rifles, their traps, and the strange stories they told of the deserts, and fierce Indians . . .

GUADALUPE VALLEJO (1890)

Perhaps such diversity was not completely new to Santa Barbara. While the likes of Don Jose de la Guerra traced his ancestry back to 14th-century Spain, other "Spaniards" traced theirs back into the timeless realm of pre-Columbian Mexico and pre-slavery Africa. With the Kentucky trappers and Boston hide traders, with the Carrillos and Ortegas, they too formed the gente de razon of Santa Barbara.

The population had grown to 1200 by the time Colonel Fremont and the California battalion raised the U.S. flag over Santa Barbara in 1846. But as Edwin Bryant tells us, it was hard to estimate the size of the town when it was "deserted of nearly all its population" and when most of its adobes were sealed tight and abandoned, with the exception of de la Guerra's. A force of Californios had planned to cut off Fremont with a Christmas Day ambush at Gaviota Pass. Forewarned by American residents, Fremont had marched his troops past Santa Ines Mission and through the treacherous San Marcos Pass instead, arriving in Santa Barbara molested by no more than torrential rains. The battalion rested a while in town, passing New Year's Day observing a Chumash procession from the mission fill "the empty and otherwise silent streets" with a rendition of *Yankee Doodle Dandy*. Finding no resistance in Santa Barbara and hearing rumors that the Californians were gathering to attack them at Buenaventura, the Americans continued down the coast. They found Ventura abandoned, too, with the exception of one unfortunate Spaniard.

About eight o'clock in the evening, while I was in my room talking with some ladies, several armed men entered it. One of them approached me, touched me on the shoulder and said 'You are a prisoner.' . . . I allowed myself to be led by these persons to the camp. What was my surprise, on my arrival there, to find that the only reception given me by Colonel Fremont was to tell me to prepare myself, for I was to be shot.

Don Jose Arnaz, 1847

After questioning Don Jose, Fremont freed the gentleman and departed from the channel coast. And so the region became part of the United States.

At first the U.S. flag brought few changes to Santa Barbara. The gold rush ended trade in otter skins and cattle hides, but it also focused American interests elsewhere. Few ships wasted time anchoring in the channel when their passengers and supplies brought heavy premiums for quick delivery to San Francisco. Although Santa Barbara was left to itself, its adobe houses with tile roofs still sheltered Spanish dons. And the dons, receiving exorbitant prices for their cattle now being sold to forty-niners as beef, lived in as lavish a style as ever. Under the golden sunshine of the south, the halcyon days of Santa Barbara lingered a few more years. Twenty-four years after his first visit as a sailor on a Boston brig, Richard Henry Dana returned, and while deploring his arrival on a "sail-less" steamship, was elated to find Santa Barbara as he remembered it.

The same bright blue ocean, and the surf making just the same monotonous, melancholy roar, and the same dreamy town, and gleaming white mission, as when we beached our boat for the first time, riding over the breakers . . .

Dana, 1859

Sights

Towering oil platforms may have replaced the masts of Boston clippers in the channel, yet sea lions continue to swim in the coves of the Channel Islands, and the weather remains as "serene and pleasant" as Archibald Menzies found it in 1793. Surviving are too few Chumash and gone are the Californian dons, but Indian paintings cover the rocks and caves of the mountains, cattle and horses still graze in the Santa Ynez valley. Earthquakes have continued to do their damage, the one in 1925 so devastated Santa Barbara that it produced a new town, one renovated and rebuilt in keeping with its Spanish past. Today the beautiful resort of Santa Barbara successfully blends the pleasures of its seaside location with handsome red-tiled adobes and a magnificent mission church. Brief excursions take you down the coast to the mission church at Ventura, and up the coast past El Refugio beach, through smugglers' canyons, and to other missions, including the completely restored and fascinating La Purisima.

Historic Santa Barbara

Although most of the historic sights cluster in the two areas of Old Town and Mission Canyon, the lovely resort certainly warrants some scenic walking along Cabrillo Boulevard by the sea, and some drives through the foothills and the posh communities of Montecito and Hope Ranch. The Santa Barbara Conference and Visitors Bureau (see "Directory") offers self-guided tours of these areas with its town maps and 12-m driving tour. Also the historical society offers **guided walks** through town (966–1601) and El Cuartel at the Presidio has self-guided tour maps on historic architecture.

★★★ El Pueblo Viejo (Old Town) □ In the center of downtown where the street names commemorate the wealthiest of the gente de razon—De la Guerra, Carrillo, and Ortega—survive the homes of comandantes and the barracks of soldiers all intermingled with art galleries, boutiques, and sidewalk cafes. Barely a block exists without historic plaques recalling the past, and two museums further bring to life the Santa Barbara of old.

Just off State Street is the 1826 home of Santa Barbara's most famous commander, Captain Jose de la Guerra, who not only defended Santa Barbara but also, according to Jose Arnaz, "was a handkerchief for the tears and the refuge of all the poor." Devoutly religious and respected by all, the captain also knew how to extend his hospitality. The **★ Casa de la Guerra** (11 and 15 De la Guerra St.) was so much the center of social life, that barely a foreign visitor failed to mention its gatherings—whether Christmas pageants in the garden or Chumash dance performances in the courtyard. Perhaps the most famous of these events was the wedding of Alfred Robinson to de la Guerra's youngest daughter. For that great event, the mission bells rang out and Robinson's company ship let off a salute of twenty-three guns that "echoed among the surrounding hills and over the bay." After the ceremony, began the fandango that continued for three days at the Casa de la Guerra.

The bride's father's house was the principal one in the place, with a large court in front, upon which a tent was built, capable of containing several hundred people. As we drew near, we heard the accustomed sound of violins and guitars and saw a great motion of people within. Going in, we found nearly all the people of the town—men, women, and children—collected and crowded together leaving barely room for the dancers . . . Our sailor dresses—and we took great pains to have them neat and shipshape—were much admired, and we were invited . . . to give them an American dance, but after the ridiculous figure some of our countrymen cut in dancing after the Mexicans, we thought it best to leave it to their imaginations. Our agent [Robinson], with a tight black swallow-tailed coat just imported from Boston, a high stiff cravat, looking as if he had been pinned and skewered, with only his feet and hands left free, took the floor just after Bandini, and we thought they had had enough of Yankee grace.

RICHARD HENRY DANA, 1836

De la Guerra's house and plaza remain central to festivities, especially each August when Santa Barbarans dress in Spanish costumes and produce pageants and parades during the **Old Spanish Days Fiesta.** The ample house now holds numerous shops and a restaurant and the core of **El Paseo,** a pedestrian arcade on De la Guerra Street that also includes the 1849 **Orena Adobe** (39 De la Guerra).

Continuing east on De la Guerra you pass a few other old adobes, now commercial establishments, before arriving at the corner of Santa Barbara Street and the ★★ **Historical Society Museum** (136 E. De la Guerra). The Spanish Room here is just filled with wonderful heirlooms, such as Anita de la Guerra's (Senora Robinson) wedding dress, portraits of Santa Barbara's finest, old silver stirrups and chests, and religious art. The museum courtyard is a reconstruction of a rancho patio, but for the real thing take a few more steps into the beautiful old

★ **patio** formed by rough beams and walls of the **Casa de Covarrubias** (715 Santa Barbara) where the last Mexican congress met and the **Historic Fremont Adobe** next door, which explains why there was a last Mexican congress at all. Actually both buildings are older than the U.S. conquest by Fremont in 1846. The Case de Covarrubias was built in 1817 by Domingo Carrillo for his married daughter, and the Historic Adobe dates from 1836 when it was occupied by Governor Pio Pico's sister. Neither building is open to the public, but a walk into the rustic patio separating them is not only permitted but worthwhile. *While the courtyard and patio can be visited at most hours, the museum is open Tues.–Fri. noon–5 p.m.; weekends 1–5 p.m.; closed holidays; tours Wed. and weekends at 1:30 p.m.; donations; 966–1601.*

Walking north on Santa Barbara Street you approach ★★ **El Presidio State Park** □ (E. Canon Perdido at Santa Barbara). Since all the California presidios had basically been lost, with the exception of a few old adobes here and the chapel in Monterey, the ongoing archaeological reconstruction of Santa Barbara's fort offers a unique opportunity to see one of early California's most important institutions. In **El Cuartel** (122 E. Canon St.) you visit the barracks that formed the west wall of the fort and that now constitute the oldest building (1788) in Santa Barbara. There is an exhibit on the soldiers' quarters, a model of the presidio, and a museum shop with good history books. Across the street is the ever developing north side of the presidio, anchored by the **Caneda Adobe** (123 E. Canon Perdido), the second oldest structure in town, and once quarters for officers and their families. Here there are some exhibits as well as a 14-minute audio visual. Next door is the padre's quarters, followed by the reconstructed chapel, complete with lively, trompe l'oeil paintings. Other parts of the presidio will be excavated and reconstructed, including the comandante's house. The only other remnant is the **Rochin Adobe** (Santa Barbara between Canon Perdido and De la Guerra) that was built from the original adobe bricks of the presidio chapel, but now is covered with wood. *The State Park is open weekdays 10:30 a.m.–4:30 p.m.; weekends noon–4 p.m.; closed major holidays; donations; 966–9719.*

A few blocks away is the ★ **Hill-Carrillo Adobe** (11 E. Carrillo St. near Anacapa), home to both Anglo-Americans and Hispano-Americans. Built in 1826 by Daniel Hill of Massachusetts for his wife Rafaela Ortega, the adobe had the first wooden floor in Santa Barbara, and today it is still elegantly furnished with many trade items. In 1833, the adobe became the birthplace of the first Californian born to Anglo-American parents (a daughter of Thomas Larkin, U.S. consult to California). Later it was owned by Guillermo Carrillo who "excelled on the guitar." *Open Tues.–Fri. noon–4 p.m.; free; 963–1873.*

There are many other adobes and more recent Spanish revival buildings to be seen as you walk around town and shop on State Street. But none warrants more of a visit than the 1929 **Santa Barbara County Courthouse** (Anacapa and Anapamu). Its architecture is one of the most striking examples of California's Spanish revival style, complete with Moorish ceilings and lavishly tiled walls. The second floor is decorated with murals of early California history, the most exceptional ones are in the beautiful *Supervisor's Room.* Up the elevator and around a small staircase you can visit the *clock tower* with its good views over the rooftops of town to the harbor. *Open 9 a.m.–4:30 p.m. daily; self-guided tour brochure for fee; donation; 962–6464).* Just a block away is the **Museum of Art** (Anapamu near State) with its diverse collection of American art, photography, and antiquities *Tues.–Sat. 11 a.m.–5 p.m.; Sunday noon–5 p.m.; closed major holidays; free; 963–4365.* And two blocks up State, past fashionable shops and restaurants is the **Arlington Theater** (1317 State St.), a thirties movie palace with a trompe l'oeil Spanish village for an interior that seems roofed only by the starry sky (open for performances; 966–4566).

Harbor □ At the foot of State and Chapala streets was the old port, lined with beaches belonging to the mission's Rancho de la Playa. Before the Spaniards, there was a Chumash village. And before the Chumash culture, a simpler one that lasted thousands of years. The mound created by ancient cultures has been covered by modern buildings; the beach remains although the mission no longer owns it. No matter the changes, you can't look at this harbor without conjuring up the beautiful ships that once arrived here.

. . . we saw a vessel under full sail, standing into the bay. The beautiful symmetry of her spars, sails, and rigging, added to the elegance of her hull, her trim appearance, her sky-sails and man-of-war semblance, called forth a variety of remarks from the bystanders . . . and as a gust of wind struck her sails, she lay over and displayed the smooth and bright appearance of her copper . . .

ROBINSON, 1832

A good place to view the harbor as well as the surrounding mountains is from the end of **Stearns Wharf,** an extension of State Street. The wharf was originally built in 1872, then restored in 1981 with shops and restaurants. (Fee for parking on wharf, but walk on for free.) To the east, Cabrillo Boulevard continues along a good expanse of beach where artists like to display their work on Sundays. Farther east, along the route of the Camino Real, is the **Andree Clark Bird Refuge** (1400 E. Cabrillo Blvd.) with walking and bike trails. To the west of State Street, the boulevard extends along yet more beach, past a *windsurfing* area and on to Cabrillo Street where you can rent a *sail boat* (962–2826), or take a *cruise* of the harbor (969–5217), or simply walk along the breakwater in the area of the Yacht Harbor.

★★★ **Mission Santa Barbara** ☐ *Laguna and Los Olivos* ☐ Once the mission lands extended from El Refugio to the west and continued east for almost 20 miles. Even today mission adobes that sheltered Chumash cowboys can be found in Hope Ranch and Montecito, and remnants of the mission's elaborate water system can be seen a few miles away in the Botanic Garden (see below). Though the mission, like all others, lost most of its land holdings as a result of secularization, Santa Barbara was the only one to be continuously owned and used by the Franciscans. As a result its church and art has been so well-preserved that today you can visit this magnificent stone church, called "Queen of the Missions," and appreciate the Frenchman Duhaut-Cilly's remark that

From the roadstead we could have taken it for a chateau of medieval times, with its lofty openings and belfry . . . We had not expected to find in this country otherwise removed from the fine things of Europe, this sort of luxury.

1827

The present church was constructed after the 1812 earthquake. Fray Antonio Ripoll found his inspiration for its neoclassical architecture from a book by Vetruvius in the mission library. From Vetruvius' drawings of Doric columns and Roman temples, and with the supervision of a carpenter and the skill of Chumash artisans, the present church was designed and built around the older, damaged ones. The unusually beautiful new church gave the Santa Barbarans an excellent excuse to express their religious devotion in a great celebration. Fray Antonio himself, arranged for a rocket-maker from San Diego to begin working months in advance of the dedication, so that there would be enough firecrackers to make a brilliant showing. Finally the 1820 dedication took place, with all in attendance—the governor from Monterey, Captain de la Guerra and all his troops, Indian musicians and dancers from nearby missions, and "food, drink, and shelter were given to all who asked."

The Te Deum was chanted . . . amid the great illumination of all the altars . . . Then, in succession, were illuminated the (azoteas) housetops, the corredors [arcades], and the tower, the last-mentioned having many flags of all colors. Immediately, the musicians of the three missions passed through the corredors, where they played at will for about two continuous hours. Meanwhile, rockets, serpents, firecrackers were fired . . . All this was repeated on the two following nights. Immediately after going out, the soldiers, cavalry, as well as infantry, continued the festivities . . . while the Indians had their dances . . . A man was appointed to serve the wine and brandy, until all had enough.

FRANCISCO SUNER, 1820
(*Englehardt*)

Today the mission facade with its rose-colored pilasters and mortar lines looks very trendy, almost like a post-modern building. In addition to the church with its wonderful trompe l'oeil altarpiece, the convento has been converted into an extensive **museum** with rooms of colonial art, mission crafts and memorabilia. Also you can still see the elaborate Moorish fountain, the peaceful garden, and the cemetery (containing the remains of many of the illustrious—de la Guerras, Covarrubias, Orenas—as well as 4000 Chumash neophytes). Or you can wander about some mission ruins nearby. In July, the **annual crafts fair** takes place here. *Open Mon.–Sat. 9 a.m.–5 p.m.; Sun. 1–5 p.m.; closed major holidays; self-guided tour materials in gift shop; fee; 682–4713. Located just over 1m from downtown, you reach the mission by following signs from Santa Barbara Street.*

Mission Canyon □ Following signs from the mission, in ½m you come to the ★ **Museum of Natural History** (2559 Puesta del Sol Rd., just off Mission Canyon Rd.). Among its many collections is an excellent one on the Chumash that includes a plank canoe and dioramas showing their lifestyle at the time of Spanish contact. (Open weekdays 9 a.m.–5 p.m.; weekends and holidays 10 a.m.–5 p.m.; closed major holidays; donation; 682–4711.) About another mile along Mission Canyon Road you come to the 75 acres of the **Botanic Garden**. The 5 miles of trails here meander among plants and trees native to California. Also here you can see the old mission dam and parts of the aqueduct that once joined it to the mission and its fields. The gardens are at their most beautiful in the spring and summer, but they're open all year 8 a.m.–sunset (free).

While out in this part of the foothills called the Riviera, you might consider taking the scenic drive through the hills covered with eucalyptus and orange trees, palms and bougainvillea, by following Alameda Padre Serra Road next to the mission, and then following **Scenic Drive** signs to Montecito. Or you might continue up Foothill Road to the oak scrub of Los Padres National Forest and the Painted Cave (see "Excursions" below).

Accommodations

Three exceptional resorts have long attracted travelers to Santa Barbara. The most famous is the exceptional **Santa Barbara Biltmore,** next to the sea in Montecito. Now owned by Marriott, the Biltmore maintains its old Spanish ambience, its warm and attentive service, its acres of beautiful gardens. The lobby contains antique furnishings, fine carpets, and old handpainted Spanish tiles. Sitting in well-proportioned lounges you can take tea, read the papers off their wooden racks, dine, dance, or just relax while looking at the sea. Most of the 230 units overlook the tranquil gardens; some have fireplaces, others terraces or balconies, some are separate cottages, and all are lovely. Three restaurants, lounges, and boutiques. Private beach club with Olympic size pool, another large pool, Jacuzzi, tennis, putting green, shuffleboard, and other games. Access to golf and horseback riding. Valet parking. ***Very expensive.*** Write 1260 Channel Drive, CA 93108; 969–2261; 800–228–9290 U.S. To reach Channel Drive, turn off Cabrillo Blvd. just past the Andree Clark Bird Refuge, or exit US 101 at Olive Mill Road. The Biltmore is 4 m from downtown.

The other two resorts are nestled in the foothills of the Santa Ynez mountains. Certainly the **San Ysidro Ranch** has to be one of the most unpretentious retreats with its homey old lounge (the only spot with a TV), its old adobe from mission days, and its dining room which once served as a citrus packing house. But the 550 delightful acres of bridle and hiking trails, the 39 very private cottages, some with Jacuzzis and all with wood-burning fireplaces, have attracted many of the famous, including John and Jackie Kennedy during their honeymoon. Restaurant (jackets required for dinner), lounge with dancing. Pool, tennis, and horseback riding. Parking. ***Very expensive.*** Write 900 San Ysidro Lane,

Montecito 93108; 969–5046. Located about 9m from downtown, 5m north of the San Ysidro Road exit of US 101.

More manicured is **El Encanto Hotel and Garden Villas** perched above Santa Barbara in the Riviera section close to the mission. The pool, lobby and restaurant have fantastic views of red-tiled roofs and the harbor, and numerous celebrities have enjoyed the privacy and quiet of the 100 cottages, found along meandering garden paths on 9 acres of grounds. Many of the cottages have kitchens and wood-burning fireplaces, and all have at least two separate rooms. Restaurant and lounge with entertainment. Pool and tennis. Parking. ***Very expensive***. Write 1900 Lasuen Road, CA 93103; 687–5000. Located ¼m from mission, just off Alameda Padre Serra.

If its even more of a mountain retreat you desire, check the inn at Los Olivos (see ''Excursions'' below). But if you prefer a location within walking distance of El Pueblo Viejo and the sophisticated shops and restaurants of upper State Street, consider the **Hotel Upham**. Established in 1871, the Upham is Santa Barbara's oldest inn. As you sit in the Victorian lobby over your complimentary breakfast, or enjoy the free wine and cheese in the garden gazebo with the cat, you can well understand how Agatha Christie and other notables chose this quiet spot for their stay in Santa Barbara. The 39 rooms all have private baths, some have gas fireplaces and four-poster beds, and some are suites. Restaurant. Parking. ***Expensive***. Write 1404 De la Vina St., CA 93101; 962–0058. Other inns are scattered in this neighborhood, so you might want to contact the Conference and Visitors Bureau for the Bed and Breakfast listing.

Certainly one of the best buys is the Motel 6 just off Cabrillo Blvd. and within a block of the east beach. But further west on Cabrillo Blvd. around lower Castillo Street are others to seek out, including a Best Western and a TraveLodge. The real **motel row,** however, is about 3m north of town on State Street.

Restaurants

There's fine food in Santa Barbara, from upper State Street all the way to the end near the harbor where former mission soup kitchens are quickly being replaced by trendy restaurants. On the upper end near the Arlington Theater is the very French, but casual **Maison Robert** (1325 State St.; lunch Mon.–Fri., dinner daily; 962–1325; ***moderately expensive***) that serves traditional duck a l'orange and seafood in pastry shells.

Toward the opposite end is the innovative **Chalkboard** (621 State St.; dinner Tues.–Sat.; 962–2773; ***moderate to moderately expensive***) that might be changing ownership. Check to see if it is still serving such nouvelle delights as rotisseried duck with apple chutney and exotic California pizza. Also very good is the **Wine Cask** (813 Anacapa St.; lunch and dinner Tues.–Sat.; 962–1128; ***moderate to moderately expensive***) with its historic location in El Paseo, its terrific wine offerings, and its fine, if limited, daily offerings of nouvelle California cuisine such as a delicious linguini with sun dried tomatoes, black olives, and pine nuts or grilled lamb with shallots, dill, and lemon demiglace. Popular with Santa Barbarans is **Louie's Restaurant** (1404 De la Vina in the Upham Hotel; dinner Tues.–Sat.; 963–7003; in the low end of ***moderately expensive***), candlelit and cozy, and serving seasonal dishes such as an appetizer of wild mushroom won tons or roast pork loin with fig sauce.

For seafood consider **Famous Enterprise Fish** (255 State St.; lunch and dinner daily; 963–8651; ***moderately expensive***) for their mesquite grilled fish. More family style is the **Moby Dick** (Stearns Wharf, open all day; 963–0549; ***moderate***) with its harbor views and local seafood. Also with views yet more elegant is **La Sala** lounge at the Biltmore with its seafood bar, complimentary appetizers, and music during cocktails (5–7:30 p.m.). Here a light dinner of shrimp cocktail or raw clams supplemented with the free hors d'oevres can be not only quite moderate, but delightful.

Also popular in Santa Barbara is Mexican food. The **Acapulco** (1114 State St; 11 a.m.–10 p.m. daily; 963–3469; ***inexpensive***), located in the swishy La Arcada mall offers a patio cantina as well as indoor dining on all sorts of Mexican dishes including tasty pork and green chile burritos with salsa ranchero. Less conveniently located but also very popular is **La Tolteca Tortilla Factory** (614 E. Haley St.; Tues.–Sat. 8 a.m.–8 p.m., Sun. till 7 p.m.; 963–0847; ***inexpensive***) with the usual choice of enchiladas, burritos and tacos and freshly made tortillas.

There are numerous spots to snack, lunch or breakfast around the historic center. Near the presidio is **Main Squeeze** (138 E. Canon Perdido; Mon.–Fri. 11 a.m.–9:30 p.m.; 966–5365; ***inexpensive***) with a juice bar and offerings such as pesto pasta salad for lunch, and vegetarian lasagna and tacos for dinner. Across from El Paseo is the pleasant patio restaurant called the **Presidio Cafe** (812 Anacapa; breakfast and lunch daily; 966–2428; ***moderate***) that serves crepes and quiche to a classical music background. Nearby on State Street you can drink a fresh juice at **Las Aguas Frescas** (#716, open 8 a.m.–7 p.m.) then head to **Ruby's Cafe** (#734; 7 a.m.–5 p.m.; ***inexpensive***) where delicious breakfast is served all day. You can also arrange a picnic by shopping at the **gourmet shop** of the Wine Cask (see above) with its delicacies like cherry tomatoes filled with pesto and excellent wine selection or order a box lunch from **Chio's** (128 A E. Canon Perdido; ***inexpensive***), where the sandwiches and very tasty gourmet salad are more than ample.

To round out your visit you might consider enjoying a cocktail hour view from the terrace of **El Encanto Hotel** or taking in the Sunday brunch at the **Biltmore.**

Excursions

Near Santa Barbara: Southeast

A trip along the lower channel coast follows much the same route as Captain Portola and Friar Crespi. And it passes near villages bearing the nicknames given them by the 1769 expedition—''Carpinteria'' recalls the boat-building witnessed there by the Spaniards and ''Pitas (whistles) Point'' the sleepless night the Spaniards passed listening to the Chumash play their ''doleful pipes.'' Today US 101 takes you to Rincon Point, then a scenic road hugs the coastline to Ventura much like the old Camino Real that often was washed out by the tides.

The road thither is partly over the hard sandy beach, and . . . when the tide is low, it is possible to perform the whole journey over this smooth level.

ROBINSON

From Ventura you can arrange trips to the Channel Islands or plan some meanderings into the Ojai Valley, returning to Santa Barbara by Lake Casitas on CA 150 and rejoining US 101 near Rincon Point. The entire land loop covers about 75 m. Pleasant restaurants can be found in Ventura and Ojai. Picknicking can be enjoyed at the beaches or in Los Padres National Forest, north of Ojai. Accommodations are convenient in Ventura.

Carpinteria □ Although modern housing has subdivided and replaced the Chumash village here, the ''magnificent valley'' described by Cabrillo remains as the **Carpinteria State Beach** (exit marked on US 101; 684–1855), a vast beach with calm swimming waters (and camping, picnicking, and fishing too). In the small town the **Carpinteria Valley Museum of History** (956 Maple Ave.) offers interesting exhibits of Chumash home furnishings and artifacts. *Open 1:30–4 p.m. except Sat. 11 a.m.–4 p.m. and closed Mon.; 684–3112. To reach the museum exit US 101 at Casitas Pass Rd., about 10m from Santa Barbara, and follow signs.*

Ventura □ It was here that Cabrillo saw his first Chumash canoes and so named the village after them, "Pueblo de las Canoas." But Ventura's history and final name came from Father Serra's founding in 1782 of his ninth and last mission, San Buenaventura. Perhaps it is only appropriate that the town bears just an abbreviated form of the mission name, because in the early years a vaster region belonged to the mission, one of the wealthiest and most productive of the chain. Only after secularization and Jose Arnaz' purchase of the mission did a town appear, but it was too tiny to be more than a hamlet—a few houses along the Camino Real (itself no more than a bridle path), that led from the mission buildings to the river, then on to Santa Barbara. And the ranches that replaced the mission were as far-flung as the mission lands had been. Today one town adobe, the ★ **Casa de Ortega** (215 W. Main St.), remains in the pleasant old section near the mission. Even it is a diminished version of the original (built in 1857) since a flood washed away the orchards that once surrounded it. You can see the rustic interior, furnished with period pieces. *Open 10 a.m.–5 p.m.; free.* There's also a ranch, now encompassed by the town golf course, that has been restored down to the family chapel and furnished. This ★ **Olivas Adobe** (4200 Olivas Park Dr.), built by Don Raymundo Olivas in 1847 for his family of 22 children, offers an earlier, smaller adobe, too, a visitors center, and pleasant grounds. *Open weekdays 10 a.m.–3 p.m.; weekends till 4 p.m.; free; 654–7837; located ¾m off E. Harbor Blvd. near harbor.* Although some of the ranch adobes in the Ojai Valley (see below) have also been refurbished, including that of Jose Arnaz, they are not open to the public.

Little remains of the ★ **Mission San Buenaventura** (211 E. Main St.; follow California St. off US 101, then left onto Main) other than the church now that Figueroa Plaza, old book shops and antique stores have replaced its once fabulous 17 acres of gardens.

The garden of Buenaventura far exceeding anything I had before met with in these regions . . . not one species having yet been sown, or planted, that had not flourished . . . apples, pears, figs, oranges, grapes, peaches and pomengranates, together with the plantain, banana, coconut, sugar cane, indigo . . . All these were flourishing in the greatest health and perfection, though separated from the seaside only by two

The Sonoma Coast

ALL PHOTOS COURTESY OF LAWRENCE FOSTER

A 19th-century clipper ship, San Diego

Chumash baskets

Mission sculpture

San Luis Rey Mission

Some 20th-century sailing vessels, Ventura

Hides drying at La Purisima Mission

Bells at San Miguel Mission

Details of San Gabriel Mission

Santa Barbara, with its modern Spanish-style architecture

or three fields of corn that were cultivated within a few yards of the surf.

CAPTAIN GEORGE VANCOUVER, 1783

Still to be enjoyed are the magnificent Moorish side door of the church and nearby garden fountain. A small **museum** contains Chumash baskets and religious relics and offers self-guided tour maps of the church and garden (open 10 a.m.–5 p.m. except Sun. till 4 p.m.; closed holidays; fee; 643–4318). Just a block from the church is the ★ **Ventura County Historical Museum** (100 E. Main) that includes Chumash and Spanish artifacts in constantly changing exhibits, as well as displays on farming and the oil industry that have become so important to the region. (Open Tues.–Sun. 10 a.m.–5 p.m.; free; 653–0323.) Across the street is the museum's ★ **Archaeological Dig** exposing not only parts of the old mission and bowls and beads obtained through the China trade, but also earlier remains of native Californians. (Same hours as museum; audio-visual shows.) A few more blocks along Main you come to the Ortega adobe mentioned above. Behind the church, you can drive on Palm St., then left onto Pole and wind your way up **La Loma de la Cruz** (Hill of the Cross) where Padre Serra erected a cross in 1782. While a new cross has replaced the original one, a visit to the hill is worthwhile for its view of the town and coast.

Closer to the sea, the **Ventura State Beach** (down California St. to Harbor Dr.) offers miles of sand and surf as well as a promenade for strolling. Traveling east on Harbor Drive for 3m you come to Spinnaker Road and the **harbor** area. On one side are the dunes of **McGrath State Beach,** a favorite morning spot with surfers, and on the other is **Harbor Village** with its yachts, restaurants, and shops. Here you can rent a boat or take a weekend harbor cruise (642–7753), or arrange for whale watching during the winter.

Hundreds of the grampus whale are sporting a mile or two distant from the land, spouting up water and spray to a great height, in columns resembling steam from the escape-pipes of steamboats.

LT. EDWIN BRYANT, 1847

Also here, at the end of Spinnaker Dr., is the headquarters of the **Channel Islands National Park** where you can visit the models of this great wilderness area and see films describing the islands (1901 Spinnaker

Dr., open 9 a.m.–5 p.m.; free). Trips to the islands are easily arranged through Island Packers (642–1393).

Brochures and maps of Ventura can be obtained at the **Visitors Center** (785 S. Seaward Ave.; 648–2075), just off US 101 at the Seaward exit. You can picnic at the beach, enjoy Mexican food at **La Mission Restaurant** just a block east of the church, or explore the many spots at Harbor Village where the northern Italian cuisine at **Berto's** (open daily lunch and dinner; the downstairs is ***moderate,*** the upstairs ***moderately expensive*** and with slightly different menu) is particularly good. The linguini with clams was one of the best I've ever tasted and the tagliarini fruitti di mare was deliciously full of seafood. Accommodations are plentiful in Ventura with a **motel row** clustering around Harbor Drive near Seaward. And the modern resort complex of **Fairfield Harbortown Hotel** offers over 200 units at its location convenient to Harbor Village. Some of the units have harbor views, some are suites with kitchenettes and fireplaces. Restaurant, lounge with entertainment and dancing. Pool, tennis, windsurfing nearby, boat rentals, beaches and golf. Parking. ***Expensive.*** Write 1050 Schooner Dr., CA 93001; 654–1212, 800–772–2243 U.S., 800–622–1212 CA.

Ventura is located on US 101, 27m southeast of Santa Barbara and 70m northwest of L.A.

Ojai Valley □ Following Ojai Freeway (CA 33) out of old Ventura, you pass through an area once very much the domain of the Buenaventura mission. Just ½m east of the road along Canada Larga Road, you can see ruins of the mission aqueduct that formerly spanned 7 miles. Staying on CA 33 you pass Casitas, named "little houses" after the Chumash village that used to cluster here around a small Spanish chapel. Eventually you pass Rancho Arnaz, where Don Jose Arnaz retired in the 1850's after being terrorized by Fremont then stripped of his ownership of the San Buenaventura mission. Don Jose later related his loss of property at the hand of the U.S. in the person of Colonel Stevenson who "even took away my saddle horse, leaving me with my family buried in poverty." It seems that years later Stevenson attempted to arrange for reparations, but the proud Spaniard "repulsed his offers."

From CA 33, turn east on CA 150 in order to reach the charming town of **Ojai** *(oh high),* 12m north of Ventura. Located at the base of the craggy foothills of the Santa Ana mountains, Ojai is home to a number of resorts and inns and boasts a flourishing art colony that mounts outdoor exhibitions for the public each Sunday. You can visit some of the artists' studios by obtaining a listing from the **Art Center** (113 S. Montgomery; 646–8117), just off the main street of E. Ojai. Or check the **visitors center** (338 E. Ojai; open daily) for local happenings and even for information on picnicking spots in **Los Padres National Forest,** just 5m further north on CA 33, through oak groves and orchards. Or simply enjoy a stroll in Ojai, relaxing with a pleasant meal at **Antonio's** (106 S. Montgomery across from the Arts Center; open lunch and dinner daily; 646–6353; ***moderate***), its patio a favorite spot for tostadas and its daily specials offering more than just Mexican fare. On Sundays there are often mariachis strolling through the restaurant.

Near Santa Barbara: West and North

When Portola set out from Santa Barbara looking for the harbor of Monterey, he forged the Camino Real along the "extremely delightful" coast, stopping at Chumash villages where today there are numerous fine state beaches—Goleta, El Refugio, and Gaviota. Near Gaviota and about 35 m west of Santa Barbara, the original Camino Real continued to where La Purisima Mission would eventually be built. Today's US 101 veres to the north and provides access to both La Purisima and Santa Ines missions, near the town of Buellton. After visiting both missions, the modern traveler can follow much of Fremont's route by looping back to Santa Barbara through Los Padres National Forest and ranch country, passing near Lake Cachuma and the Chumash Painted Cave on CA 154, and reentering town via the San Marcos Pass. Here Lt. Bryant forgot his soldiery duties in 1846 to exclaim, "A lovely and more picturesque landscape I never beheld." The entire trip, including backtracking from La Purisima, covers a distance of about 120m and can be traveled in a day trip, in either direction, of course. Or a mountain retreat can be planned at the lovely inn in Los Olivos. There's picnicking at the beaches and La Purisima, bakeries and delicatessens in Solvang. And there's fine dining in Los Olivos.

El Refugio □ The Ortegas moved their adobes into the safety of the surrounding canyons after Bouchard's raid, leaving the beach free for its current state facilities of camping and picnicking. The surrounding land remains much as Padre Crespi described it in 1769.

We traveled about a league along the beach, but afterward left it and made the rest of the march, which covered about three leagues, over high hilles, cut off from the sea in some places; and we were frequently interrupted by ravines and gullies by which the mountains discharge waters.

Today US 101 spans the canyons, bypassing the rugged terrain used by friars and neophytes, smugglers and soldiers, and even the more recent stagecoaches. Never does old California seem so removed as when US 101 provides a view of the little that remains of the famous old ranch house, nestled in the canyon far from today's byways and yesteryear's pirates (about 2½ m north of Lompoc exit, 5 m south of Buellton).

★★★ **La Purisima Concepcion Mission** □ After the earthquake of 1812 destroyed the first of La Purisima's buildings, the mission was moved a bit to the north, right on the Camino Real as it passed north to San Luis Obispo. Disaster struck the new mission again, in the form of drought; then again, in the form of fire; and then again with the 1824 uprisings when the military repeatedly battered the adobe walls with a four-pounder.

Protected by thirty-three infantrymen, they began firing at about 8 a.m. always advancing until we reached within range of our muskets. From their loopholes the Indians poured out a lively gun-fire at us with their one pound cannon, and also sent out a shower of arrows. Boldly despising that resistance, the artillery replied with brilliantly directed shots.

JOSE MARIA ESTRADA, 1824

Perhaps so many disasters prevented the friars from ever completing their building plan, because La Purisima is the only mission not arranged around a quadrangle. Secularization brought about further destruction as sheep grazed in the gardens and gathered in the church, and rain melted away the roofless adobe walls. By the turn of the century La Purisima appeared no more than a ruin with a few arches standing brave and birds nesting in the church. Today it is the most authentically reconstructed mission and boasts not only the church and friary, but also the soldiers' barracks, the soap factory and tannery, the shops and resevoirs so essential to the self-sustaining missions (see background to *Along the Camino Real: Mission Life*).

. . . the Mission now has 10,000 sheep and as many cattle, that is to say, much wool for clothing, much meat to eat in the pozole *and rations, much tallow for sale, and money to obtain invoices and so forth. We count on $5,000 for goods from Mexico this year, and some for securing statues for saints . . .*

FRAY MARIANO PAYERAS, 1810

At La Purisima not only has each part of the mission been reconstructed, but it has been furnished to the original use even down to livestock in the corrals.

This eleventh of the missions, founded by Friar Laseun in 1787, now is a state historic park with a 1-mile self-guided tour, museum, and picnicking facilities in a beautiful rural valley dominated by the Santa Ynez mountains. In the summer two **special events** take place: Mission Life Days (end of May usually) and Living History Tours. On December 8, the celebration of the mission's founding occurs with an evening service during which *luminarias,* candles glowing through paper bags, light the pathways and old church. (Open daily 9 a.m.–5 p.m.; closed major holidays; fee; 733–3713; or write RFD Box 102, Purisima Rd., Lompoc 93436.)

Ruins of the **old Purisima** can be found in the nearby town of Lompoc. At the south end of F Street, evidence of the great 1812 earthquake can be seen in a gash through a nearby hill. Also there's the small **Lompoc Museum** (200 S. H St.) with exhibits on California Indians and local history (Tues.–Fri. 1–5 p.m.; weekends 1–4 p.m.; donations; 736–3888). The real reason to visit Lompoc, however, is to see the vast fields of flowers that bloom spring and summer around this town that produces half the flower seeds in the U.S. (**Flower Festival** held last week in June. Write the Chamber of Commerce, 119 E. Cypress Ave., CA 93436; 736–4567, located just across from the museum.)

The mission can be reached by exiting west at Buellton from US 101 and continuing 15m. Or you can approach from the Lompoc exit on 101, continuing on CA 1 for 19m to Lompoc, then turning east and traveling 2m to the mission.

★ **Mission Santa Ines** □ In 1804 when the other Channel missions were flourishing, Santa Ines was established to convert those Chumash living in the beautiful mountain valleys away from the coast.

. . . this mission will be less visited than the others, because it will be necessary to pass the Sierra . . . or to go by way of the rancho of the Ortegas. The one as well as the other is more inconvenient and difficult than the road along the beach to Monterey.

Friar Estevan Tapis, 1803

Vaqueros driving herds eventually beat a path to the other missions and a few visitors did make their way to Santa Ines, including Joseph Chapman who after pirating with Bouchard became a jack of all trades at the mission, building a grist mill here in 1820. Yet the mission remained isolated and small, even though its cattle herds flourished, ranging over a vast plain protected by two chains of the sierras. The region remains great ranching country and each spring the Spanish tradition of the round-up is commemorated by **Los Rancheros Visitadores**—a group of ranchers and famous people (Ronald Reagan is an honorary member)—who end their annual riding and camping trek in the Santa Ynes mountains with a blessing from the priest of this mission.

More easily visited by todays highways, the mission rewards its many visitors with a fine church interior decorated with trompe l'oeil paintings of false doors and balustrades, of pretend marble and ornate refinements so otherwise unavailable. The museum contains some manuscripts of the music performed by the neophyte choir and orchestra. Here, as in all the missions, the descendants of those Chumash who caused Portola a sleepless night by their flute playing

. . . the hole of the flute is the pathway to thought

FERNANDO LIBRADA
A Chumash, born 1804

and who so entertained the first Spaniards with their chanting and dancing, learned the refinements of the Catholic liturgy.

They no longer hear their chants nor instruments, but in their place are heard devout songs and harmonized instruments. The violin, *the* baja de violin, *the violin (instruments made by the neophytes themselves, as also the* tambora*), the sweet German flute, the trompa, the bandola, are those they know and use in the functions of the Church. They are fond of music, and they learn easily by memory the sonatas which they hear, or which are taught them*

TAPIS, 1814

There's a recorded self-guided tour to the facilities here that some find jarring, but you can also proceed on your own. *Open Mon.–Sat. 9:30 a.m.–4:30 p.m., till 5 p.m. in summer; Sun. noon–5 p.m.; closed major holidays; fee; 688–4815. The mission is located at 1760 Mission Dr., just a few blocks east of downtown* **Solvang,** a larger than real Danish community—built in storybook-style architecture with windmills seemingly surmounting every building. If you're not going on to more elegant dining at Los Olivos, consider one of the many restaurants in Solvang, or shop for your picnic supplies at the Danish bakeries and delicatessens lining the main street of Mission Drive (CA 246). *Solvang lies 35m via CA 154 and 45m via US 101 from Santa Barbara.*

Santa Ynez Indian Reservation □ Just 3m east of the old mission along CA 246, you pass near the old reservation belonging to the formerly numerous Chumash whose approximately 15,000 people occupied this valley and the Channel coast. In 1972 this reservation was one of the smallest in the U.S. with a mere 75 acres of land and shockingly few residents—forty, no more. So admiringly described by the early Spaniards, so industrious and talented in building missions, painting murals, carving pulpits, and singing mass, and still so ever present in the museum exhibits of the region, the Chumash themselves have barely survived the epidemics and displacement brought on by the arrival of Spaniards and Anglos. Their plight recalls the words of a California Indian from the north.

I am very old . . . my people were once around me like the sands of the shore . . . many . . . many. They have all passed away. They have died like the grass . . . They have gone to the mountains. I do not complain, the antelope falls with the arrow. I had a son. I loved him. When the palefaces came he went away. I do not know where he is. I am a Christian Indian, I am all that is left of my people. I am alone.

EX-NEOPHYTE, 1850 *(Castillo)*

Los Olivos □ Going a few miles farther on CA 246 you come to the junction of 246 and 154. Just west on CA 154, about 35 m from Santa Barbara via the San Marcos Pass, lies the tiny village of Los Olivos. You can visit Los Olivos to stroll its few streets, looking into art galleries and visiting the tasting room of Austin Cellars (292 Grand Ave.). Or you can tour the surrounding mountains to visit other wineries and Arabian horse ranches. Or you can just relax and enjoy the good mountain air, for there's not much else to distract you. The best place to do this is at **Los Olivos Grand Hotel,** carefully designed to re-create the tranquility of a country inn, with each of its 21 suites decorated in distinctive French provincial furnishings keyed to the prints of American and Impressionist artists. While each elegant room varies, all offer gas fireplaces, double sinks, and down comforters. Some have private Jacuzzis. Excellent restaurant. Lounge. Garden. Pool and Jacuzzi. Parking. ***Very expensive*** (includes continental breakfast, newspaper each morning, and a bottle of wine). Contact Box 526, 2860 Grand Ave., CA 93441; 688–7788, 800–626–7249 U.S., or 800–654–7263 CA. Many come to the hotel for an overnight just to enjoy the French food at its **Remington's** restaurant (reserve through hotel; Sun. brunch, Mon.–Sat. lunch, daily for dinner; ***very expensive***) where the seafood is rich (consider lobster in basil cream sauce) and the entrees inventive (venison with a wild lingonberry sauce). Less elegant, but good is the historic **Mattei's Tavern** (CA 154 at Los Olivos; dinner only; 688–4820; ***moderate***), an 1886 stagecoach stop on the Butterfield Line and now a steakhouse with a very Victorian setting, down to lace curtains, antiques, and large fireplace.

★ **Chumash Painted Cave** □ Friar Payeras recounted in 1810 that he had found "traces and signs of superstitions, witchcraft, and even idolatry" among the Chumash. After baptism, their "extravagant" worship ended, or at least took place out of his sight in the mountains. The brilliantly colored, sophisticated, and mostly abstract designs seen at this cave represent one of those ceremonies that disappeared with the conversion of the Chumash. Unfortunately, neither Payeras nor other friars described the rituals involved with such cave paintings that appear throughout the region, and date from A.D. 1000 to 1800. While you can't enter the cave, you can glimpse the paintings through a screen at the entrance.

Reaching the cave can be a bit confusing since it isn't marked, but the drive along the winding, tortuous lane (Painted Cave Rd.) that curls through Los Padres National Forest is well worth the effort for the views alone. *About 25m from Los Olivos on the San Marcos Pass Road (CA 154), or about 1½m from the sign for W. Camino Cielo Road, turn left onto Painted Cave Rd. Or from Santa Barbara, turn right 10m north of town. Then just under 2m, park where the narrow road permits as you enter a heavily forested canopy. Climb up the rocks to the left where you can see the screened entrance to the cave.*

Suggestions

Directory □ The zip code varies throughout the region, but the 805 area code applies even to numbers on the excursion routes, except for 800 toll-free numbers. ★ *Santa Barbara Conference and Visitors Bureau* at 1330 State Street, Suite 200, Box 299, CA 93102; 965–3023.

Getting Around □ Downtown sights are manageable on foot and bike paths line the harbor with rentals found along the way, but the **Metropolitan Transit Company** has a brochure explaining how to use their services (Carrillo and Chapala sts., CA 93101; 683–3702) and the *Santa Barbara Trolley Company* provides another alternative for touring town sights and beach drives (564–4315). ★ Car rentals are available as are taxis (965–5111). ★ Tours include very personalized **limousines** (969–9072), the **Touring Taxi** (962–2344), the **Travel Gallery** (687–0721), and others.

Arriving □ The Santa Barbara Municipal **Airport** is just 8 m from downtown and includes the service of commuter and national airlines. Car rentals, including **Avis** (964–4848) and **National** (967–1202) can be arranged and **Airport Express** (965–1611) provides scheduled bus service into town. ★ Scheduled buses also link Santa Barbara with the L.A. airport less than 100m away. Contact **Santa Barbara Airbus** (964–7374). ★ **Amtrak** is at 209 State St. (687–6848). ★ **Greyhound** can be found at Carrillo and Chapala (966–3962).

Weather □ Summers and fall find Santa Barbara hotels booked in advance, yet the weather is truly a delight year round. ★ The average daily high in January is 63° F; the low is 41° F. ★ The average daily high in July is 76° F; the low 56° F.

ALONG THE CAMINO REAL: MISSION LIFE

. . . come, oh come to the Holy Church! . . . I would that this bell might be heard in all the world . . . or at least . . . by all the pagan people who live in this sierra.

FRAY JUNIPERO SERRA, 1771
(Palou)

So Father Serra announced the founding of San Antonio de Padua, the third mission, by ringing the mission bell from a tree and readying an arbor for the first chapel. His wish to be heard by the pagans of the Santa Lucia mountains was granted, at least partially, when one fearless Indian came to get a closer look at the curious bells. By the beginning of the 1800s San Antonio had nearly 1300 neophytes, and the entire mission system begun by Serra was flourishing. Enough years had passed for the construction of dams and aquaducts to water the finally productive fields of wheat, the maturing orchards of pears and pomegranates, and the gardens of European vegetables and herbs. The cattle, sheep and horses, so arduously brought up from Baja California, had multiplied, then multiplied again into vast herds that covered thousands of acres of land.

First attracted by pealing bells, then impressed by the increasing bounty of the missions even at times of drought, more and more native Californians moved to the missions and converted to the Catholic faith. Sometimes, however, years would lapse before the Indians could be enticed away from their traditional villages and lifestyle.

They lived without king and without law. They maintained themselves with acorns, seeds, and herbs . . . They knew no labor than that of the dance, play, and hunting.

FRIAR ESTEVAN TAPIS, 1814

The friars, seeing their reluctance, would give them gifts of clothes "which they like and desire very much" and impress them with the ceremonies of the church, with orchestras and choirs, and with processions and fireworks. And if they became neophytes, the mission would care for them with daily rations of food, with clothing, and shelter. Some Spaniards feared the Indians abandoned "their savage life" to improve their social condition rather than to save their souls, or as Hugo Reid so bluntly put it

The priest having converted *some few by giving them cloth and ribbons, and taught them to say* Amar a Dios, *they were baptized. . .*

As the missions thrived, their buildings improved and grew in number. Adobe bricks, and sometimes even stone, replaced the earlier reed-and-log structures; red clay tiles, so characteristic of the California missions, replaced the dried grasses of thatched roofs. Whitewash brightened mud facades; Indian paintings and imported ones adorned church interiors. And mission San Miguel even boasted a spa at its Rancho Paso Robles.

. . . we reached a place where a sulphurous hot spring boiled up from the ground, and formed a rivulet which crossed the road. Father Juan had erected a small house over the spot for the purpose of shelter, and convenience for bathing . . .

ALFRED ROBINSON, 1830

Adobe houses for both cowboys and shepherds dotted the ranches far from the monastery, such as the one near the beach at Rancho San Simeon—and San Luis Obispo built a particularly fine *assistencia,* or branch chapel, granary, and friary at Rancho Santa Margarita where the padres spent a good deal of time during the harvest. And the monasteries themselves underwent extensive renovation.

Large soap works were erected; tanning yards established; tallow works, bakery, cooper, blacksmith, carpenter, and other shops; large spinning rooms where might be seen 50 or 60 women turning their spindles merrily; and looms for weaving wool, flax, and cotton. The large store rooms were allotted to the various articles . . . wheat, barley, peas, beans, lentils, chickpeas, butter and cheese, soap, candles, wool, leather, flour, lime, salt, horsehair, wine and spirits, fruits &c, &c.

HUGO REID (1852)

Mention should be made of the residences, too: the guardhouse; the friars' quarters often with a library, yet always with extra rooms for visitors; the *monjerio,* or "nunnery" for unmarried girls who were kept separate from the barracks of the unmarried boys under rules, which Augustias de la Guerra Ord tells us were "not more strict . . . than still prevail in some of the Spanish-American countries in much higher classes." And to the side of the monastery quadrangle could be found the Indian village where the families lived. Such were the great mission estates.

The Indian neophytes were the laborers who made the mission possible, the blacksmiths and weavers, the vaqueros and carpenters, even the candlestick makers. They tended the crops, ground the grain, and they cooked. They carved the pulpits, sang mass in their "clear and sonorous voices," and formed the processions on feast days—the senoritas in "red flannel petticoats," the men with "red and blue ribbons" flowing from their hats. These neophytes regulated their lives to the ringing of the mission bells morning, noon, and night. But as one neophyte describes his life, he clearly enjoyed the routine.

When the sun rises and the stars and moon fall down, then the eldest of the house awakens everyone to begin their breakfast of juiuis *heated, and meat and tortillas . . . this over, he takes his bow and arrows and leaves the house . . . He goes off to the distant woods full of bears and rabbits, deer and thousands of birds. Here He spends the day hunting and returns happy, loaded with hares. But when wood is needed, then he leaves the house in the morning . . . with companions who can help him when the load is very heavy . . . His wife would stay home making the meal, his older son would work with the men. His daughter stays with the women making shirts, and if these also have sons and daughters, they stay in the mission. The sons at school to learn the alphabet, and if they already know it, to learn the catechism . . . At midday all eat together, seated around the fire . . . While they eat, talk and laugh, too bad if the closed door causes the smoke to thicken and them to cry without wanting to . . . The meal over, all return to their work . . . till later, before going to bed, they again eat.*

Pablo Tac
A Luiseno born in 1822

Not all was regimented. The mission food of porridge and stew could be supplemented with favorite berries collected in the forests, with herbs grown in neophyte gardens, and with fish caught in their canoes. Evenings and Sundays—after mass, of course—were times the neophytes had to themselves.

. . . the Indians assembled, on Sunday afternoons, to indulge in their favorite sports and pursue their chief amusement—gambling [on a ball game] . . . at least two or three hundred Indians of both sexes were engaged in the game . . . Great excitement prevailed and immense exertion was manifested on both sides, so that it was not till late in the afternoon that the game was decided. . .

ROBINSON (1846)

Many Indians continued to enjoy their *temescal,* or sauna-style bath, during leisure moments, and most were permitted a few weeks leave to visit relatives in other missions or even faraway, and still heathen, villages. There were relaxing times at the ranches when, during roundups, the neophyte *vaqueros* displayed their talents lassoing and branding calves. And memberships in the mission band and choir were so valued that many would forego alcohol on a Saturday eve in order to be ready to perform at Sunday mass. Even the most Catholic of entertainments, feast days, permitted the converted Indians to perform dances of their own choosing, dances that expressed according to one French observer "many of their old beliefs, which the padres, from policy, pretended not to know."

The grotesque costume of the dancers, adorned with feathers and painted in all sorts of colors, lends to their features so wild an appearance and so strange a character that one would be tempted to believe they were arousing themselves to battle rather than pleasure.

A. DUHAUT-CILLY, 1827

Mission life didn't suit all the neophytes. Many accustomed to the carefree lifestyle of their tribes, couldn't tolerate the routine. Others couldn't bear the interference in their personal and family lives, with daughters locked into monjerios and all denied expressions of what the friars called "their lewdness." Some, brought considerable distance from their villages to live at the mission, were homesick and used every occasion to request permission to return.

On one of these occasions . . . I answered with a certain annoyance: "Well, you make me realize now that, although you were given a steer, a mutton, and a fanega of grain every day, you would, despite all this, long for your woods and your shores." Then the keenest-witted Indian . . . replied, somewhat shamefacedly, "It is so Father, as you say, it is so."

FRIAR FERMIN LASUEN, 1800
(Cook)

Unfortunately the neophytes found more serious reasons for discontent. "Among themselves they employ no kind of chastisement," but the friars often found that "inclination to lewdness and theft" demanded punishment. Perhaps most missionaries followed Lasuen's admonition that "the first principle is patience, and the second is patience, and the third is patience, and so are all the others." But after all the principles were considered, a padre might feel that a neophyte who had run away most certainly deserved twenty lashes or so. And the more neophytes that ran away, the more soldiers were sent to bring them back to the mission and a flogging or two.

And if they alleged, as proof of cruelty, the number of Indians who had fled . . . I had the satisfaction of replying that they were already coming back and that they assured me that none had gone for fear of work, nor punishment, but because of fear of the disease . . .

LASUEN, 1801

Disease, in fact, seemed an excellent reason for running to the wilderness. Epidemic after epidemic hit the dense populations of the missions and rapidly spread through the confined quarters for unmarried neophytes. Some governors thought the climate of the missions might be at fault—so near the sea and so damp and foggy, or with extremes of heat and cold—like at San Antonio where there had been "frequent illness and deaths." In 1802 the epidemics continued, with pneumonia and diphtheria killing several hundred in the missions from Carmel to San Luis Obispo, and devastating Mission Soledad with the death of 70 children. Just a few years later scarlet fever struck, taking its toll of 1600. Yet the frightened neophytes were not free to return to villages in the healthier environment of the wilderness. Some tried anyway.

Indians of course deserted. Who would not have deserted? Still, those who did had hard times of it. If they proceeded to other missions, they were . . . flogged . . . If they stowed themselves away in any of the rancherias [villages], the soldiers were monthly in the habit of visiting them . . . the only alternative left them was to take to the mountains . . .

REID (1852)

About four percent of the entire mission population succeeded in becoming permanent fugitives, finding refuge with the unconverted tribes in the interior region of the San Joaquin valley.

Along with their failures and their human tragedies, the missions achieved much. Over 83,000 Indians were baptized in just over 50 years, and while a friar could not always provide them with a deep understanding of their new faith

He gave them . . . an insight of the Catholic religion, but did not in one iota alter their own.

REID (1852)

A few exceptional neophytes actually went to Rome to study for the priesthood. And a few neophytes were adequately trained and ''civilized'' to gain the freedom to live along the gente de razon.

Citizen Gil, native of Mission San Diego and carpenter by trade, desires to separate himself from said Mission . . . in order to go where he can exercise this trade with adequate profit . . . he maintains himself in some comfort. Therefore he has our leave to separate himself from the Mission.

FRIARS FERNANDO MARTIN AND
PASQUAL OLIVA, 1826

Although mission life oppressed some and nurtured to independence too few, it did feed, clothe, and house thousands of neophytes and protect them from exploitation by the gente de razon, an exploitation that would become all too prevalent with the end of the missions.

Sights

The four missions found on and around the Camino Real in the region from San Luis Obispo up to Monterey, provide interesting diversions along US 101, a ranching and farming region amid rolling hills. But it is the scenic coastline here that attracts many tourists along spectacular Big Sur, from El Morro to Point Lobos, a coastline the early explorers found forbidding with few coves in which to seek safe refuge.

. . . the coast is bold, rugged, and without shelter.

CABRILLO EXPEDITION, 1542

The very difficulty of the coast forced the Camino Real inland, approximately along the route of US 101. If you're driving through the area only once, you probably plan to explore the coastal road (CA 1). Since you need at least several hours to visit Hearst Castle, and a good 3 hours just to drive along the 100 miles to Monterey via Big Sur, you might treat yourself to at least an overnight or two in the region, and add time to visit the town of San Luis Obispo, San Miguel Mission, and San Antonio de Padua. And the wineries around Paso Robles as well as the beaches near San Luis Obispo and Morro Bay offer diversified pleasures in this beautiful region.

Driving along the Camino Real (US 101) you pass through some old ranch lands. Just south of San Luis Obispo was the **Rancho Nipomo** (1837), owned by the New England captain William Dana and his wife, Maria Josefa Carrillo. The Rancho Nipomo was an important stop on the Camino Real, and during the early American period it was critical to the first postal system.

Governor Kearny has established a semi-monthly mail . . . to be carried on horseback, by a party consisting of two soldiers. Starting every other Monday from San Diego and San Francisco, the parties meet at Captain Dana's rancho the next Sunday, to exchange mail.

California Star, 1847

Once the Dana adobe dominated the Camino Real in the Nipomo area, but today you must take the Nipomo/Thompson Street exit from US 101, make an early right onto Oakglen and continue 1m to #673. (When last visited, the adobe was closed for repairs. Check in advance as to its scheduled opening: 805–543–7896.) Just north of the exit for the town of Santa Margarita, you can see to the east the modernized and expanded adobe *asistencia* that belonged to Mission San Luis Obispo. The barn here was built around the nave of the old Spanish building where padres once took their retreats. And if you're driving to or from Santa Barbara, visit La Purisima Mission (see Index) for the best example of how the old mission functioned.

Mission San Luis Obispo

The Mission is situated in a beautiful place on a slight elevation close by an arroyo . . . near the Sierra de Santa Lucia and about three leagues from the ocean. The land is very fine and fertile.

FRAY PEDRO FONT, 1776

The modern town of San Luis Obispo has grown and flourished around the fifth of the missions founded (1772) by Junipero Serra. But in the early days, the mission was located in a sparsely populated area along the Camino Real. Few converts were attracted to the mission, the local Indians finding they were comfortable enough living as they always had. Once the mission did get started, its converts numbered in the hundreds rather than thousands. Although never populous, this mission grew prosperous for its size, with bountiful crops and large herds of horses, mules, and sheep. A good deal of San Luis Obispo's success derived from its energetic missionary, Friar Luis Martinez, who, we are told, was of brown complexion and had "a very large nose which had been twisted from an injury."

In his robe he was a poor Franciscan and always fulfilled faithfully his duties as a priest. But he had vanity in his vaqueros and mules. He desired that no one should surpass the vaqueros and mules of Mission "San Luisito" as he called San Luis Obispo. There cotton was loomed with perfection. They made shawls, quilts and other articles from this material.

ANGUSTIAS DE LA GUERRA ORD
(1878)

Father Martinez administered San Luisito for over thirty years, years in which he not only made the mission ranches productive, but ones in which he explored the unknown interior region seeking runaways and potential new converts. Located right on the Camino Real, the mission was a favorite stopping place for travelers, and the friar became known for the "neatness" of his table as well as for his practical jokes, called throughout California "Fray Luises." Nearly a half-century later the priest inspired a novelist to relate what may have been a real "Fray Luis" still circulating among storytellers. The story goes that a general and his bride on their wedding tour had stopped at the mission.

On the morning of their departure, the good padre, having exhausted all his resources for entertaining his distinguished guests, caused to be driven past . . . for their inspection all the poultry belonging to the Mission. The procession took an hour to pass. For music there was squeaking, cackling, hissing, gobbling, crowing, and quacking of the fowls, combined with the screaming, scolding, and whip cracking of the excited Indian marshals of the lines.

HELEN HUNT JACKSON in *Ramona* (1884)

Unfortunately, Friar Martinez also felt free to criticize some of the policies of the newly independent Mexican government and found himself accused of fomenting sympathy for Spain. He was arrested in front of an assembly of all the neophytes, then expelled.

Soon after the departure of Padre Martinez, the mission fell into ruin. But the good land attracted its rancheros and continued to support bountiful crops, and even poultry farms. A small town crowded about the mission church that continued to function for the parish that eventually was composed of Spaniards, Mexicans, the first French vineyardist, Scots, Anglo-Americans and Chinese. Today the *town of* **San Luis Obispo** offers more than the little that remains of its mission. Enjoyable town walks, such as the self-guided ★ **Paths of History,** take you along some of the blocks around the mission church—to old adobes and Victorian brick buildings (on Chorro and Monterey sts.), to nostalgic 19th-century stores like an old cigar factory now a restaurant, and to **Ah Louis General Store** (800 Palm St. at Chorro; 2–5:30 p.m.) opened to serve Chinese railroad laborers in 1874. (Either stroll on our own reading and markers along the way or pick up, for a fee, the *Visitors Guide* containing a self-guided walking tour at the Chamber of Commerce office just a block from the mission at 1039 Chorro St.; 805–543–1323.) The old **mission church,** found in the center of town near Chorro and Monterey streets, continues to serve its parishioners. Although it retains its handsome wooden door studded and arched, the church is not among the most impressive, having lost most of its authentic furnishings during years that saw it transformed into something Gothic. Next door, a part of the convento has been refurbished into a museum (open 9 a.m.–4 p.m. daily; closed major holidays; donations; 805–543–8563). In front of the church and situated around the old mission creek is **Mission Plaza,** a fine park with picnicking and a bustling town gathering place, particularly in mid-May during the **Fiesta** de San Luis, and also in August during the Mozart Festival when concerts sometimes take place in the church here as well as at the mission San Miguel. (Write Box 311 CA 93401 or call 805–543–4580.) At the other end of the plaza is the **County Historical Museum** (696 Monterey St.) with exhibits on the Indians of the region and memorabilia donated by local residents (Wed.–Sun. 10 a.m.–4 p.m.; free). More walking gives you a good sense of this pleasant college town (Cal Polytech and Cuesta College), and 8 blocks east of the mission down Pacific takes you by the 1853 **Dallidet Adobe** (Pacific and Toro St.), a picturesque spot once home to the first Frenchman in town, as well as to the old **Ramona Depot,** and even to a Frank Lloyd Wright-designed medical building (1106 Pacific).

While I don't think the central coast beaches can compete in quality with those to the south, they still offer the sounds of gulls and the roar of the sea. There're some popular beaches near San Luis Obispo, particularly **Avila Beach** 9m to the south with its funky boardwalk and nearby padre's landing (now Port Luis), where two-masted brigs traded with Friar Martinez. More isolated beaches at **Montana de Oro State Park** are found at the end of Los Osos Valley Road from San Luis. Other beaches can be found 12m to the north at Morro Bay where the surfing at **Atascadero State Beach,** and the boat trips out to a sand spit in the bay dominated by Morro Rock, are popular pastimes.

San Luis Obispo is located 110m north of Santa Barbara on US 101 (take the Broad Street exit to the mission), and 145m south of Monterey via CA 1, 100m via US 101.

★★ **Mission San Miguel** □ With lands that once included the productive agricultural area and vineyards around Paso Robles, and with an estate that extended thirty miles to the Pacific Ocean near Hearst Castle, the Mission San Miguel was quite capable of supporting itself up to the time of secularization.

. . . San Miguel which in 1833 was very rich. Padre Juan Cabot showed me all of its warehouses. They were full of goods, grain, etc., and also had a goodly sum of money belonging to the Mission. When I returned there in 1835 I found not even a glass in which to drink water and had

to drink from a cup I had brought myself. All of the assets of the Mission, herds, etc., had disappeared.

ANGUSTIAS DE LA GUERRA ORD
(1878)

The mission lost not only its assets, but its missionaries as well. Abandoned, and located right on the Camino Real between San Francisco and Los Angeles, the mission became during the gold rush a haunt for gamblers and wanderers, and a convenient spot for the opportunistic salesperson to make a pitch. Until almost the end of the 19th century, a saloon and a mail order sewing machine store occupied the convento.

Throughout its years of ruin and misfortune, the church itself remained untouched and today offers one of the most colorful and delightful interiors to be found in any of the missions. While some paintings were imported to San Miguel, as they were at all the missions

. . . *for the purpose of stimulating devotion among the converts.* . . .

FRIAR JOSE SENAN, 1806

the missionaries weren't always able to purchase the adornment deemed necessary for their churches. When glass wasn't available, then windows would be made of rawhide scraped thin and oiled until translucent. And when fine marble and European sculptures could not be obtained, when archways and balconies demanded more skill than locally available, then they would be achieved through trompe l'oeil murals. Under the direction of Estevan Munras, an artisan from Monterey, and with hide stencils cut into the classical patterns found in books from the mission library, the neophytes of San Miguel transformed plain walls into a properly inspirational church (1820).

Since 1928 the mission has once again belonged to the Franciscans who have restored the quadrangle, and turned the former workshops into living quarters and classrooms for a retreat house. The convento has been converted into a **museum** that contain an interesting sculpture of San Miguel slaying Lucifer, as well as exhibits on mission life. Although still right next to the highway, the mission is surprisingly tranquil, a wonderful worn complex that is perfect for picnicking or visiting on the **Fiesta** of San Miguel, the third Sunday in September, and during the Christmas season for the performance of *posadas,* the reenactment of Mary and Joseph's search for lodging. *Museum open 9:30 a.m.–4* *p.m., the church 9 a.m.–5 p.m.; closed major holidays; donations; 805–467–3256. The mission is located about 10m north of Paso Robles, 38m north of San Luis Obispo just off US 101.*

Across from the mission is the Monterey colonial style ★ **Rios Caledonia Adobe** (1850), once the Caledonia stagecoach inn and before that the home of Petronillo Rios who owned the secularized San Miguel Mission (Wed.–Sun. 10 a.m.–4 p.m.; donation; 805–467–3357).

★★ **Mission San Antonio de Padua** □ Off the Camino Real, the San Antonio mission remains, even today, somewhat isolated in its lovely valley surrounded by the Santa Lucia mountains.

We descended a slope at the foot of which flowed a considerable stream of water [San Antonio River] . . . The whole country over which we travelled, especially from this stream onward, was covered on both sides with white oaks and live oaks, as high and of as great girth as can be found in the finest parks of Europe.

FRAY JUAN CRESPI, 1769

The very isolation of San Antonio has protected it. No settlers expropriated its bricks for new construction; no town took over its land. Enough remained over the years so that the ruins of the mission could be studied and replicated. Extensively reconstructed, surrounded by wilderness, and still a Franciscan retreat, San Antonio today gives you a good sense of its separateness and vastness a century and a half ago.

A visit to the mission includes not only the church, but ruins of the soldiers' barracks, the friary now museum, the old wine vat and grist mill, and the padre's garden. On June 2, the church celebrates the **feast day** of San Antonio. *Open Mon.–Sat. 9:30 a.m.–4:30 p.m.; Sun. 11 a.m.–5 p.m.; closed major holidays; donation; 408–385–4478. The mission is near the village of Jolon on Fort Hunter Liggett military reservation, 43m south of Soledad (exit US 101 at Jolon Rd. north of King City), and 38m north of San Miguel (exit US 101 at Fort Hunter Liggett).* Both routes take you through about 20m of open country still much the same as in mission days. Just before reaching the mission, there's a tempting sign for the Nacimiento-Ferguson Road that leads through the Santa Lucia mountains to Big Sur.

Mission La Soledad □ Named in honor of "the Sorrowful Virgin of Solitude," this 13th of the missions never quite overcame its difficult location. While some believe the mission received its name from Portola, who is said to have met an Indian with a name sounding like "Soledad," others are convinced that the mission's desolate setting inspired the name.

It was near sundown when we arrived and dismounted at the door of La Soledad. The gloomiest, bleakest, and most abject-looking spot in all California.

ALFRED ROBINSON, 1830

Perhaps it was the difficult soil, so much better for grazing herds than growing crops, that lent the mission its bleak aspect. Or perhaps the mission's most virtuous priest, Friar Vicente Sarria, joined his guests too often on the night of a fast, confining himself to "a dish of herbs dipped in flour and fruit, and a little water." The mission did support itself, tapping the Salinas river to irrigate the formerly recalcitrant fields. But the river, too, turned against the mission, flooding it three times. The last flood, in 1831, washed away the church. Not too many years later, Friar Sarria himself passed away having survived "toil and apostolic hardships" as well as the "frugality of his food," to reach his 68th year.

Today the Salinas valley flourishes as a very rich agricultural area, but all that remains of La Soledad is a **replica** of the 1832 church, part of the friary, now used as a small museum, and a self-guided walk through adobe ruins. More than anything, this is a nice picnicking spot. *Open 10 a.m.–4 p.m.; closed Tues. and major holidays; 408–678–2586. Located 3m off the Arroyo Seco exit of 101, south of the town of Soledad and 17m north of King City; 40m south of Monterey via US 101.*

San Simeon □ Where missions like San Miguel struggled with trompe l'oeil paintings to create the slightest suggestion of European opulence, William Randolph Hearst simply bought and transported Gothic fireplaces and Italian marbles, choir stalls and medieval tapestries, in order to decorate the extravagant re-creation of a Spanish-style cathedral he called home. What he couldn't import, he had replicated in concrete. Though Hearst's land was part of the Mission San Miguel, his sumptuous estate, complete with pseudo-Greek temples, Renaissance gardens, and the castle itself, seems light years distant from such simple beginnings.

From the Mission [San Miguel] to the beach the land consists almost entirely of mountain ridges, devoid of permanent water. For this reason the region is not occupied until one reached the coast where the mission has a house of adobe . . . some clear land for planting grain . . . 800 cattle, some tame horses and breeding mares are kept at said Rancho, which is called San Simeon.

FRIAR JUAN CABOT, 1827

Visiting the Hearst Castle, most officially known as the **Hearst-San Simeon State Historic Monument,** requires taking one or more of the nearly 2-hour walking tours (a sizable fee for each). Tour 1 provides an overview, including the downstairs castle, gardens and pool; Tour 2 includes Hearst's private quarters and library in the castle; Tour 3 includes the new wing; and Tour 4, primarily the gardens. The visitor center opens at 8 a.m. when tour tickets for that day go on sale. However, it's advisable to secure tickets in advance by picking them up at your local Ticketron office, or writing for them 1 month in advance (800–952–5580 CA or 916–445–8828 for forms and information). *Tours leave at least once every hour from 8:20 a.m.–3 p.m. in the winter, and more frequently in the summer and on holidays (closed major holidays). The entrance to the castle grounds is just off CA 1, 42m north of San Luis Obispo, 96m south of Monterey via Big Sur, and 44m from San Miguel at US 101 (follow CA 46 west from Paso Robles to CA 1).*

The **San Simeon-Hearst State Beach** (5m south) offers swimming (and campsites) while further south in Cambria the scenic drive along **Moonstone Beach** is a worthwhile detour involving little extra time.

Big Sur □ The scenic road north from San Simeon to Monterey 100 miles away, is narrow and spectacular, tortuous and wildly beautiful. Clinging to cliffs, the road travels through a region that, despite such contemporary presences as Esalen and a Zen monastery, remains most like the coast explored by the first seafaring Spaniards. Sea otter swim the Pacific here and beaches remain unimproved; the redwoods named by Portola cluster in their magnificent stands, and wild boar and fox alike frequent the wilderness. On one side of the road are the Santa Lucia mountains, with the Ventana wilderness and giant redwoods to explore. On the other side, far below, is the Pacific Ocean.

. . . the sea has a heavy swell, and the coast is very high. There are mountains which reach the sky, and the sea beats on them.

CABRILLO EXPEDITION, 1542

While some simply drive CA 1, perhaps pulling into the state parks for a picnic lunch or just enjoying the numerous observation points along the way, most visitors come to explore the region more thoroughly. About 10 m south of Big Sur Village is the **Julia Pfeiffer Burns State Park,** with redwood groves and waterfalls, whale-watching stations and picnicking facilities (summer; weekends spring and fall). Just north of Big Sur Village is the **Pfeiffer-Big Sur State Park** with trails into the Ventana wilderness (permits required), picnicking and hiking, river swimming and fishing. (For information on permits and camping, contact the park [408–667–2315], or stop at the Big Sur visitor center just 2½ m north of Big Sur Village on CA 1.) Although the park may not have a beach, just to its south you find the road leading to lovely **Pfeiffer Beach.** Several miles even farther north is the **Andrew Molera State Park,** closed to motor vehicles but with a beach, bluffs and forest for campers and picnickers to enjoy. Just 2½ m south of Carmel is **Point Lobos Reserve,** a wildlife sanctuary covering nearly 1500 acres. Here you can hike through cypress forests, skin dive in the sea, and along the 6 miles of coastline you can watch otters, sea lions, and pelicans (bring binoculars). Beginning in November, the vantage points here are good for winter whale watching. Also, there are picnic facilities. (Open during daylight each day; fee; 408–624–4909.)

Suggestions

Getting There ☐ The easiest way to pick and choose your sightseeing in this region is to have your own car or to rent one (Monterey or San Luis Obispo). However, in the summer **bus tours** operate out of Monterey (408–899–2555) and provide visits to Big Sur and Hearst Castle. ★ Commuter and regional airlines connect major cities with both San Luis Obispo and Monterey. ★ **Amtrak** (805–541–0505) and **Greyhound** (805–543–2121) operate out of San Luis Obispo to the major cities. ★ The 100m drive along Big Sur is more dramatic from the north when you skirt the open-cliff side of the road; some prefer driving from the south, enjoying the views at turnoffs, but feeling safer hugging the mountains. ★ San Luis Obispo is approximately at the midpoint of the California coast. ★ Big Sur is 155m south of San Francisco and 290 m north of L.A.

Weather Tips ☐ Most of this region enjoys weather in the 70s during the summer and in the 60s during the winter, but there are variations and the evenings can be cool all over. ★ Big Sur has hot summer days, cool nights, and congested weekend traffic; the winter often brings sudden rain storms; summer fog can obscure the views. ★ Inland temperatures can soar during the summer at places like Mission San Miguel, and on exceptionally hot days

. . . *fleas cannot endure the summer months and during the heat of the day they may be seen gasping upon the brick pavements.*

ALFRED ROBINSON, 1830

Along the coast at San Luis Obispo the average high in July is 77° F, the low 52° F; the average high in January is 62° F, the low 41° F.

Restaurants

There are pleasant picnicking facilities in this region—at some of the missions, along the Big Sur coast, and even across from the access road to Hearst Castle. To purchase your picnic supplies there are general stores on the coastal road, including one in Big Sur Village, and the Chamber of Commerce in San Luis Obispo has a listing of farmers markets where you can buy fresh produce in the summer and fall. Restaurant facilities are plentiful, from the fast food restaurants on US 101 and the many offerings in San Luis Obispo and Morro Bay, to the patio restaurant across from Hearst Castle, the little dining spot at the junction in isolated Jolon, and the beautiful restaurants on the Big Sur road. I found the most convenient places to be in San Luis Obispo, Morro Bay, and Big Sur.

Just a mile south of *Big Sur Village* is the road leading to one of California's most dramatic spots for dining, **Ventana** (noon–3 p.m. except Sun. 1:30–3:50 p.m.; 6–10 p.m. daily; 408–667–2331; ***moderate to moderately expensive***). Perched in the hills 1,000 feet above the sea, Ventana has created a serene environment within its breathtaking location. Rustic and sophisticated at the same time, soothing even to harp music on some Sundays, you can soar here with red-tail hawks and flutter with humming birds. Lunch on the outdoor patio brings the best sense of the Santa Lucias, and waiting in the outdoor lounge (no reservations for lunch) provides the best views of the Pacific. Fortunately, the food makes the visit even more worthwhile, whether you lunch on a lovely smoked prawn salad surrounded by radicchio, kiwi, and raspberries or dine on pasta with grilled scallops and red pepper sauce. Less than a mile south is another Big Sur favorite, **Nepenthe** (11:30 a.m.–4:30 p.m. lunch; dinner 5–10:30 p.m.; 408–667–2345; ***moderate to moderately expensive***) serving more traditional American food—heaps of french fries, quiche, salads, and steaks, and without the mellow ambience of Ventana. But the views here are spectacular, too; the music country western.

At *Morro Bay* you can enjoy some fresh local seafood while viewing dramatic Morro Rock looming over the bay. **Galley Restaurant** (899 Embarcadero; 11 a.m.–9 p.m.; reserve at 805–772–2806; ***moderate***) is a very popular restaurant with warm service and complete dinners arranged around local specialties such as rock cod. Following Main Street out to the state park and bird preserve, you come to the restaurant at **The Inn at Morro Bay** (lunch and dinner; reserve at 805–772–5651; sunset specials ***moderate,*** otherwise ***moderately expensive;*** jackets required for men at dinner) with its tranquil views and continental cuisine that includes steak au poivre as well as seafood.

In *San Luis Obispo* there are a number of pleasant restaurants in historic buildings dotting the central area around the mission. For lunching on salads and sandwiches in oak paneled booths, stop by **J.P. Andrews Saloon** (Monterey at Osos; lunch daily; dinner Wed.–Sun.; 805–541–1888; ***inexpensive to moderate***) situated in a handsome bank building dating from 1893. Or try the Mexican food, particularly the delicious *salsa,* at **Tortilla Flats** (Higuera and Nipomo; 11 a.m.–9 p.m. daily; 805–544–7575; ***inexpensive***) located in the attractively renovated turn-of-the-century Creamery Building. Just a few steps from the mission and looking very much like a picturesque old adobe is **Sebastian's** (1023 Chorro St.; 11 a.m.–3 p.m. lunch, 4–9 p.m. dinner; entertainment Thurs.–Sun.; 805–544–5666; ***moderate***). The outdoor patio and tavern here are very popular for soup and salad at lunch, for seafood and prime ribs at dinner. If you're in the mood for northern Italian cuisine, head out to the southern end of Osos Street to **Cafe Roma** (1819 Osos St.; 5:30–9 p.m.; 805–541–6800; ***moderate to moderately expensive***) where the daily specials can be very good, including the homemade linguini with scallops or the marinated and mesquite grilled swordfish. You might want to stop by the **Madonna Inn** (100 Madonna Rd. just off US 101; 7 a.m.–10 p.m.; 805–543–3000; ***moderate***) even if you aren't tempted to eat the breakfasts and cream pies served in its coffee shop. Only seeing the Madonna Inn will make you believe its outlandish decor, a hot pink concotion of flowery fabrics and gingerbread ostentation that covers every surface. Given the crowds, it's obvious that not only the color blind can eat here.

Accommodations

There are three fine inns that take advantage of the beauty of this central coast. **Ventana** has the same exceptional location as its restaurant along Big Sur. The 28 units scattered among the hills offer privacy and tranquility. Designed in cedar wood, and taking the most advantage of their environment in the mountains overlooking the sea, most units have fireplaces, some have hot tubs. The quiet, introspective atmosphere maintained here results in the inn's request that children not be brought as guests. Restaurant and lounge. Pool, sauna, and whirlpool. Parking. ***Very expensive,*** price includes continental breakfast and afternoon cheese and wine. Write Ventana, Big Sur, CA 93920; 408–667–2331 or 800–628–6500 CA. **The Inn at Morro Bay** has a prime location away from the motel bustle of the Embarcadero; it's just at the entrance of Morro Bay State Park with a golf course across from it, the woods and a blue heron sanctuary next door, and the bay right in front. The gray clapboard lodges have 100 tastefully designed rooms with cathedral ceilings, brass beds, refrigerators (stocked with a complementary bottle of wine), and furnished balconies (some with views of the wildlife on the bay and in the park, others of the pool). Some rooms have fireplaces. Restaurants and lounge (entertainment) with great bay views. Pool, bicycles, Jacuzzi, and sundeck. Parking. ***Moderate*** (pool view) to ***very expensive*** (bay view suites). Contact at Morro Bay, CA 93442; 805–772–5651, 800–321–9566 CA, or 800–772–5651 elsewhere in the U.S. Located 1m past the Embarcadero on Main Street. The **San Luis Bay Inn** has an exceptional location overlooking Port Luis at the end of Avila Beach. From your balcony you watch the gulls over the sea, deer wandering the neighboring hills, and drowse to the sound of fog horns. This very informal resort offers 76 unusually large, casually decorated rooms. While there is no true lobby, there are two restaurants, a lounge with entertainment, pool, tennis, 18-holes of golf, bicycles, aerobics, and nature walks. Parking. Courtesy airport and Amtrak transfers. ***Very expensive*** with ocean view. Contact Box 189, Avila Beach 93424; 805–595–2333 or 800–592–5928 CA. Located 3m west of US 101 (exit Avila Beach from south, San Luis Bay Dr. from the north) and 7m south of San Luis Obispo.

There are plenty of accommodations along the highways, with a Motel 6 in San Luis Obispo and another on CA 1 around Morro Bay. There are ***motel rows*** in San Luis Obispo (8 blocks from center on Monterey St. with a TraveLodge and Quality Inn), Morro Bay (around the Embarcadero and Main St. with numerous Best Westerns), near Hearst Castle at both Cambria (the small establishments fronting Moonstone Beach are particularly nice) and San Simeon.

THE SPANISH CAPITAL: MONTEREY

. . . we found ourselves to be in the best port that could be desired, for besides being sheltered from all the winds, it has many pines for masts and yards, and live oaks and white oaks, and water in great quantity, all near the shore.

SEBASTIAN VIZCAINO, 1602

The magnificent Monterey Bay, often shrouded by fog, was not easily discovered. Blown off the coast by a storm, the earliest explorer Cabrillo may have missed the port entirely. And long after Vizcaino's discovery, when Spain decided to defend the bay against the Russians and English, the Portola expedition struggled to find it. No matter how persistently Portola led his soldiers through the Santa Lucias and around the Monterey peninsula, he discovered only a little stream for "what should be the Rio Carmelo," a mere cove for "what should be a port." Whether Vizcaino's radiant description misled them, whether weariness and hunger blurred their vision, or dense fog deceived them, the Spaniards, as their chaplain explains, wondered if Vizcaino's port had simply disappeared.

However, . . . [the port] of Monterey has become invisible to us, and we did not find it anywhere throughout the journey . . . Therefore, the best and most careful conclusion that we could come to is that Monterey has been lost, or the land swallowed up . . .

FRAY JUAN CRESPI, 1769

The loss was not only a body of water discovered more than a century and a half before them. The very reason for the expedition, for the months of hunger and the deaths of too many friends, was to establish the primary fort and mission of Alta California at the apparently vanished bay. They continued to search. Months later, after discovering the bay at San Francisco if not the one at Monterey, the expedition returned. The day was clear, revealing the immense bay formed by Point Pinos and Point Ano Nuevo and enabling the expedition to recognize the body of water as the one described by Vizcaino, the so desperately sought after bay of Monterey. Messengers were sent down the barely forged Camino Real, past the reed chapel and tiny garrison already established at San Diego, and continuing on a two month journey through Baja and over to Mexico City, where their good news was greeted with the joyful pealing of church bells. And in Monterey, the Spaniards founded both the mission of San Carlos Borromeo and a royal presidio to defend the king's bay and territory.

A chapel and altar were constructed next to the same ravine and oak tree, adjoining the beach, where it is said that Mass was celebrated at the beginning of the past century [by Vizcaino] . . . after the Mass . . . the officers conducted the ceremony of taking possession of that land in the name of His Catholic Majesty . . . accompanied by shouts of "Viva!," the clangor of bells, and musket shots. After this we all ate together along the beach and walked along it during the afternoon.

PADRE JUNIPERO SERRA, 1770

Celebrations eventually would become more elaborate as Monterey grew into a capital city. Yet the early years remained as austere as the founding ceremonies, as frustrating as the search for the elusive bay. At this provincial capital the Manila galleons, laden with silks and porcelain, were to stop on their way to Acapulco; yet captains of the China trade more often preferred fines to detours to so remote a place. To this provincial capital, Spain ordered the annual supply ships, but supplies arrived so infrequently the Spaniards were left "without a tortilla." Only Commander Pedro Fages' bear hunts saved the colony from starvation. And the land around the presidio though perfectly located for fortifying the bay, couldn't support adequate crops, forcing Father Serra to rebuild the thatched mission nearer the Carmel River. As for the presidio, it did boast a chapel and house for the comandante, although most buildings were constructed of logs and mud. Perhaps the soldiers and their families were too discourged to build a fine fort, for their efforts certainly failed to impress the Anza expedition.

It is all a very small affair, and for lack of houses the people live in great discomfort. Nor is this for want of materials, for there is lime and timber to spare . . . The commander [Anza] indeed had to lodge in the storehouse, and I in a dirty little room full of lime, while the rest of the people accommodated themselves in the plaza with their tents . . .

FRIAR PEDRO FONT, 1775

Not too surprisingly the first *gobernadora,* or governor's wife to live in the capital, Dona Eulalia de Fages, found it intolerable. No shops and too few entertainments, the shocking nakedness of the Indians, all drove this refined woman from Catalonia, Spain, to spend her years in Monterey plotting a way to leave. First she had to convince her husband to abandon his valuable post. So she shunned his affections for months. When that didn't work, she shocked this Catholic community by suing for divorce. Then she changed her mind.

Suddenly one morning Eulalia with a thousand protests summoned me, and amid tears humbly sought pardon for all the past . . . Gracias a Dios *that now we dwell in union and harmony.*

PEDRO FAGES, 1787
(Richman)

Reconciled with her husband but not to Monterey, Dona Eulalia secretly petitioned Mexico City to recall him for his alleged ill-health. Although this plot also failed, she eventually succeeded in forcing Don Pedro's resignation. In 1791, after nine years as governor and many others spent in the exploration and conquest of California, Pedro Fages sailed to Mexico to live contentedly, we presume, with Monterey's first *gobernadora.*

If Dona Eulalia had just been more patient, she could have joined in the excitement generated in Monterey as foreign ships began to visit the capital. She may have been present when the first foreign vessel, carrying the Frenchman Laperouse, was guided to its anchorage, "which the fog was hiding from us," by the firing of guns every quarter hour. But it was Governor Arrillaga's wife who replaced her aboard Vancouver's ship for an evening of dining and dancing that was so unfortunately cut short.

. . . the motion of the ship, though very inconsiderable, greatly to my disappointment obliged the ladies, and indeed some of the gentlemen, very soon to retire.

GEORGE VANCOUVER, 1792

Although Vancouver did find Monterey still "lonely," and not too interesting, he noted that the officer's quarters at least were roofed with red tiles and that the padres were building "a church with stone and mortar." Within a few years, Monterey's population would reach 400 to form a town that, despite its shortcomings, was a town of

liberal-minded, generous people, each of whom endeavored to surpass the other in manifesting an interest in our welfare.

VANCOUVER, 1792

The capital city grew, but its fortifications crumbled. As early as Vancouver's visit the presidio was seen to be in a "defenseless state." By the early 1800s a mere storm destroyed the main gate and no money could be found for rebuilding it. Not only was the presidio in no condition to provide protection, its soldiers became increasingly demoralized during the years of war between Spain and Mexico. As Spain fought the insurgents in Mexico, it forgot its faraway province. No supply ships arrived after 1811. No funds for soldiers' salaries were received. The missions sustained the province with their crops and livestock, but suppliers of ammunition and even blankets were harder to find.

In the last years of Spanish government . . . I personally saw . . . four soldiers going to bed in a big tub make of skins, covering themselves with dry hay because they had absolutely nothing else with which to protect themselves from the cold.

PIO PICO (1877)

It was in such a sorry state that the Monterey presidio found itself challenged, for the first time, to protect Spain's territory. Hippolyte Bouchard, pirate and self-proclaimed liberator, arrived to free Monterey from its Spanish bondage with 600 men, over 60 cannon and two howitzers. The Monterey presidio matched up with only 8 heavy guns, not all serviceable, and 40 soldiers. Instead of coming ashore to discuss principles of independence, Bouchard opened fire. Monterey responded heroically and for two hours its defenders

. . . kept up a constant and effective fire, doing much damage to the frigate, aided by the soldiers of the presidial company, who bore themselves at the battery with an unspeakable serenity despite the balls that were falling around them.

GOVERNOR PABLO VICENTE DE SOLA
1818
(Bancroft)

Bouchard pretended to surrender, sending ashore a few prisoners to show his good faith. But a bit later he landed hundreds of men on the beach and Monterey, already evacuated by its women and children, and now deserted by its soldiers. The pirates held Monterey for a week, sleeping on the landing beach near the customs house. As one of them explains, they had no problem occupying their time.

The Sandwich Islanders [Hawaiians], who were quite naked when they landed, were soon dressed in the Spanish fashion, and all the sailors were employed in searching the houses for money, breaking and ruining everything.

PETER CORNEY, 1818

When the Californians, who had only one drunken citizen captured refused an exchange of prisoners, Bouchard burnt Monterey and sailed off. Not till months later were all the settlers able to return, their houses rebuilt, the presidio chapel purified, and the presidio itself finally refortified, even if its battery was reduced to only two cannon.

Only too soon foreign war ships, this time from the United States, would again challenge Monterey. But the struggle against Bouchard would be the capital's last and only defense of Spain. In 1822 the governor and comandantes, the prefect of the missions, and other notables gathered in the presidio plaza and celebrated Mexico's liberation from Spain with the thundering of the few cannon left to them. They agreed to

. . . at once recognize that this Province is solely dependent on the Imperial government of Mexico and independent of Spanish domination.

CALIFORNIA ARCHIVES, 1822
(Englehardt)

Mexican independence hardly solved the problems of the presidio, since paychecks continued to exist only in memory. While 1828, and nearly twenty years without pay, brought the first mutiny at the presidio, it was "easily quelled without serious consequence." The presidio never would recover from its problems, but Monterey as a town was coming into its own. After Corporal Manuel Boronda and a few others dared to build their adobes outside the presidio walls, others left their cramped quarters inside the fort and lived in homes, often no more than straw huts, scattered haphazardly about the surrounding plain because there were no streets. Although one French visitor, Duhaut-Cilly, thought anyone expecting to see a substantial capital city might think he had made a mistake "as to the true anchorage," Monterey had grown large enough to warrant some ordinances from the town council.

Church duties must be strictly performed; nor must any one leave church when the sermon begins, as is customary . . .

Liquor not to be sold on dias festivas *[holidays] before mass, nor after the drum-beat at night . . .*

Entering taverns or houses on horseback strictly prohibited.

MONTEREY, ORDENANZAS
MUNICIPALES, 1828
(Bancroft)

A few years later the municipality instituted fines for owners who allowed their hogs to roam the streets, such as they were.

In the last decades of the Mexican period, Monterey more proudly wore the title of capital city. Commerce brought affluence, and straw huts became quaint adobe cottages, white-washed and roofed with California tiles. Although enormous quantities of silver were in circulation, there was no fear of thieves. Money was carelessly "tied up in a handerchief" and adobe doors were always left open in welcome.

Nothing is more common than to see a woman living in a house of only two rooms, and the ground for a floor, dressed in spangled satin shoes, silk gown, high comb, and gilt, if not gold ear-rings and necklace.

RICHARD HENRY DANA, 1835

And the duties earned from the customs house enabled even the long-suffering presidio officers to dress lavishly in silk jackets and brocaded vests, velvet pants and broad sombreros "with a gilt or figured band."

They have no suspenders, but always wear a sash round the waist, which is generally red.

DANA, 1835

Over forty foreigners established themselves here in order to carry on trade, finding the proximity of the governor and customs house useful. One of the most influential of these merchants was the Bostonian Thomas Larkin. This enterprising businessman started the first lumbering of redwoods for export, and his contacts within California and from around the world—Valparaiso, Mazatlan, Honolulu, and Canton—not only stimulated local commerce, but also led to the building of a new wharf and an expanded customs house. As Monterey prospered so did Larkin who decided to build a home appropriate to his wealth. With a redwood frame, Irish carpenters, and 5000 dollars he constructed the first two-story home in California, encircled it with verandas, walled it with adobe, and topped it off with a hipped roof. It was so smashing that Governor Alvarado built a second one, and soon anyone of consequence wanted a house in the "Monterey style."

. . . the newly-constructed buildings which give this town an air of youth and freshness, which charms and seduces as much as the amiable hospitality of its inhabitants.

GABRIEL LAFOND, 1843
(Crouch)

Another settler, one of the first, was the Englishman William Hartnell who traded the usual tools and cottons in addition to holy pictures and altar lace for mission cattle. Not completely successful in commerce, Hartnell later founded the first *colegio* in the province for the education of the sons of the illustrious Estradas, Soberanes and Arguellos.

The terms of enrollment are as follows: the fee for each student for room and board, laundry and tuition, is 200 pesos a year . . . the student must bring with him at least four changes of underwear and two sets of wearing apparel, bed linen, two towels, two napkins, and a set of silver.

WILLIAM HARTNELL, 1833

Unfortunately the first families more often than not preferred to educate their sons abroad—or in the saddle, perfecting their horsemanship if not their command of math. The colegio floundered with 11 borders, six of them mission educated neophytes.

As for the daughters of the gente de razon, they learned sewing, embroidery, and music and, marrying in their teens, rarely received a formal education. When they did go to school, as Prudencia Higuera recalled, the teacher told them the earth was round and "we all laughed out loud, and were much ashamed." Whatever they lacked in formal education, however, they made up for in dancing, religion, and amiability—what some called their orthodox occupations. Hartnell, like many foreign residents, became captivated by one such adolescent belle, Teresa de la Guerra who married the Englishman and bore him twenty children.

My husband gives me everything that I want. I give him myself and his children. There is an Indian girl for every baby born as soon as it born; I have only to bear and love them.

TERESA DE LA GUERRA HARTNELL

Although all the ladies did indeed seem charming, not all were so retiring. Governor Arguello's daughter was known for her horsemanship, and was said to lasso a cow "the same as men." And Dona Teresa's sister, Angustias, was of a different mold even if she, too, eventually married a foreigner, the American Ord. Dona Angustias was considered "the prettiest woman in the place," but she was equally well known for her penetrating wit and intelligence, so much so that more than one Yankee visitor commented on the "justness and elegance" of her remarks. And far from being a helpless belle, Angustias was bold and, as she herself said, "not frightened by anything."

[Monterey] was the place most frequently visited by ships of different nations, especially warships, whose distinguished officials served as a model in manners. It consequently resulted that people of the better class in Monterey had finer manners than those of any other place, not even excepting Los Angeles, where there was a very select society.

JOSE ARNAZ (1878)

Monterey society may have been the most refined in this Mexican territory—in fact, only here could be heard the melodious notes of a piano. Yet political intrique often led members of the elite to forget their manners, such as Juan Bautista Alvarado, the local favorite son who so rudely fired a cannon shot at the governor's mansion, thereby deposing the Mexican appointee. Perhaps these flaws in good society reflected shortcomings of some of the dignified foreign visitors who served as "a model in manners." The French Count Duflot de Mofras could hardly be said to have set a perfect example while dining at the Hartnell house.

. . . he found fault with every one of our dishes, however, he did full justice to the wine.

DONA TERESA, 1842

Certainly the count offended all sense of propriety when he retired to his room after dinner and, finding a barrel of the choicest wine stored there, proceeded to drink himself into oblivion.

Next morning at breakfast my guest, not making an appearance . . . I ordered the door [to the guest room] to be broken; and there stretched upon the floor my Frenchman lay drunk . . .

DONA TERESA, 1842

In the 1840s the foreign vessels, especially warships, anchored even more frequently at Monterey not only to enjoy the lavish balls—"Dances were given continuously in Monterey"—but also to spy for their governments. Count Duflot was a spy in addition to being arrogant, and after his many flirtations and free dinners he wrote his government saying it would be advantageous to establish a French colony on the Pacific Coast. Other nations eyed California for annexation as Mexico's control over its territory weakened. Some even made threatening approaches, such as the British man-of-war that anchored at Monterey, hopeful that Mexican debts might be paid in full with the aquisition of California. No government, however, was more determined than the United States to possess California.

We must have it, others must not.

THOMAS LARKIN, 1846
(Hammond)

So anxious was the United States to secure California that Thomas Ap Catsby Jones, commander of the Pacific fleet, created an international incident by prematurely sailing into port and demanding the surrender of Monterey. As the 44-gun frigate *United States* took aim on the defenseless capital, the Californios met in Governor Alvarado's house.

The entire night was spent in discussing projects and arguing about what was best to do. Finally the decision was reached to transfer the government to Mission San Antonio de Padua, taking the archives in carretas *[carts] . . . Afterward the plaza was surrendered without resistance, for there was no means of defense.*

JOSE ARNAZ, 1842

Unfortunately for the American commander, there was no state of war between Mexico and the United States, at least not yet. Soon after taking possession of the presidio, Commodore Jones learned of his mistake.

The American forces returned to their ship, our soldiers returned to their stations, the American flag was lowered, and the Mexican flag was hoisted and saluted by the Commodore with 21 guns.

ANGUSTIAS DE LA GUERRA ORD, 1842

The embarrassed American soldier ordered to lower the U.S. flag, promptly got drunk and nearly fell off a cliff. The Californios merrily celebrated their quickly regained freedom. And the commodore awaited his recall to Washington.

More discreet methods were needed. Thomas Larkin was appointed U.S. consul in 1843, and then at the request of Secretary of State Buchanan, he became a secret agent with instructions to work toward the peaceful annexation of California. Californians were tiring of the political confusions of the time, and knowing that Mexico could not offer stability, many wished for independence. And there were so many Americans living in the territory, not only in Monterey, but also in other coastal cities and the interior, that they quite possibly could influence the loyalties of the Californios. Already Monterey celebrated the 4th of July because its jubilant dances and fireworks coincided with the solemn religious services of the feast day of Our Lady of Refuge.

. . . they usually had salutes, a dance, etc. It was a great fiesta day.

ORD, 1846

One July 4th, that in the year 1846, U.S. warships were anchored in the bay. All of Monterey anxiously suspected a U.S. takeover, so much so that during the services for Our Lady of Refuge rumors spread that the Americans were disembarking. All the parishioners rushed out of the presidio chapel, and in their panic some were injured. Local suspicions certainly were warranted. In the preceding months, hadn't the interloper Fremont audaciously raised the American flag on California soil? Hadn't another warship, the U.S.S. *Portsmouth* pulled into San Francisco Bay? And hadn't Consul Larken held a ball for that so-called invalid Archibald Gillepsi, saying that he was in Monterey "to improve his health?"

. . . we found it difficult to believe that the government of the United States would send a ship of war solely to bring a young invalid to California.

ORD, 1846

For Dona Angustias, surely Gillepsi was "an emissary who came for no good." Indeed he came with orders for Larkin and Fremont. As Larkin reported ". . . the pear is near ripe for falling." The Californios had good reasons for their suspicions, yet they anticipated the takeover three days too early. Not till July 7th did Commodore Sloat land his troops.

Once again California was threatened. This time the presidio was not simply ill-prepared, it had just about disappeared, its adobes reused in other building projects. A few cannon did pretend to protect the town, but by the time the American fleet arrived all the artillerymen to fire them were gone. In fact, the entire army had retreated to positions in the countryside. Not even a Mexican flag could be found to make its proclamation flying over the city. Troops landed, and the United States took possession of Monterey, defenseless yet again.

There was no garrison, and I believe that the only Mexican officer present was old Captain Mariano Silva.

ORD, 1846

Although Monterey surrendered without a fight, Larkin's dream of the peaceful annexation was not to be realized. Californios organized against the U.S. invasion, and fought hard with few resources. But not in Monterey. Monterey surrendered, and for the last time.

The Spanish capital, then Mexican capital, became an American headquarters. Governors established themselves in Larkin's two-story adobe; troops bunked in the customs house while other troops like the New York Volunteers performed *Henry IV* in Jack Swan's boarding house. But change in possession brought only too few changes in politics. The petty feuds and political coups of the Mexican period persisted under the Americans who appointed five different governors in the first months, and at times two of these gentlemen simultaneously claimed the honor. At least Rev. Walter Colton, the first U.S. mayor of Monterey, achieved some semblance of government when he convened the Constitutional Convention of 1849. With the discovery of gold the presidio again was deserted, this time by U.S. soldiers gone to make their fortunes. Even Larkin took advantage of the boom in the north, selling out his Monterey properties for land in San Francisco. Soon the capital would move north, too, leaving behind the settlement founded with such difficulty by Gaspar de Portola in 1770.

Monterey, the prettiest town on the coast, and its capital and seat of customs, had got no advantage from the great changes, was out of way of commerce and of the travel to the mines . . . and not worth stopping at . . .

RICHARD HENRY DANA, 1859

Sights

The bay is still magnificent, otter and sea lions glide through its waters. The town has grown, of course, but the Custom House and Larkin's two-story home continue to grace the maze of streets left from the old capital town. Even the presidio chapel, the only one still in use, can be visited along with numerous other adobes and historical museums, as well as an exceptional new aquarium. The Monterey Peninsula includes more than the town of Monterey, it includes half-day bike rides or scenic car trips around 17-mile drive. It includes the Monarch butterflies at Pacific Grove (Lighthouse Ave., Oct.–Mar.), wind-gnarled cypress trees and mansions at Pebble Beach, and Serra's mission at Carmel. North around the bay were the cattle ranches and retreats of the wealthy, now mostly replaced by artichoke fields and the farms clustered near Salinas.

Town Sights

Although many Anglo-Americans attempted to straighten the tangle of Monterey "streets," they remain tangled and are also complicated now by car traffic if not by wandering pigs. It's best to park your car (in the Fisherman's Wharf area, if you can) and follow the self-guided walking tours available: The **Monterey State Historic Park** (MSHP, Visitors Center at Pacific House, Scott St. at Custom House Plaza; 649–2836; open daily 10 a.m.–5 p.m.; closed Christmas and Thanksgiving; set fee for all monuments mentioned below as part of MSHP); or the **Path of History,** a self-guided tour that encompasses more sights than the park, including many privately owned adobes closed to the public. You can obtain maps of the Path of History at many of the sites belonging to MSHP, as well as at the Chamber of Commerce (see "Directory"). *Tips:* Many of the MSHP adobes can be visited only on regularly scheduled tours; check the daily schedule for these house tours before planning your day. Also, in the summer you might want to sign up in advance at the houses that interest you most, because the tours, limited in size, are often full. Some of the privately owned adobes open for the **Spring Adobe Tour;** seasonal events mark **Christmas in the Adobes** (for details on both, contact the Chamber of Commerce).

★★★ Historic Monterey □ Starting at the Custom House Plaza near Fisherman's Wharf and spreading over the neighboring downtown streets, are many carefully preserved buildings from the period when Monterey flourished as a capital. The best place to begin is **Pacific House** (at Scott St.) where you can easily pick up information at the visitors center. The enterprising Larkin built Pacific House in 1843 in order to supply anchored ships with water. After the U.S. takeover, Pacific House became the official naval depot and the fortunate Larkin took the opportunity to enlarge it. Later the depot became a sailor's boarding house, then a saloon with bull and bear fights in the backyard now transformed into the beautiful Memory Garden, where each June Monterey celebrates its founding with a *merienda,* or picnic (MSHP fee and hours). Behind Pacific House is Joseph Boston's shop **Casa de Oro** (Scott at Olivier), called "house of gold" not for its appearance but for rumors that this general store once secured forty-niners' gold dust in its safe. The renovated store continues to boast the iron safe, its shelves are again full of merchandise—now souvenirs for travelers (Wed.–Sat. 10 a.m.–5 p.m.; Sun. noon–5 p.m.; free). The **★★ Custom House** (Custom House Plaza near Fisherman's Wharf) is the oldest of California public buildings (parts of it date from 1827), and it once stood on the very edge of the harbor. Here, all ships wanting to trade along the coast had to pull into port and register their cargoes. From Russia, England, Hawaii, and France came sailing brigs eager to do business. Often the captains' names were simply incomprehensible to the customs officials, so more convenient nicknames, like "four-eyes" for the New Englander who wore glasses, were used to open accounts. Just as often, the traders avoided paying duties by smuggling along the coast or hiding their goods from officials

It was then considered as no disgrace for a merchant to evade the revenue laws . . . When the vessel reached the port of entry, the customs officers would go through the formality of making an examination of the ship, but did it in quite a superficial way. They were so exceedingly well-mannered that they did not wish to appear impolite . . .

WILLIAM HEATH DAVIS, 1843

Those taxes that were collected supported almost the entire California government. Larkin reported that, on the average, $86,000 was collected annually. The Custom House today is cleverly restored to look as it originally did, piled with the merchandise once brought from around the world in exchange for California hides and tallow. (MSHP fee; open daily 10 a.m.–5 p.m.). Walking around Heritage Harbor and following Scott Street west, you come to Pacific Street and Monterey's ★ **First Theater,** the first in California to dare charge admission (1847). Although mostly Anglo-melodramas provided the entertainment, after the U.S. conquest the New York Volunteers did put together a performance of Shakespeare. Year round you can walk through the exhibits that include, it's claimed, a chair carved from the oak tree under which Vizcaino said the first mass in Monterey. On summer weekends you can enjoy a play preceded by a visit to **Jack Swan's Tavern,** still serving up food and drink as well as being part of the exhibition here. (MSHP Wed.–Sun. 11:30 a.m.–5 p.m., later when performances; tavern open daily in summer; 375–4916).

Just down Pacific Street, around the outside of Heritage Harbor, you come to the entrance of the **Monterey Presidio,** still in use but by the U.S. Army. Near the main gate, Vizcaino landed and Serra and Portola celebrated their arrival at Monterey. Although the original presidio was built on the other side of town where the chapel still stands (see below), the presidio was moved to this more strategic location atop the hill in the Mexican period.

"El Presidio," or town of Monterey, is situated on the declivity of a beautiful rising ground, the top of which is crowned with stately pines. The gradual ascent to its elevated summit is covered with scattered woods and rich and varied flowers.

ALFRED ROBINSON (1846)

The battery is gone, along with all other fortifications, but here and there are plaques and monuments to the likes of Friar Serra, as well as Commodore Sloat. (Map available at museum.) The ★ **museum** tells the history of presidio hill from the time of early Indian settlements to the present, with dioramas and interesting artifacts, particularly those from Governor Arguello's estate. (Mon.–Fri. 9 a.m.–11:45 a.m.; 12:30–4 p.m.; closed major holidays; free; 242–8414.)

Retracing your steps on Pacific past the First Theater, you come to the first of the old houses, the 1830s ★ **Casa Soberanes** (336 Pacific at Del Monte). Originally built by Jose Raphael Estrada, member of one of Monterey's first families and whose step-brother, Governor Alvarado, was able to secure for him the special town lot overlooking the bay. When the Estradas needed to sell the house, their cousin Ezequel Soberanes gladly purchased it, raising his seven children here and preparing them for their proper place in Monterey society.

This piano the secretary of the government Don Manuel Jimeno, played at dances. The Senoritas Soberanes, knowing nothing about music, sang harmoniously nevertheless and in perfect time.

JOSE ARNAZ, 1840s

Until 1922 Soberanes' descendants lived in the house; today the Monterey colonial style home is furnished to a later period, but the adobe construction and garden provide period interest. (MSHP fee; by tour only; 10 a.m.–1 p.m., 2–4 p.m.; closed Thurs.) Further up Pacific you pass other adobes, including the **Casa Serrano** (#412; open weekends 2–4 p.m.), on your way to the historic area around Civic Plaza.

Above Jefferson on Pacific Street is Civic Plaza, a fine town park surrounded by a number of old adobes. The **Casa Gutierrez** presents an especially picturesque garden patio, and even though now a restaurant, it preserves the rustic interior of what was in 1841 a simple Californian home. Also here is the **Monterey Peninsula Museum of Art** (559 Pacific St.) with its collection of Asian art, photography, and regional and folk art (Tue.–Sat. 10 a.m.–4 p.m.; Sun. 1–4 p.m.; closed some holidays; free; 372–7591). Overlooking all of this is ★★ **Colton Hall** (522 Pacific St.) built by Walter Colton, Monterey's first Anglo-mayor, and the site of the 1849 Constitutional Convention. This historic building, now the museum of the city, contains a wonderful display of the convention, with papers and memorabilia strewn across the convention tables as if readied for the delegates to return from lunch to begin anew their debates on California's first constitution. On October 13 the exhibit becomes even livelier as school children reenact the debates. In another part of the building you can visit what remains of a much deteriorated 1854 jail. (Open daily 10 a.m.–noon, 1–5 p.m.; closed major holidays; free; 375–9944.)

Just a few more steps up Pacific, turn left on Madison and come to the busy intersection of Calle Principal, Hartnell and Polk. Here in the small but attractive **De la Torre Adobe** (599 Polk, closed to public) Juana de la Torre practiced her expert midwifery on women from as far away as Salinas. Across the street at the **Stokes Adobe** (500 Hartnell) could be found the printing press for the first newspaper, *The Californian,* as well as patients waiting to receive medical advice from acting pharmacist—"doctor" James Stokes. Stokes also had in his home here a popular general store called "La Gran Barata," or the great bargain. Today the adobe is a French restaurant.

Dropping down on historic Calle Principal you can see models of sailing brigs and exhibits on the whaling industry at the **Allen Knight Maritime Museum** (550 Calle Principal; Tues.–Fri. 1–4 p.m.; weekends 2–4 p.m.; closed holidays; free; 375–2553) and enjoy the facades of buildings until you come to the next corner and house of one of the foremost Americans, Thomas Larkin. The ★★★ **Larkin House** (Calle Principal and Jefferson), with its combination of Spanish adobe and New England styles, became the archtype for fashionable Monterey homes during the Mexican period. It also was the focus for important events leading to the U.S. conquest. Here Archibald Gillespi came, invalid or not, carrying his dispatches, so secret they could be committed only to memory, never to paper. Here Commodore Sloat held meetings and General Kearney established his headquarters. As for Larkin during those turbulent times, he was held hostage by the *Californios.* Upon returning to this house he wrote his friends and left a record of hospitality that persevered even in war.

I am happy to inform you I am home again . . . I've had as you may imagine some ups and downs. Twice aimed at to be shot . . . I was closely confined, more so than the others, but had never less than 4 or 5 meals sent to me a day, 4 or 5 courses each . . .

LARKIN, 1847

In one of the earliest California real estate deals, Larkin converted his initial $5000 investment in the house into a $30,000 sale after only 14 years. The house now is restored and resplendent with Larkin family antiques—Baccarat chandeliers, Hepplewhite furnishings—as well as the original redwood floors, glass windows, and crooked door frames. (MSHP fee; by guided tour only; 10 a.m.–5 p.m.; closed Tues.)

Near the Larkin House clustered numerous historic adobes. Around Alvarado, Polk and Munras streets the houses of old Monterey's elite once entertained visiting capitans from around the world, dining them at their rosewood tables and honoring them with dances in their second-floor ballrooms.

The houses of Don Juan Cooper, Don Jose Amesti, and Don Jose Abrego, were generally the centers of familiar reunions, and dances were commonly held at one or the other of these houses on the afternoons and evenings of fiestas.

JOSE ARNAZ, 1840s

Although the home of the impetuous Governor Alvarado and the adobe of the Englishman Harknell are gone, and the **Estrada Adobes** (456 Tyler near Bonifacio) now form part of the Monterey Savings Bank (at least their facades form a lovely and public patio), the ★ **Casa Amesti** (516 Polk St.), elegant and retaining its beautiful gardens can still be seen (open weekends 2–4 p.m.; fee; 372–2608) and the **Casa Abrego** (Webster and Abrego) stands restored, though greatly diminished in size and now bereft of its piano (closed to public). And two other adobes are refurbished and regularly open to the public: the ★ **Stevenson House** (530 Houston St., off Pearl) with one room well furnished to the period of the 1830s, and the rest with memorabilia of Robert Louis Stevenson commemorating his brief stay here (MSHP fee; by tour only; 1–4 p.m.; closed Wed.); and the Cooper-Molera Adobe.

One of the largest homes was the ★★ **Cooper-Molera Adobe** (508 Munras), really a complex of buildings that included store fronts (still standing on Polk St., dating from 1826) and private dwellings built by

Captain John Rogers Cooper, who after his marriage to the illustrious Encarnacion Vallejo was known as Don Juan Bautista. Half-brother to Larkin, it was Cooper who encouraged his relative to come to California to make his fortune. The last Cooper descendant to live here was Frances Molera, who died in 1968. Today the home fronting Munras Street has been restored to the period of the Coopers' greatest wealth, around 1860. The shop now functions as one, with souvenirs and historical materials; there's a museum room as well as a brief slide show on the history of the house; there're barns and other functional areas restored to just as they were when they were an integral part of a gentlemanly Californian's home. (MSHP fee; by tour only; open 10 a.m.–4 p.m., except till 5 p.m. in summers.)

As you walk over to the east side of town to the presidio chapel, you pass even more adobes. Not only did the sturdy townhouses line Alvarado and Calle Principal all the way down to the harbor, but they crossed over Munras, Webster and other streets. The earliest enclave of adobes was built outside the presidio walls just a few blocks south of the presidio church where the first of them all, the 1817 **Casa Boronda** (end of Boronda Lane off Fremont; closed to public) still stands, now hidden by the car repair shops lining Fremont Street. The Boronda Adobe and the six others that joined it here were most certainly looted by the pirate Bouchard.

Near Lake Estero where the presidio was originally established is the **Royal Presidio Chapel** (550 Church St. near Figueroa). Although founded by Serra in 1770 as the San Carlos Borromeo Mission, the sanctified ground became the *capilla real* for the governor and presidio soldiers once that mission was moved to Carmel. The present building dates from 1794 when master mason Manuel Ruiz finished the supervision of its construction. A chapel fit for the king's representatives, its facade of neoclassic and baroque motifs is among the most elaborate in California. Yet, it was a provincial chapel without all the refinements that could be found in Madrid, say, or even Mexico City.

We used to go to church attended by our (Indian) servants who carried small mats for us to kneel upon, as there were no seats. A tasteful little rug was considered an indispensable part of our belongings, and every young lady embroidered her own. The church floors were cold, hard, and damp, and even the poorer classes managed to use mats of some kind, usually the tule woven by the Indians.

BRIGADA BRIONES, 1828

Today the parish church has become the San Carlos Cathedral where services continue the tradition begun by Padre Serra (open daily 8 a.m.–6 p.m. except during mass; free; 373–2628).

The Bay □ While the whaling industry that flourished in Monterey during the 1850s is no more, and while the fishermen who later caught the sardines that supported the local economy have moved up the coast, **Fisherman's Wharf** survives full of curio shops, food stands, restaurants and a few fish markets. It is near here that Larkin built his wharf, and it is here you come to arrange sports fishing, tours of the harbor, or winter whale watching cruises. Also, it is here that you feed the always hungry and honking sea lions.

At **Cannery Row** the sardine packing factories have been transformed into galleries and restaurants, banishing to the past the tawdriness immortalized by John Steinbeck. One of the most inventive transformations has been of the former Portola Sardine Factory into the **Monterey Bay Aquarium** (866 Cannery Row), one of the largest aquatic museums in the world and a superb place to understand the role of the bay in sea oriented Monterey.

It is a merry sight to behold, on a bright sunny day, the joy of the Indians, at the landing place, as they scoop with their nets the leaping of the silvery fish [sardines] that are thrown upon the rocks—the darting of the birds, the splashing of the water as they pounce upon their prey—the jumping porpoise—the spouting whale, all of which attract hundreds of spectators to the beach, and keep them there for hours beholders of the scene.

ALFRED ROBINSON, 1834

The aquarium has developed its exhibits ingeniously, from constructing an artificial tidal pool right on the bay to re-creating a kelp forest in a two-story tank. A tank of the once nearly extinct sea otter that first attracted foreign ships to the coast, is accompanied by a feeding time talk that allows you to stroke an unbelievably plush otter pelt. (Open daily 10 a.m.–6 p.m. except Christmas; fee; weekends and holidays reservations recommended through Ticketron; 375–3333). Parking is limited at Cannery Row so on weekends and peak season you might want to park at the Convention Center near Fisherman's Wharf and take the free shuttle bus here. Inside the aquarium is a museum shop and very pleasant restaurant, the Portola Cafe, serving seafood, of course.

Scenic Drives □ The drive from Monterey to the open sea along

Ocean View Boulevard takes you past the charming Victorian and old Methodist retreat cottages of **Pacific Grove** to the **Point Pinos Lighthouse,** dating from 1855 and containing a few exhibits on its history (open weekends 1–4 p.m.; free). It was from Point Pinos that the Portola expedition first recognized Monterey Bay.

There we began to see thousands of sea lions that looked like a pavement a hundred yards from land, we saw two whales together, the sea being very quiet as though calm with oil.

FRIAR CRESPI, 1770

Continuing around the coast from Point Pinos is **Asilomar State Beach** with its miles of rocky shore and chaparral covered dunes wonderful for beachcombing.

From Asilomar State Beach, you come to Sunset Drive and one of the four entrances into **17-Mile Drive.** This bike (limited hours) and car road through the Del Monte Forest and along the coast travels in a loop that goes to Carmel and back. You can picnic in Monterey cypress groves, or at Spanish Bay from where Portola returned so disappointed to San Diego, or at Seal and Bird Rocks, wonderful points for viewing coastal wildlife. Or you might be looking for one of the six golf courses located on this drive, the most famous one being that at Pebble Beach. (Pick up self-guided tour maps at entrance gates; fee for cars; 372–5813). However you enjoy it, this route between Monterey and Carmel has been popular for centuries.

The road between them lies over some steep hills and hollow vallies, interspersed with many trees; the surface was covered over with an agreeable verdure; the general character of the country was lively, and our journey altogether was very pleasant.

VANCOUVER, 1792

Carmel

George Vancouver, riding his horse over part of what would become 17-mile Drive, became the second foreign visitor to mission headquarters at ★★★ **San Carlos Borremeo Mission.** A few years earlier Laperouse had journeyed to this second of Serra's missions, and finding the neophyte women tediously grinding wheat with stone mortars, he left them an iron mill. Upon his arrival Vancouver discovered that progress is not simply opportunity, for the mill had been discarded, the women preferring "their own methods." The mission was, nonetheless, progressing and Vancouver noted that the beginnings of a stone church was replacing Serra's earlier adobe chapel.

Manuel Estevan Ruiz, a master-mason and stone cutter, has agreed to teach his trades to the natives and to practice them therein, in consideration of 18 reales ($2.25) a day for a term of four years.

FRIAR FERMIN LASUEN, 1795
(Englehardt)

It is this same stone church today, with its massive simplicity, romantic Moorish dome and window, and beautiful setting near the sea, that pleases so many travelers. Yet Serra chose for his headquarters a mission that would struggle to sustain itself and its too few neophytes. After Serra died here in 1784, after the deaths of the other great and early missionaries Friar Crespi and Father Lasuen, the mission headquarters were moved to Santa Barbara. Left behind were traces of earliest California and a monument befitting Padre Serra: the first library, now re-created with Serra's own books; religious art brought from Baja California on the Portola expedition, including what Serra described as "a very beautiful statue of Our Lady which stood on the altar" at the founding of San Carlos church in Monterey (now in the side chapel at Carmel); and Serra's barren living quarters, no more than a cell revealing the sacrifices necessitated by life on the frontier. Serra's death bed

. . . consisted of a few hard boards roughly hewn and covered with only a blanket, which he used rather to cover himself with than to soften his couch for resting, and he did not even have a sheep skin as is the custom . . .

PADRE FRANCISCO PALOU, 1784

Also to be seen in the *museum* with its extensive collections including William Harknell's mementos on the colegio at Alisal; the Indian cemetery with its marker for Old Gabriel, dead at 151 years of age (Serra's baptism records indicate that in fact Gabriel lived a mere 140 years); and the gardens, among the loveliest in the mission chain. To the rear of the mission quadrangle is the ★ **Munras Memorial** presenting antique furnishings of the Munras family as they would have looked in their Monterey adobe that no longer stands. In September you can enjoy the annual San Carlos **festival.** *Open Mon.–Sat. 9:30 a.m.–4:30* *p.m.; Sun. and holidays 10:30 a.m.–4:30 p.m.; closed major holidays; donations; map; 624–3600. The mission is 5m from Monterey on CA 1, on the southern edge of Carmel at 3080 Rio Road.*

Apart from the mission, old Carmel had few occupants. Some ranches ranged inland along the river, but the only one still standing is the privately owned Boronda Adobe (Boronda Rd., just south of Carmel Valley Rd.; closed to public). It is here that the son of Monterey's Corporal Boronda built his home in 1840 by adding to an Indian adobe. His wife Juana made a yellow cheese from the surplus milk on their farm, and the later commercial dairy farm that replaced them made Dona Juana's cheese in greater quantities and spread the fame of what has become known as Monterey Jack. But apart from the few who grazed cattle in the Carmel Valley, and apart from the five or six soldiers and their families at San Carlos Borromeo with the missionaries, it can be said that for colonial Carmel

The remainder of the population consists of full blooded Indians.

FRIAR JUAN AMOROS, 1814
(*Englehardt*)

There may be no historic sights to tempt you down **Carmel Valley Road,** but a drive through this rustic area dominated by mountains and dotted with ranches is satisfying nonetheless. And you can continue back to Monterey on the beautiful country road through Laurales Canyon, off Carmel Valley Road about 10m from CA 1. (At the end of the canyon road turn left onto CA 68 for Monterey.)

Back around Carmel Bay, the steep shore and gullies didn't do much to attract the ranchero and his cattle. But the picturesque spot became the favorite retreat of San Francisco writers and artists at the beginning of this century. What was good enough for Jack London and Mary Austin, became home to later generations of poets and painters. Today, **Carmel-by-the-Sea** no longer is quiet, even if its residents attempt to preserve its picturesque cottages and village ambience. On weekends the shops and galleries are filled to capacity, and even more people flock to town in July for the two week long **Bach Festival** (Carmel Bach Festival, Box 575, CA 93932; 624–1521), and the **town beach** (at the end of Ocean Ave., the main street) has the whitest of white sand, fine for walking and sunbathing, though its clear waters are too cold for swimming. For swimming (with caution for there's a rip tide) and picnicking drive to the southern end of Scenic Drive to the **Carmel**

River State Beach. For more information on art galleries and cultural events write Carmel-by-the-Sea Business Association, Box 5433, CA 93921, or visit on San Carlos Street at Vandevort Court; 624–2522.

Salinas

As Bouchard sacked Monterey, the soldiers and government retreated to Salinas. Here with a few ranch buildings, built to shelter the vaqueros who managed the Rancho Nacional, the presidio grazing lands. In later years, many of the gente de razon petitioned for ranch lands in the vicinity of the river and creeks and built their country homes here. The Soberanes family received the *Rancho de Alisal* in the foothills of the Salinas. Later they gave part of their land to William Hartnell.

At last I have become a ranchero . . . The Soberanes have granted me an equal right with them in the Alisal property, giving me permission to pasture as many cattle as I consider advisable, to build a house and to plant as many [grape] vines and orchard trees as we need . . .

WILLIAM HARTNELL, 1831

Hartnell did build a home as well as California's first *colegio*. Later, during the American period, ex-Governor Alvarado retired to another part of the ranch, disillusioned and on the verge of leaving California forever, forsaking it for Mexico. Politics, he said, brings only unhappiness, it's "the most ungrateful career that a man can follow." Although cattle range the Salinas Valley, only fragments of the Soberanes Adobe still stand (private residence on Old Stage Road, about 5m east of Salinas). Gone are the orchards, gone is the first colegio (although some of its memorabilia can be seen at the Carmel Mission), gone are the homes of Alvarado and Hartnell (once located near 955 Old State Coach Road), gone is El Alisal.

A romantic stop, in a valley, between large hills covered with trees. In the center a fine stream winds its way towards an excessive plain . . .

ALFRED ROBINSON (1846)

Given the too few historic sights left from early California, it's only correct that the **city of Salinas** is best remembered as the birthplace of author John Steinbeck. But if you are in the area around the third weekend in July you might check out one tradition very reminiscent of ranching days, the **Salinas California Rodeo** (Box 1648, CA 93902 or 757–

2951 for information). For the other reminder of the Mexican past you needn't enter town, just follow signs off US 101 to the **Casa Boronda** (333 Boronda Rd. at W. Laurel). Boronda was never a wealthy man, and his adobe with a few simple furnishings reflects his status. The best part of this adobe is the enthusiasm of the volunteers from the local historical society. There's an annual *merienda,* or cook-out in September. (Open only Sun. 1–4 p.m.; free; 757–8085.) If you are driving through town, enjoy the art deco signs along Main Street, before turning west on to Central in order to see the Victorian house that John Steinbeck grew up in (132 Central Ave.; a restaurant serving lunch; reservations required 424–2735).

Salinas lies just off US 101, less than 20m east of Monterey on CA 68.

Accommodations

Some hotels have taken particularly good advantage of Monterey's beautiful bay and historic ambience. The **Monterey Plaza** has an exceptional setting overlooking the bay and is conveniently located at Cannery Row. Views of the bay, where otter bask in kelp outcroppings and sea lions swim, dominate the common areas as well as most of the 290 exceptionally large rooms and suites, but the interior here is noteworthy too. Red Portuguese marble, Oriental carpets and antique screens enrich the elegant lobby areas; the tea room and lounge offer a warming fireplace as well as piano music. The rooms are handsomely decorated with teak furniture, the bathrooms have Italian marble floors and shower stalls. Fine Italian restaurant, lounge, and shops. Exercise bikes, concierge for arrangements for golf and other sports, and health spa planned. Valet parking. ***Very expensive.*** Write 400 Cannery Row, CA 93940; 646–1700, 800–334–3999 CA, or 900–631–1339 elsewhere in the U.S.

The **Spindrift Inn** is located more in the heart of Cannery Row, but its intimate lobby and those of its 42 junior suites (with bay views) offer incredible tranquility. Each unit has window seats, canopied beds, and wood burning fireplaces. The ***very expensive*** price includes continental breakfast, afternoon tea, and valet parking. Write 652 Cannery Row, CA 93940; 646–8900, 800–841–1879 CA, 800–225–2901 elsewhere in the U.S. Away from the bay is another intimate establishment, the **Hotel Pacific** right along the Path of History and with sea views from its upper level garden terrace. The 100 suites here are found in various levels of contemporary, but historically inspired rambling adobe building. The lobby is small, like a living room; each suite has a fireplace and terrace or patio. Jacuzzi. ***Very expensive*** price includes continental breakfast, afternoon wine and cheese, and parking. Write 300 Pacific Street, CA 93940; 373–5700; 800–554–5542 CA; 800–225–2903 elsewhere in the U.S. My favorite of these intimate inns is **Merritt House**, the renovated 1830 adobe that later becomes the dignified home fronted with two-story columns of Judge Josiah Merritt. The 25 units of this inn can be found in the old Merritt house as well as in a more recent addition; all are surrounded by lovely gardens. The rooms vary, but are furnished handsomely to the period, and even the smallest ones offer fireplaces and terraces or balconies overlooking the garden. The suites are enormous, with full living room and bedroom, each with wood burning fireplaces. The ***expensive*** range for regular rooms, ***very expensive*** for suites, include a continental breakfast in the homey Common Room. Write 386 Pacific Street, CA 93940; 646–9686. Located conveniently on the Path of History.

If you're looking for a resort, the peninsula has many options starting with the **Lodge at Pebble Beach**, a completely self-contained resort surrounded by the manicured lawns of its championship golf course and overlooking Carmel Bay. The Lodge is really a series of two-story complexes housing 160 units, many of them suites, that more often than not have sea views and fireplaces. The main "lodge" contains the elegant lobby and terrace bar as well as some of the 4 restaurants; there're other lounges, some with entertainment; a village with numerous shops. The pool is 25 meters in length, there are tennis courts, Jacuzzis, and access to other sports besides golf. Valet parking. Rates begin at ***very expensive*** and go up considerably. Write Box 1128, Pebble Beach 93953; 624–3811. Located along 17-Mile Drive. The **Quail Lodge** has more of a mountain setting at its location on the Carmel Valley Golf and Country Club. The lodge is rustic and tranquil, modern in design with stained wood cathedral ceilings and thick carpeting. There are 100 units here, some with fireplaces, some found in patio cottages or pool and lakeside lodges. Elegant restaurant and lounge. Pool, tennis, 18-hole golf course and health spa. Valet parking. ***Very expensive.*** Write 8205 Valley Greens Dr., Carmel 93923; 624–1581, 800–682–9303 CA, or 800–538–9516 within the U.S. Located 3½m down Carmel Valley Road (turn right to hotel), within 10 minutes of Carmel-by-the-Sea. Less sumptuous but a wonderfully comfortable place to relax is the **Valley Lodge**, deep into the mountain serenity of Carmel Valley. The well-landscaped grounds are dotted with 31 homey units, some patio rooms, others containing fireplace suites with kitchenettes and porches. Although there is a hearty continental breakfast that comes with your room, other meals can be cooked from purchases in the nearby village or enjoyed in Carmel. Good swimming pool and hot tub; fitness center and sauna. Helpful management. Parking. ***Moderate to expensive.*** Write Box 93, Carmel Valley 93924; 659–2261; reservations in peak season require a 2 night minimum on weekends. Located 11m down Carmel Valley Road from CA 1, ½m from Carmel Valley Village.

There are a number of other pleasant establishments in the moderate to expensive range, particularly the intimate inns of Carmel with their fireplaces and complimentary breakfasts, such as **Lobos Lodge** (27 rooms; Ocean and Monte Verde; Drawer L-1, CA 93921; 624–3874) and **Vagabond House** (12 rooms; Delores and 4th; Box 2747, CA 93921; 624–7738). Victorian bed and breakfast establishments can be found in Pacific Grove, such as the noteworthy **Gosby House Inn** (22 rooms; 643 Lighthouse Ave., CA 93950; 375–1287), and in Carmel and Monterey. For more information on such places, contact the Monterey Chamber of Commerce.

Many of the large chain hotels are located in the region, Hilton, Hyatt, and Holiday Inn among them. At the Monterey Conference Center next to Fisherman's Wharf there are two establishments, a Sheraton a block inland and the **Doubletree Hotel** (374 rooms; 2 Portola Plaza, CA 93940; 649–4511, 800–528–0444). A **motel row** of sorts is found just off the Munras exit of CA 1 with a number of Best Westerns and local establishments; the TraveLodge is located near the Path of History.

Restaurants

The bay provides not only views for hotels and a place in history for Monterey, but also the bay prawns, rock cod, abalone, squid and salmon served fresh and well-prepared in so many local restaurants. With a prime location on the bay, **Domenico's** (50 Fisherman's Wharf, lunch and dinner daily; ***moderate-moderately expensive;*** reserve at 372–3655) is one of the finest for the traditional Monterey style of Italian seafood. Here you can dine not only on pasta with clams, but on crab cioppino and clams oreganato as well as mesquite grilled prawns. The oyster bar is wonderful for a light meal; if available make sure you try the marinated Dungeness crab cocktail. Overlooking Cannery Row is another large and extremely popular restaurant, the more pretentious **Sardine Factory** (701 Wave St.; Mon.–Thurs. opens at 4 p.m.; weekends at 2 p.m.; ***moderately expensive*** for hearty fixed-price dinner, up to ***expensive*** a la carte; reserve at 373–3775). This continental restaurant offers a variety of meat and seafood entrees but abalone is a specialty here—made from the delicate appetizer of cultured abalone with ginger sauce, to the house specialty abalone cream soup and main course of abalone. When available, try the delicious appetizer of Monterey prawns with their own caviar. The ambience here varies with the room, from the informality of the old bar room and the bustling of the large glass domed Conservatory Room, to the more intimate and formal Captain's Room. There is an extensive selection of California wines.

There are many more casual and modestly priced seafood establishments. The **Old Row Cafe** (807 Cannery Row; 9 a.m.–9:30 p.m. daily; ***moderate***; 372–7003) with its ceiling made from sardine tins offers good food, such as its hand-rolled ravioli stuffed with crab and covered with cream sauce and its fresh squid, lightly battered and delicious. Down on the Municipal Wharf where the fishing boats bring in their haul each day is **Sandbar & Grill** (on wharf off Figueroa St., 11:30 a.m.–11 p.m.; 10:30 a.m. for weekend brunch; ***moderate***; no reservations; 373–2818). While eating spinach salad with prawns or fried oysters and squid at this casual, local establishment, you can enjoy good views of the bay. In the evening there's piano music. Also with good bay views, at the very tip of Fisherman's Wharf, is **Rappa's** (11 a.m.–10 p.m.; ***moderate,*** with early bird specials bordering on the inexpensive; no reservations; 372–7562), a tidy restaurant offering fresh fish, baked cod bouillabaisse, and Italian-style squid.

Of course there are many cuisines to enjoy in this region. Next to Monterey Bay in the Heritage Harbor complex is the distinguished restaurant **Fresh Cream** (Scott and Pacific; Tues.–Sun. 6–9:30 p.m.; ***expensive*** reserve at 375–9798). Very well respected for its nouvelle cuisine, this small restaurant offers a new menu daily that, though limited, should please you with its carefully prepared French offerings. Usually you can choose a wonderful fish entree as well as duck or tournedos. Carmel, with its many quaint restaurants, is a favorite spot to dine and **L'Escargot** (Mission and 4th; dinner 6–9:30 p.m., closed Sun.; ***moderately expensive to expensive***; reserve at 624–4914) has long been one of its most popular for French provincial cuisine—escargots, smoked salmon, poulet chausseur, and chicken with fois gras and truffles. Also in Carmel is the **Gold Fork** (Ocean between Dolores and Lincoln; dinner 5–11 p.m., closed Mon.; ***expensive***; reserve at 624–2569), offering more continental and regional cuisine than traditional French. Decorated in ''California Provincial'' with floral carpeting, light paneling and Western style chandeliers, this restaurant has created a warm and comfortable ambience that is very popular. The specialty of the house is artichoke bisque and it's delicious. I also enjoyed the duckling here and found the rack of lamb very tender, if not cooked traditionally. There're some nouvelle offerings, too, like fresh agnolotti filled with Dungeness crabmeat and served with a sun dried tomato sauce.

A wonderful spot for casual dining and very good Italian food is Carmel's **Casanova** (5th between San Carlos and Mission; open 8 a.m.–dinner; ***moderate to moderately expensive;*** 625–0501). Here you can enjoy excellent canneloni (ricotta and sun dried tomatoes), linguini with scampi, or just a light salad of avocado stuffed with shrimp while you dine in one of the cozy indoor rooms or on the outdoor patio of this country cottage. Also popular, and attractive with its Carmel garden setting, is **Forge in the Forest** (5th at Junipero; lunch and dinner daily; bar menu Mon.–Thurs. 3–11:30 p.m.) where you can have cocktails with snacks of nachos or Chinese chicken salad, next to a handsome old wooden bar. In Monterey you should try the Mexican food in the picturesque **Sancho Panza** (590 Calle Principal; 11 a.m.–10 p.m.; ***inexpensive to moderate***; no reservations; 375–0095), located in the historic Casa Gutierrez, with indoor and patio dining.

With absolutely no ambience to recommend it, indeed you must place your orders at one of several food and bar stations so that it will be delivered to your table, is Monterey's **Gianni's Pizza** (725 Lighthouse Ave.; open 4 p.m. daily except Fri. and Sat. at 11:30 a.m.; ***inexpensive***; no reservations, some take-out; 649–1500). This is no ordinary pizza parlor, for in addition to the large, freshly prepared pizza you can also have cold pasta salads or lasagna, pastry and cappuccino. (Located a few blocks above Cannery Row.) In Monterey inexpensive sandwich and breakfast spots can be found along Alvardo Street, **Belleci's Deli** (#470; closed Sun.) being one of the cheapest, yet still good. In Carmel, check out **Le Bistro** (San Carlos, between Ocean and 7th).

There are a few places that belong in no particular category. The selection of gourmet prepared foods and take out deli at the **Mediterranean Market** in Carmel (Ocean at Mission) is terrific for snacking, eating in your room, or picnicking. The elegant breakfast at **Delfino's** (in the Monterey Plaza Hotel, 400 Cannery Row; 646–1700) should be planned one morning when you want to contemplate the beautiful bay and pamper yourself with good service, refined table settings, and lovely fresh fruit and a spinach omlette with sour cream. And mention must be made of Clint Eastwood's restaurant in Carmel where tourists line up just to have their pictures taken. If you want to eat at Eastwood's

Hog's Breath Inn (San Carlos between 5th and 6th; open daily lunch and dinner; ***moderate to moderately expensive***; 625–1044), you can try a reuben sandwich, a steak dinner, or Dirty Harry's Special.

Suggestions

Directory □ The zip code varies over the peninsula, but the area code is 408 except for toll-free numbers. ★ For helpful information contact *Monterey Peninsula Chamber of Commerce* (Box 1770, Monterey 93942; 649–1700) or visit during standard business hours for a copy of their excellent map at 380 Alvarado Street, near Custom House Plaza.

Getting Around □ Walking is highly recommended in Monterey along the Path of History and in Carmel-by-the-Sea. ★ Car rentals, taxis and bicycle rentals (373–3855) are available. ★ A free **shuttle bus** skirts the Path of History, Fisherman's Wharf, and Cannery Row during most weekends, holidays and holiday seasons, and daily in the summer (9 a.m.–10 p.m.; 899–2555). ★ Also there is **bus service** between Monterey, Carmel, and Salinas (899–2555). ★ Tours for sightseeing in town and around the peninsula, as well as to Hearst Castle, are offered by **Classic Tours** (372–3044) and, in the summer, **Gray Line** (373–4989).

Arrival □ The Monterey **airport** (373–3731) is just on the outskirts of town. Both regional and national airlines provide service here; **National** and **Budget** car rentals, taxis, and a limousine service are available. ★ The nearest **Amtrak** station is in Salinas (40 Railroad Ave.; 422–7458). ★ **Greyhound** operates out of Monterey (351 Del Monte Ave.; 373–4735). ★ Monterey is located 125m south of San Francisco and 320m north of L.A.

Weather Tips □ Although summer is the peak season here, so are spring and fall (when the **Monterey Jazz Festival,** Box JAZZ, CA 93940, takes place). ★ Year-round cold seas make for acceptable surfing and scuba diving if not pleasant swimming for everyone (and strong currents might deter others). ★ Summer fog and romantic mists are part of Monterey's charm. ★ In January the average high is 53° F; low 36° F. ★ In July the average high is 71° F, low 52° F.

ALONG THE CAMINO REAL: END OF THE MISSIONS

. . . those poor men [neophytes] are being freed from the clutches of the missionaries, who will at last finally lose their swarms of people and pesos.

MARIANO VALLEJO, 1833
(*Hutchinson*)

Humane ideals of equality and liberty swept newly independent Mexico, reaching its California outpost in the guise of secularization, called "confiscation" by some, of the missions. For decades the friars had taught the California Indians the fundamentals of Christianity, trained them in the mechanical arts, and disciplined them. After so many years, surely the neophytes should be ready to take their place as useful and devout citizens in the society of gente de razon. Only the padres' desire for power, it was said, only their enjoyment of personal riches gained from the missions and Indian labor, could explain their resistance to secularization. Why else would they be against the emancipation of the Indians and against turning mission lands into Indian pueblos?

. . . The truth is, that the labor of the missionaries to make men of them [the neophytes] is the most laborious in the world.

PADRE NARCISO DURAN, 1833

The missionaries did, indeed, argue against secularization. To them, emancipation meant only that their neophytes would revert to "wild" habits of roaming about. In no way would they behave as proud property owners, carefully tending their gardens for the good of the province. Their neophytes were childlike and not accustomed to the settled ways of civilization. For them, freedom meant returning to the millennia-old traditions of hunting and gathering in the wilderness. And if they did not revert to paganism in the mountains, their mingling with the gente de razon in the towns could lead only to their debauchery. Since the founding of the Pueblo San Jose near Mission Santa Clara, there had been problems protecting the neophytes. At Mission Santa Cruz, too, with the Villa de Branciforte just a mile away, the padres had struggled to protect their charges from the vices of the colonists. Finally the governor had to forbid the gente de razon from "trafficking" with any Indian, male or female.

The only thing in which the Indians . . . have made progress from their intercourse with the whites is that they have become experts in playing cards.

PADRE ESTEVAN TAPIS, 1800
(*Englehardt*)

So the missionaries argued against secularization. Only they could nurture the neophytes toward civilization, a state they had yet to attain.

. . . the advance made by the Indians . . . from day to day it grows as well in dealing with the people as in clothing and eating; for they deal and salute with urbanity . . . They are careful to cover themselves, . . . [but] they are not very dainty in eating.

FRIARS JUAN BAUTISTA GANCHO
and PEDRO CABOT, 1814

A compromise was reached. An experiment in secularization would prove who was right—the missionaries or the gente de razon. Only the most advanced neophytes would participate, those who were long confirmed as practicing Catholics, those married and with families, and those with trades to support themselves; the carpenters, blacksmiths, and masons would be free to leave the missions. With considerable fanfare, the governor announced their emancipation only to find few were interested.

. . . these unfortunates are so prejudiced and incapable of thinking that many of them refused to accept the favor.

GOVERNOR JOSE FIGUEROA, 1833
(*Engelhardt*)

Perhaps they were unthinking, as the padres also had argued. Or perhaps these neophytes had already worked on special projects in the towns and presidios, with the permission of the friars, and knew their treatment would be only worse. Others had accepted their freedom, however. Released from the constant vigilance of the missionaries, they indulged in all those things so long denied them.

. . . many having gambled away their clothes, implements, and even their land, were compelled to beg or plunder in order to support life. They at length became so obnoxious to the peaceable inhabitants that the padres were requested to take some . . . back to the missions.

FREDERICK WILLIAM BEECHEY,
1827

Secularization was far from dead. Whether or not the Indians were ready to be emancipated, they soon would be. The authorities had too long been forced to rely on the missions to support them. Throughout the Mexican period, no salaries came from the impoverished capital in Mexico City and the California outpost had to support itself. Soldiers needed to be fed and outfitted, governors' guests needed to be feted. Demands were made on the missions to provide what couldn't be obtained from Mexico, demands that led to grumbling by the friars and their increasingly discontented charges.

. . . If now, besides supplying 300 blankets and 300 yards of serge to the troops alone, not counting the very many pieces of both kinds . . . furnished the needy people of the adjoining town of San Jose, we must produce forty more for the infantry, we shall have to overwork the unfortunate neophytes whose lot is to go naked.

FRIARS MARGIN CATALA and
JOSE VIADER, MISSION SANTA
CLARA, 1821
(*Englehardt*)

The government's debt to the mission accumulated to nearly a million dollars. The grumbling increased, sometimes the neophytes rebelled, and friction with the authorities intensified. At the same time the number of gente de razon grew rapidly so that more and more individuals required land—particularly the already cultivated, rich lands belonging to the missions. Tired of missionary complaining, greedy for mission lands, the government ordered the missions secularized.

A law was passed stripping the missions of all their possessions, and confining the priests to their spiritual duties, at the same time declaring all the Indians free and independent rancheros.

RICHARD HENRY DANA, 1835

Mission Santa Cruz became the Indian village of Pueblo de Figueroa, named in honor of the governor. Mission San Jose, too, became a pueblo, and like the others its affairs were managed by an illustrious member of the gente de razon, in this case Jose de Jesus Vallejo. At Mission San Juan Bautista the Castros administered the new and ''free'' pueblo for the former neophytes, who by law owned the mission lands and proceeds. An inventory made by Senor Castro in 1835 indicated the mission properties were worth nearly $140,000. To the Indians he gave some tools, seeds, and plots of land—a value of about $8500. Over half the land he held in trust as ''community lands.'' By the end of 1836, the records for the free pueblo indicated a debt of $1300. The same was true at Santa Cruz and at all the missions

. . . many administrators took advantage of the opportunity presented them for enrichment. They robbed with impunity even to the extent of stealing dishes and pots, the doors, tiles and other things belonging to the Missions.

ANGUSTIAS DE LA GUERRA ORD,
1839

After assessing the liberated Indians' needs, the administrators found nine million ''extra'' acres for themselves and other petitioners to the government. At the time of secularization, there were only 51 land grants in California. Six years later there were over 300. Some individuals owned more than 25 million acres of land. Administrator Jose de Jesus Vallejo managed his vast rancho, comprised of mission lands, from an 18-room mansion located in front of the mission church. Jose Castro, sometimes acting governor and eventually comandante general, made his headquarters at San Juan Bautista, the pueblo by then devoid of Indians and renamed it San Juan de Castro.

. . . wealth, instead of being confined to the monastic institutions, as before, has been distributed among the people.

ALFRED ROBINSON (1846)

Not all the Indians accepted this "redistribution" of their wealth passively. Some rebelled, and at Santa Cruz they demanded land. Most fled to the interior and joined pagan tribes in raiding the new ranch lands of the gente de razon, stealing horses, and rustling cattle to satisfy their mission acquired taste for beef.

It is said that last Saturday certain Indians . . . swooped down and took the rest of the horses which belonged to the pueblo. They had to be pursued on horses from the mill and could not be reached . . . The pueblo is in a lamentable condition, having no way to round up its cattle . . .

ALCALDE OF SAN JOSE 1835
(*Winther*)

Others did try to work in the towns or on the ranches, but they found their pay next to nothing—often just food and clothing, and that for no longer than a few months each year. When wages were offered, they rarely came to more than half that of the gente de razon for the same work. A few did remain near the missions, especially when the padres remained as well. Their lives were far from easy, in fact they were "reduced to a state of misery" as the lands that once supported them no longer were theirs—at Carmel, land was granted right up to the threshold of the San Carlos church, making attendance at mass an act of trespassing. And those trusted neophytes who had worked in the friary rather than on the land, found the adjustment to their "freed" status unbearable.

. . . one Indian barber, named Telequis, felt the change in his position so much that when he was ordered out to the field with the others he committed suicide by eating the root of a poisonous wild plant, a species of celery.

GUADALUPE VALLEJO (1890)

At the peak of the mission period, the padres succored tens of thousands neophytes, harvested over a hundred thousand bushels of grain a year, and managed hundreds of thousands of livestock. They entertained every traveler along the Camino Real, not only with hearty meals from mission products and wines from their vineyards, but also with fireworks, dances, and concerts like the one supervised by Padre Duran at Mission San Jose.

The number of the musicians was about thirty; the instruments performed upon were violins, flutes, trumpets, and drums . . .

ALFRED ROBINSON, 1831

After secularization, they too were dispossessed. Frequently they were refused the shelter of their old friaries and forced, instead, to live in adobes once reserved for *vaqueros*. Just as often they weren't even paid the salary due them as parish priests. At San Juan Bautista, Friar Anzar complained that "so far as I see I am to be paid with meat and grain," not with money to pay for candles, clothes, or services. And his 76-year-old colleague, Padre Abella, had only an oxhide for his bed, only jerked beef for food—his total reward for having served 42 years in California.

Your Paternity is not ignorant of the critical situation in which this poor church and its priest find themselves, since they are without funds and even without an Indian to ring the bells.

FRAY ANTONIO REAL, 1843
(*Englehardt*)

The padres lingered as long as they could, impoverished just like the Indians who remained with them, and then they died, not to be replaced. And the churches, with no one to repair them, decayed. Their tiled roofs went to hacendados, their wooden floors found other homes. The wind and rain melted adobe bricks of workshops, corrals, and church alike. Less then a century after Friar Serra founded the first church at San Diego, the missions were no more than ruins.

Some missions . . . are almost as though they had ceased to exist.

FRIAR GONZALEZ RUBIO, 1840
(*Englehardt*)

Sights

From Monterey the Camino Real continued inland around Gavilan Peak to Mission San Juan Bautista, then headed north to the Pueblo San Jose and Mission Santa Clara. Between the missions and official towns, the Camino Real's course was often a lonely one through wilderness, with mountains covered with pines and flocks of antelope ranging the valleys. The regions off the ancient road were even more remote. Mission Santa Cruz was more easily reached by boat at its position on the Monterey Bay. And Mission San Jose, along the barely explored region east of San Francisco Bay, most often was reached through its *embarcadero,* or boat landing. Apparently San Jose owned many large boats capable of carrying a thousand hides to trading brigs anchored miles away. Yet land routes to such mission outposts were in place, and the friar from Santa Clara used just such a route on his visit to Mission San Jose for a festival.

. . . the Padre's carriage was brought to the door. It was a singular contrivance, invented by himself, and built by the Indian mechanics under his direction—The carriage was drawn by a fine black mule . . . a fiery black steed, led the mule with a "reata" fastened about his neck. On each side were two "vaqueros," with lassos fixed to the axletree, by which they facilitated the movement over the road . . . Three of the priest's four pages attended him also . . .

ROBINSON, 1831

On its final push from Santa Clara north to the San Francisco presidio, the Camino Real passed through a land inhabited only by native Californians, a land awaiting the decades to lapse before the Palo Altos, Menlo Parks and Bayshore Drives would transform its natural beauty into modern cities. Today paved roads circle Monterey Bay and pass the beaches that lead to Santa Cruz and on up the coast to San Francisco. US 101 more closely approximates the route of the old Mission Trail and takes you to the best preserved sights of this section, those at San Juan Bautista. Because so many of the historic buildings mentioned for this region have collapsed, only to be replaced by replicas, or nothing at all, it's best to be selective in your sightseeing. Old adobes in San Jose and Santa Cruz really are excuses for enjoying local history, best suited for the aficionado unless the other considerable pleasures of these towns are the reason for your visit.

★★ **San Juan Bautista** □ Several miles off US 101 is the pleasantly tranquil and historic pueblo of San Juan. Around its very Spanish plaza you can visit the mission church and later buildings of secularized San Juan de Castro.

The one who squandered much was Jose Castro. He lived at San Juan Bautista, or San Juan de Castro (as it was later called) and used up the goods of the mission.

ORD, 1846

Today some of Don Jose's personal possessions can be seen in the ★★ **Castro-Breen Adobe** (Second St. and Washington), on the south side of the plaza. One of the best preserved adobes in California, you can visit this well-furnished, two-story Monterey colonial building on a self-guided tour. But before visiting Castro's former home, you might want to visit next door, the headquarters of the **San Juan Bautista State Historic Park** (open 9:30 a.m.–4 p.m.; closed major holidays; small fee for all buildings around the plaza, except mission which is separately administered; 408–623–4881; self-guided tour pamphlet; 12-minute video of town's history). The headquarters is located in the 1858 ★ **Plaza Hotel,** originally a one-story saloon (don't miss the barroom) operating out of the old mission barracks (1813), then when the arrival of stagecoaches stimulated the growth of San Juan, Angelo Zanetta added a second story and opened the town's first hotel. Over on the east side of the plaza is the **Plaza Stable** (Second and Washington) with some of the horse-drawn carriages from the 1850s and 60s as well as a blacksmith's shop. As the town continued to grow as a stage stop between San Francisco and Los Angeles, Zanetta decided to build a public hall next to the stable, on the site of the former mission nunnery. This ★ **Plaza Hall** (1868) hosted dances and political gatherings on its second floor; the Zanetta's made their home on the first floor, still fully furnished. Other adobes and later wooden Anglo-American buildings can be seen while strolling around the surrounding streets. (The state park brochure guides you to these sites as does a more elaborate book sold at the mission shop.)

Before its 1835 secularization, ★★ **San Juan Bautista Mission** (Second and Mariposa) controlled not only what now is the town, but also the surrounding land on which grazed 6000 cattle and an equal number of sheep. Just northeast of the plaza was the orchard where pear trees continue to thrive.

An alameda, *or shaded walk, of some length, gave access to the establishment, on each side of which were gardens and cultivated fields.*

ROBINSON, 1831

Founded in 1797 as a buffer against unconverted and often raiding tribes from the interior, the mission did occasionally suffer from its position. During one attack, it's said that the heathens were forestalled by Padre Arroyo de la Cuesta's playing of a hurley gurley left behind by British sailors. So popular were the reels and ditties, such as "Go to the Devil," that the belligerents put down their bows and arrows to enjoy the music instead. Although the story might be entirely apocryphal, Friar Arroyo was quite enterprising in other instances as well. Apparently he was the inventor of

. . . a water clock which communicated with a bell by his bedside, which by being arranged at night could be made to give an alarm at any stated hour.

BEECHEY, 1826

The present church, handsomely restored and still providing services from its location on the west side of the plaza, was dedicated in 1812. Unusually wide and with three naves, it also has the only altarpiece painted by an American, Thomas Doaks, believed to be the first Anglo-settler in California. Apparently Doaks was a stranded Boston sailor who in 1818 received room and board in exchange for his art. Later baptized and known as Felipe Santiago, he had the good fortune of marrying into the Castro family. There's a museum in the friary with a particularly well-furnished sala and music room containing mission instruments and old scores of religious hymns. (Open 10 a.m.–4:30 p.m.; Mar.–Oct. 9:30 a.m.–5:30 p.m.; closed Christmas; donation; 408–623–4528.)

There are a number of **special events** to arrange a visit around. The first Saturday of each month (noon–4 p.m.) is living history day with crafts exhibits, villagers in period dress, and, sometimes, historical reenactments. The feast of St. John the Baptist is celebrated on the Sunday nearest June 24th with Mexican dances and music. And there's a nearby Fiesta Rodeo in July, arts and crafts shows in September, and the feast day of our Lady of Guadalupe in December. For more information on these events write the Chamber of Commerce, 201 Third St., CA 95045; 408–623–2454.

The historic plaza is at Second Street, just 3m south of US 101. It lies 30m northeast of Monterey on CA 156 and 45m south of San Jose on US 101, 95m south of San Francisco.

Santa Cruz □ The coastal location of the modern town of Santa Cruz once boasted not only the twelth of the California missions, but also the Villa de Branciforte, founded in 1797 in an attempt to people the region and further secure it for Spain. A *villa* was no mere pueblo, or village, such as Los Angeles and San Jose were. A *villa* was a town of at least 100 individuals. However, Branciforte didn't live up to its title. Only 17 individuals arrived from Mexico to colonize it, individuals that scandalized the neighboring padres at Mission Santa Cruz although one Californio was gentler in his reaction, describing the settlers as "not so bad as the other convicts sent to California." Soldiers assigned to oversee the villa soon found their jobs unexpectedly demanding. As the cattle stock suspiciously increased, with decreases at the mission, the governor ordered weekly inspections so that all stolen goods could be returned to their rightful owners. The town never succeeded, reaching the proper *villa* population only twenty-five years after its founding. After the mission was secularized in 1834, the mission and villa eventually merged, bridging the San Lorenzo River that had so long divided them.

Little remains of the early period. In the heart of the old villa (at the intersection of Branciforte Ave. and Water St.) no reminder has survived the years. Even the mission church finally collapsed from years of abandonment and from earthquakes. Today on Mission Hill (exit CA 1 at Central District, turn left onto Water then follow signs), you can visit a small scale replica of the church of **Mission Santa Cruz** (Emmett at High St.) and the museum store that contains some of the original altar furnishings and vestments. (Open 2:30–5 p.m. weekdays; Sat. noon–5:30; Sun. after masses; donation; 408–426–5685.) But the best reminder of early Santa Cruz can be found around the corner on School Street, down the block and past the **Neary-Hopcroft House** (130 School; supposedly under reconstruction), the oldest building in Santa Cruz and once the mission soldiers' barracks, and on to the end of the street where a view out toward the sea is most reminiscent of an early description of the mission.

No situation is prettier than that of this Mission. From the shore the ground rises so regularly by steps that they might be said to be the symmetrical terraces of a fortification. I know not even if the grassy covering of an artificial work could ever equal the beauty of green sward clothing them like the carpet of green velvet. The buildings are placed

. . . fronting the sea, and backed against a thick forest of large fir trees, which lend a new brillance to the whiteness of their walls.

A. DUHAUT-CILLY, 1827

Although much of the past has been lost, the modern college town of Santa Cruz offers its own funky charms, beguiling people with its **Pacific Garden Mall** (follow Mission St. to the area of Church and Pacific), a shady pedestrian area lined with boutiques and restaurants in renovated old buildings and enlived with street musicians and student cafes; enticing many on the weekends to its 1907 **Boardwalk** (400 Beach St.) with arcades, big bands, and famous roller coaster. But many tourists are attracted here by the surroundings that have survived the years of change so well. The coastal redwoods seen by Portola and lumbered by the sawmills of Thomas Larkin of Monterey are protected at **Henry Cowell Redwoods Park** (5m north on CA 9; horseback riding, swimming, fishing, picnicking, hiking and camping; 408–335–4598) and **Big Basin Redwoods** (20m north on CA 9; hiking, riding, picnicking, and camping; fees; 408–338–6132). And along the coast are nearly 30 miles of beaches, most better for surfing than swimming, and still much as Duhaut-Cilly described them in 1827.

The coast . . . everywhere covered with forests of fir trees . . . descends finally to the sea, now bathing the foot of vertical rock cliffs, now gliding in sheets of foam over sandy or pebbly beaches.

Santa Cruz is located on the northern end of Monterey Bay on CA 1, just 42m north of Monterey. About midway you pass Watsonville where the Brancifortian soldier Jose Joaquim Castro made his home. Just to the north, Castro's daughter Martina had her land at Soquel, now known for its wineries. *From Santa Cruz it's 70m to San Francisco along CA 1 or CA 9, or just about 30m to San Jose on CA 17.*

Lower Bay Area □ In 1777 the first settlement apart from those at presidios was established at the pueblo San Jose de Guadalupe. Just 3 miles away was the Mission Santa Clara, joined to the pueblo by an alameda of ''large and stately'' black willow trees.

It is frequented generally on the Sabbath or feast days, when all the town repair to the church at Santa Clara. On a Sunday may be seen hundreds of persons . . . gaily attired in silks and satins, mounted on their finest horses, and proceeding leisurely up the road.

ROBINSON, 1831

Farther north, and east of San Francisco Bay, the Mission San Jose was founded on the ''frontier'' to act as buffer against unconverted tribes. These three establishments all were part of the plan to colonize the bay region, in order to defend it and to supply the San Francisco presidio with foodstuffs and supplies. Both of the missions succeeded in converting thousands of native Californians, and in producing vast quantities of agricultural products as well as cattle herds numbering over 10,000. As for the Pueblo San Jose, it too prospered in the fertile Santa Clara Valley, and grew from its founding population of 68 to about 900 in the Mexican period. Despite these accomplishments, the region mostly was known for the aguardiente [brandy] shacks and gambling dens of San Jose. As early as 1800 new stocks were added to the plaza, ''big and strong'' ones to deal with the disorderly population. Even as late as the Mexican period, when Los Angeles and Monterey were renown for their elegant balls, San Jose remained backward.

The men indulged in the rude custom of riding their horses up on the platform where the people were dancing, where they made them give turns and dance also.

JOSE ARNAZ, 1840S

The region today remains a center of Hispanic culture. The vineyards of Alameda and other notable wineries can be viewed as inheriting the old pueblo's preference for peach brandy production. Yet, despite the size of the old establishments, few original adobe buildings have survived to the present day. Floods, earthquakes, and even fires destroyed the little that remained after mission secularization and the destruction of gold rush squatters. At ★ **Mission San Jose** (15m northeast of San Jose to Fremont on I-280 south and I-680 north; Mission Blvd. exit to 43300 Mission Blvd.) only parts of the friary withstood the ravages of time.

The Mission of San Jose . . . possesses some of the best lands in the country for agricultural purposes . . . In point of beauty, the buildings here were very inferior to those of the southern missions.

ROBINSON, 1831

Today the friary has been made into a museum, and a chapel has been carefully reconstructed down to the rough buttresses and leather tied beams of the original frontier church. (Open 10 a.m.–5 p.m.; closed major holidays; donations; 415–657–1797.) Across from the church stood the mansion of Jose de Jesus Vallejo, administrator of the secularized mission and once commander of the Pueblo San Jose. For his services Vallejo received nearly 18,000 acres of fertile mission lands. The sole reminder of this Rancho Arroyo de la Alameda is the unadorned, one-room overseers house in the Niles district of Fremont (on grounds of California Nursery Company, off Niles Blvd.). Another rustic example of the ranchero lifestyle is the replica of the **Higuera Adobe** (47300 Rancho Higuera Rd., Fremont), with its earthen floors and simple architecture recalling its 1842 origin as part of the Rancho Agua Caliente, once belonging to a family well-represented in the mission cemetery. (Open 10 a.m.–1 p.m. third Sat. of every month; 415–657–2010 for directions from mission.)

As for the **Pueblo San Jose,** now the pulse center of Silicon Valley, the downtown is reviving with glass tower office buildings, an expanded convention center, and a vibrant **Museum of Art** (110 Market St.; 11–5 p.m. weekdays except Mon.; noon–4 p.m. weekends; free; 408–294–2787) and **Institute of Contemporary Art** (377 S. First St., Tues.–Sat. 11 a.m.–4 p.m.; free; 408–998–4310). Although this new town is anchored to the past by some handsomely refurbished and historic buildings, most of early San Jose has disappeared. Yet the old center is marked by St. Joseph's Church (Market at San Fernando) that replaced the pueblo chapel in 1877. And tucked away behind the high-rises near St. James Square is the oldest building in San Jose, the **Peralta Adobe** (184 W. St. John St. between Almaden and San Pedro). Set back from the street and in a small patio, this simple adobe dating from 1804 was owned by the Peralta family whose Rancho San Antonio covered 43,000 acres where now sprawl Oakland, Alameda, Berkeley, and other cities. In the days of the pueblo, Don Luis Peralta was a local official and his home was right in the center of town. A map of the pueblo here indicates its original layout, and by pushing a button you can activate a historical tape. (Patio open 9 a.m.–sunset.) There is little else to see of the old town—a few markers here and there, the California Room with its historical exhibits at the **San Jose Public Library** (San Carlos at Market), and the dioramas of early San Jose in the Pacific Hotel at the **San Jose Historical Museum** (635 Phelan Ave., a few miles south of town on 10th Ave. then left onto Phelan) where many 19th-century buildings have been moved to a park setting. (Mon.

to Fri. 10 a.m.–4:30 p.m.; weekends noon–4:30 p.m.; closed major holidays; fee; 408–287–2290.) The *San Jose Convention & Visitors Bureau* (One Paseo de San Antonio; Box 6299, CA 95113; 408–295–9600) offers maps and other useful materials on the Santa Clara Valley; for information on walking tours of the historic sites call 408–287–2290.

Three miles west of the pueblo, along the beautiful alameda once part of the Camino Real, stood the ★ **Mission Santa Clara**. Now part of State Highway 82, and its grove of willows long gone, the street called "The Alameda" leads to what remains of the mission on the University of Santa Clara campus (between Franklin and Bellamy). In 1851 a Jesuit college, and the first institution of higher learning in the state, took over the old mission buildings. But classroom needs transformed the architecture, and fire destroyed the mission church. Although much has been lost, the integration of what remains into the university campus has been skillfully and attractively accomplished. The reconstructed mission church, roofed with the original tiles and surrounded by lovely gardens, is the central focus of the campus. (Open daily; 408–984–4256 for campus information.) Just to the left of the church is the old quadrangle area with a map indicating the location of mission ruins—those incorporated into the Adobe Lodge Faculty Club as dining rooms retain handsome old beams and wooden floors. Some of the mission artifacts have been preserved in the permanent ★ California History Collection of the **De Saisset Art Gallery and Museum** (at entrance to campus; Tues.–Fri. 10 a.m.–5 p.m.; weekends 1 p.m.–5 p.m.; closed August and holidays; free). Across from the campus and up a block stands the **Jose Pena Adobe** (3260 The Alameda between Franklin and Burton) that originally may have been a neophyte's home as early as 1792, making it the oldest building in the Santa Clara Valley. Today the adobe is set back from the street and shaded by fruit trees (not open to public).

While you're driving along The Alameda in San Jose, consider a detour to the **Rosicrucian Egyptian Museum** (Park and Naglee Ave., off The Alameda) with its extensive collection of Egyptian, Babylonian and Assyrian art, said to be the largest such collection in the western United States. (Tues. to Fri. 9 a.m.–4:45 p.m.; Sat.–Mon. noon–4:45 p.m.; fee; 408–287–9171.)

San Jose lies 50m south of San Francisco on highways running both east and west of the bay, but I-280 on the west avoids the congested Bay Bridge. Fremont, on the eastern shore, lies 35m south of San Francisco on I-880.

Suggestions

Getting There ☐ From either San Francisco or Monterey, you can choose a route according to the sights you most wish to see, taking a day excursion from San Francisco to the Santa Clara Valley, perhaps following I-880 south so you can include the mission at Fremont, or simply enjoying the redwoods and coastal scenery along CA 1 to Santa Cruz. But the most historic route is also the most convenient, traveling the 125m between Monterey and San Francisco on US 101 via San Juan Bautista and San Jose, then proceeding on I-280 into San Francisco. ★ **Amtrak** connects Salinas, San Jose (408–287–7462), and San Francisco. ★ **Greyhound** runs this route, too (408–297–8890 in San Jose) and provides more local service out of Santa Cruz (408–423–1800). ★ There's an international airport in San Jose with more regional airlines service, too. ★ BART, the rapid transit system of San Francisco connects with San Jose.

Weather Tips ☐ The inland towns often have sunnier skies and warmer summer days than the coast. ★ San Jose's average high temperature in January is about 60° F, low 41° F; in July the high is 81° F; low 55° F.

Restaurants

There are a number of restaurants both pleasant and convenient along this route. *San Juan Bautista* has two restaurants located in historic adobes, both just a block south of the plaza. **Jardines de San Juan** (115 Third St.; open daily 11:30 a.m.–10 p.m.; 408–623–4466; ***inexpensive to moderate***) is fronted by an 1850s adobe but most of the dining here is done in a more modern pavilion surrounded by gardens. The Mexican food is good, whether you try the weekend specialty dinner of carne asada or the daily chicken tostada. Nearby is **La Casa Rosa** (107 Third St.; 11:30 a.m.–3:30 p.m.; 408–623–4563; ***inexpensive***), an early adobe now covered with pink clapboard and serving luncheons of casseroles and salad either indoors or in a patio. In *Santa Cruz* you can stroll along the Pacific Garden Mall to select one of the small, inexpensive restaurants lining it, such as **Lilly Marlene** (1363 Pacific Ave.; breakfast-dinner; ***inexpensive***) where a turn of the century setting, including an old soda fountain counter, can be enjoyed along with a pound of spaghetti, soup, and salad for a price you won't believe. Or for steaks and seafood with a view of the bay, try the **Crow's Nest** (2218 East Cliff Dr. at 5th Ave.; lunch and dinner daily; 408–476–4560; ***moderate***). In *San Jose,* the **Garden Cafe** (N. Market at St. John; ***inexpensive***) is right in the heart of downtown, and offers sandwiches and espresso. For more elegant dining there's the wonderful Italian cuisine at **Paolo's** (520 E. Santa Clara; Mon. to Sat. lunch and dinner; reserve at 408–294–2558; ***expensive***), where the delicate capellini and ravioli make the short trip east of downtown to 12th Street well worthwhile. Or if you find yourself hungry while visiting the university in *Santa Clara,* nearby is the sophisticated natural food of **The Good Earth** (The Alameda at Bellamy; 9 a.m.–11 p.m.; no reservations; ***moderate***) where you can enjoy sourdough hot cakes at breakfast or a rich lasagna at dinner. Picnicking opportunities can be found along this route in the historic park of San Juan Bautista and in the redwood forests north of Santa Cruz.

Accommodations

Although you probably will be staying in either Monterey or San Francisco, your schedule might make it more convenient to look for accommodations along the roads between them. San Jose, in particular, is convenient if you wish to avoid the traffic of San Francisco or use the San Jose Airport. Near the airport and highways is the **Hyatt San Jose,** a fine corporate hotel with many amenities and efficient service. The 475 units sit on 18 acres. All the rooms are ample and comfortably furnished, but those in the Regency section—slightly more expensive but with a special living room style lounge, and complimentary breakfast and evening appetizers—are particularly recommended. Three restaurants, one open 24 hours; lounge with entertainment. Large pool, spa, and fitness track. Parking. Courtesy limousine service. ***Expensive;*** weekend rates ***moderate***. Write 1740 N. First St., CA 95112; 298–0300 or 800–228–9001. Located at the junction of US 101 and 17 near I-280. Downtown you can find the **Sainte Claire Hilton,** a refurbished 1930s hotel with chandeliers, mahogany fireplace and 184 guest rooms. Restaurant, lounge with entertainment. Valet parking. Airport transportation. ***Expensive***. Contact at 302 S. Market St. at San Carlos, CA 95113; 408–295–2000 or 800–HILTONS.

Of course there are plenty of **motels** in this region, particularly on

The Alameda in both Santa Clara and San Jose, and clustered just north of I-880. Santa Cruz, too, has a motel row, including a Best Western, along Ocean Street near CA 1 at the Central District exit. And a few **bed and breakfasts** are available in the village of San Juan Bautista (write the Chamber of Commerce, Box 1037, CA 95045, for a listing).

FOREIGN THREATS: SAN FRANCISCO BAY REGION

We all hold the opinion, without any doubt that this is a very great and magnificent port . . .

FRAY JUAN CRESPI, 1769

The Portola expedition stumbled upon the bay of San Francisco in 1769, but theirs was far from an ecstatic discovery. They had, in fact, been seeking Monterey Bay and had blazed their trail north in hunger, surviving each day on five tortillas garnished with the seeds given them by friendly Indians encountered on the way. Their sufferings from "indigestion and fever" were somewhat stayed by the abundant mussel supply found "on the rocks along the shore." Still, they were at the wrong bay. And worse, having no idea they were the first explorers to reach the "harbor of all harbors," fate deprived them of the thrill of discovery.

The famous port of San Francisco named in the itinerary of Admiral Cabrera Bueno, and in the expedition of General Don Sebastian Vizcayno, as lying between Monterey and Cape Mendocino, was seen confusedly by those who went on the expedition of the year 1769.

CRESPI, 1769

Portola mistakenly thought he was at Drake's Bay, long known to the Spaniards as "San Francisco Bay." Enough exploring expeditions and Manila galleons had tacked their way along the Pacific Coast since Cabrillo's 1542 voyage that no one expected to make so momentous a discovery as a harbor capable of sheltering "all the armadas" of Europe. But Cabrillo missed the Golden Gate entirely, seeing only a continuous coastline from his position a few miles out to sea. Sir Francis Drake, after repairing the *Golden Hind,* so laden with gold and silver robbed from the Spanish galleon, missed the narrow entrance into the harbor, too. And Rodriguez Cermeno, after his ship from Manila crashed in Drake's Bay in 1595, hugged the coast in his small, newly constructed launch and, passing near the Golden Gate, just didn't see "anything worth noting down." Vizcaino sailed by and he, too, could find nothing better than Monterey Bay. It took a land expedition to find the great bay of California, hidden as it was from the sea by cliffs and the narrow passage of the Golden Gate.

. . . and within there is a very large harbor between mountains, of such a sort that it is like a box locked by many keys, which made me recognize the fact that if the depth is in proportion my master [Carlos III] has no other like it.

SERGEANT JOSE ORTEGA, 1770
(Treutlein)

No matter how great the discovered bay, Spain didn't need it. Already the empire stretched over continents. But what it had, it intended to keep—particularly the silver mines in northern Mexico and the Pacific Ocean itself, necessary for the safe passage of the Manila galleon. Foreign powers had encroached on the Pacific, first Drake and his fellow pirates representing the British, then the Russians with their explorations of the Northwest coast. Monterey had been colonized simply in response to these threats. Now, with Russian otter hunting extending all the way to Alaska, and possibly even to the American coast, San Francisco would be fortified against this growing Russian menace.

. . . I hold the occupation of [the Port of San Francisco] to be indispensable and to effect it Don Juan Bautista de Anza . . . will return . . . conducting troops required to support the two new missions, and as a symbol of defense in that port.

ANTONIO MARIA BUCARELI,
VICEROY, 1774
(Treutlein)

In 1775, Captain Anza shepherded 240 colonists destined for San Francisco along the 1500 mile trail he had pioneered from the Spanish fort at Tubac, Arizona to the one at Monterey. The expedition would be Spain's first attempt to supply its Pacific province by land from Mexico; it would be the first and nearly the last such attempt, as Indian uprisings would block off the route for decades. But this time the soldiers and their wives and children would succeed, traveling along the Gila River then crossing the mighty Colorado before suffering endless sand dunes and waterless days, in what is now known as the Anza-Borrega Desert. And they would be the first colonists to cross the cold and snow-covered Sierra before reaching the shelter of Mission San Gabriel near the Pueblo of Los Angeles. They crossed a wilderness peopled by Pimas, Papagos, Apaches, and Yumas, a wilderness bordered by tiny outposts of the Spanish empire totaling fewer than one hundred Europeans. Only one colonist, a woman in childbirth, died. Three children were born and added their numbers to the colony. It was a miraculous journey, one that eventually resulted in the founding of San Francisco.

Indeed, although in my travels I saw very good sites and beautiful country, I saw none which pleased me so much as this. And I think that if it could be well settled like Europe there would not be anything more beautiful in all the world, for it has the best advantages . . . with all the conveniences desired, by land as well as by sea.

FRAY PEDRO FONT, 1776

Over the early years five missions—Santa Clara, San Jose (see ''End of the Missions''), Dolores, Solano, and San Rafael—would be founded in order to support and protect the port of San Francisco from the Russians. Even a civilian pueblo, the first in California, was created at San Jose to further declare the region under the rule of Spain. Yet the presidio, the primary fortification against foreign incursions, initially received too few funds to even withstand the destructive forces of fog and rain. Although Lt. Jose Joaquin Moraga had carefully selected the site of the fort, near a spring for water and not too far from ''a lake suitable for washing the clothing,'' the lack of timber and supplies, and the misfortune of both the carpenter and blacksmith being disabled, resulted in a presidio ''not finished and secure.'' One presidio captain so despaired of the rains and isolation that he dared to recommend the fort be abandoned. As late as 1793 when Vancouver anchored in San Francisco Bay, the fort posed little threat to his ships and only one cannon boomed a greeting at his arrival.

. . . instead of a city or town, whose lights we had so anxiously looked for on the night of arrival, we were conducted into a spacious verdant plain, surrounded by hills on sides, excepting that fronting the port

. . . The only object of human industry which presented itself, was a square area, whose sides were about two hundred yards in length enclosed by a mud wall, and resembling a pound for cattle.

GEORGE VANCOUVER, 1792

Vancouver's arrival on the coast represented Britain's increasing commercial interests in the Pacific, in particular its settlement on what now is called Vancouver Island. Still worried about the Russians, Spain now feared that Britain too would become a problem, especially since Vancouver had witnessed the weakness of its defenses. In a rush of alarm, Spain explored Bodega Bay for yet another fort in the north—and rejected it. Funds poured into the colony's defenses, and master gunners and fortifications experts were sent to the San Francisco presidio. In less than a year of Vancouver's first visit, the Castillo San Joaquin was well under way at its strategic position on Fort Point, overlooking the sea and the Golden Gate. By the end of 1794, the timber hauled from the San Mateo hills and the 1500-a-day adobe bricks produced by recalcitrant Indians had been assembled into a 12-cannon battery protected by a 10-foot thick wall. Within two years, reinforcements arrived, nearly doubling the number of soldiers, and a year later, with Spain at war with England, the Yerba Buena battery was created with five cannon at the site of what is now Fort Mason. As the first Russian expedition to visit the bay explains, Spain had indeed improved its fortifications.

An enemy's ship attempting to run into the harbor, and deeming itself safe by steering out of range of the guns of the entrance [Castillo San Joaquin], will receive an unexpected surprise by this cannon salvo [Yerba Buena battery] at a moment when . . . least expected.

GEORGE HEINRICH VON LANGSDORFF, 1806

However, with time Langsdorff figured a way to enter the bay securely "against all attacks by the Spaniards." Ironically, these strategems would never be tested, not by the English or the Russians, for California would fall to others who came by land, not just by sea.

In 1806 the feared Russians finally arrived. But this first Russian encounter in California pleasantly diverged from Spain's worst expectations. No gun boats sailed through the Golden Gate. No soldiers, but rather scientists and diplomats, arrived on this expedition of Count Rezanov. And although the count, chamberlain to the Tsar, had strong political motives for his visit, his entire stay has been transformed over time into one of the most romantic of California episodes, a story of unrequited love, a tale of heroic death in Siberian snows.

Winds and low provisions forced Rezanov to anchor at San Francisco rather than at the Monterey capital. Such forces of fate introduced him to the family of Jose Dario Arguello, *comandante* of an establishment that had "the look of a German farmstead."

The house of the comandante is small and mean. A whitewashed room, half of the floor of which was covered with straw matting, had but little furniture . . . We enjoyed an excellent repast, and, to our great surprise, the poor quality of the house furniture considered, in a rich service of silver tableware.

LANGSDORFF

The Russians enjoyed enough meals at the Arguello home to come to appreciate the silver service. And the straw matting on the floor served well enough for evenings of dancing to tunes played on soldiers' violins and guitars. Such pleasures overcame the Spaniards hesitations toward the Russians,

. . . they suspected our coming was with sinister intentions . . .

COUNT NIKOLAI REZANOV, 1806

and eventually flirtations occurred despite the formality of conversing in Latin, the only language common to them all.

Our intimate association daily with the Arguello family . . . aroused in the mind of Rezanov some new and important speculations . . . The bright sparkling eyes of Dona Concepcion had made upon him a deep inpression, and pierced his innermost soul.

LANGSDORFF

Dona Concepcion, "the universally recognized beauty of Nueva California," awakened in the count "remnants of feelings" that had brought happiness to him in the past. Too old to be passionate, Rezanov thought, he nonetheless succumbed to the charms of Concepcion, a rare presence in so remote a spot. Other, less romantic ideas, preoccupied the count, ideas about trade and foodstuffs for the bleak Russian fur hunting outposts in Alaska.

He conceived the idea that through a marriage with the daughter of the comandante of the Presidio de San Francisco a close bond would be formed for future business . . .

LANGSDORFF

As for Dona Concepcion, Rezanov enchanted her with stories about the imperial court in St. Petersburg, its glittering balls and elegant castles. Merely fifteen, Concepcion soon yearned for such refinements and expressed a dissatisfaction with her humble existence in California.

She always referred to it jokingly thus, as a ''beautiful country, a warm climate, and abundant grain and cattle,—and nothing else.''

REZANOV

When Rezanov proposed marriage, Concepcion was all too ready to accept. Little did it matter that others in this Catholic community opposed it most adamantly, on religious grounds. Nor did it matter that her parents begged her to consider the consequences—the long, cold Russian winters, the loneliness without her family. Despite all opposition, Dona Concepcion and the Russian count were formally bethrothed, their marriage to await approval from the pope. In the interim, the count would return to his homeland in case ''fate should decree the completion of my romance,'' he could then make arrangements with the Tsar for trade with the Spanish province. His financee would await his return.

. . . [Rezanov] had . . . decided to sacrifice himself, by wedding Dona Concepcion, to the welfare of his country.

LANGSDORFF

It would be Dona Concepcion who would make the ultimate sacrifice. Count Rezanov never returned. Concepcion waited. She waited yet more years, spurning all other offers of marriage. Instead of the Tsar's court she went to Baja California where her father was made governor. She still heard no news, but waited. She returned to California where she led a religious life of performing works of charity. She waited for

36 years before she learned the count had died soon after his departure from California. While returning to St. Petersburg in 1807, and in ill health, Rezanov had ridden his horse across dreaded Siberia in winter and suffered a fall from which he never recovered. When George Simpson finally recounted to Concepcion these details of the count's death, he found that she still "loved to dwell on the story of her blighted affections" and

. . . notwithstanding the ungracefulness of her conventional costume and the ravages of an interval of time, which had tripled her years, we could still discover in her face and figure, in her manners and conversation the remains of those charms which had won for the youthful beauty the enthusiastic love of Rezanof . . .

GEORGE SIMPSON, 1842

If death took from Count Rezanov the opportunity to establish the Russian American Company on the California coast, the advantages of such a scheme were far from lost. The reports of the Rezanov voyage, that the bay was so full of sea otter that they could easily be found sunning themselves on the muddy shores, eventually attracted Russians and their Aleut hunters, who made night forays into the Spanish channel in their silent kayaks. Finding the valuable sea otter plentiful indeed, the Russians awaited the proper moment and, seeing Spain distracted by wars of independence in its colonies, established itself at Bodega Bay just north of San Francisco. In 1812 the Russian American Company built a substantial settlement farther north, above what is now called the Russian River, fortified it, and securely based its commercial operations just out of reach of Spanish California. From this Fort Ross hunters on the Farallones and Bodega Bay were supplied, and to this fort they could retreat for protection against Spanish authorities.

This citadel is constructed upon the edge of the wall of rock, on a high ground about two hundred feet above the level of the sea; to right and left are gorges protecting it . . . while the rocky wall and the sea defend it on the side to the west.

A. DUHAUT-CILLY, 1828

First Spain, then Mexico, protested the Russian presence. But the Tzar didn't deign to reply. No troops or armaments adequate to the task of dislodging them could be mounted. And perhaps, there was no will to do so, especially in the early years. Just as all supplies from Spain stopped because of the independence wars, the Russians appeared with offers to trade tea samovars and Siberian boots, Flemish linen, and needles and axes for California wheat and jerked meat. Even when California became determined to block further infiltration from the north and so established the last of all the missions at Sonoma, the Russians provided the bell to ring-in the neophytes for evening prayers. And when Comandante Mariano Vallejo transferred the San Francisco garrison north in response to new Russian settlements in the Santa Rosa Valley,

General Figueroa ordered me to proceed to found the town of Sonoma and following his orders in June 1834 I embarked 80 cavalrymen in two schooners and set out for the Sonoma landing but because we did not know the Bay currents very well, the trip took us fourteen days.

MARIANO GUADALUPE VALLEJO,
1834

bay area residents, including the comandante, still planted wheat for export to the Russians. For years the Russians and Californians coexisted peacefully, if uneasily.

Until 1846, the bay settlements successfully warded off foreign conquest, if not foreign visitors. The vast harbor attracted its share of Yankee and Hawaiian brigs, of French expeditions and English ones, of Peruvian vessels and most certainly Russian ones. Those trading for hides and tallow anchored at Yerba Buena Cove, then took launches up the creeks and rivers to missions and ranches collecting the hides called "California dollars."

In the autumn of 1840 . . . I was then about twelve years old, and I remember the time because it was then that we saw the first American vessel that traded along the shores of San Pablo Bay . . . My brother had traded some deerskins for a gun and four tooth-brushes, the first ones I had ever seen. I remember that we children rubbed them on our teeth till the blood came, and then concluded that after all we liked best the bits of pounded willow root that we had used for brushes before . . .

PRUDENCIA HIGUERA (1890)

Whaling ships anchored across the bay at Sausalito, where they could stock up on supplies and water while enjoying the local grog houses.

Numerous seamen, after so long on the Pacific whaling circuit, found the region enticing enough to jump ship; once left behind, some made themselves "obnoxious to the Mexican Government." So great was the internationalism around the bay, that Comandante Ignacio Martinez spoke a polyglot language comprised of English, Russian, Spanish, and French words, all fused into "a jargon which no one could understand but himself."

All nationalities came to the bay. Yet few *Californios* resided there. San Francisco was the frontier of the province, lacking the comforts of Monterey or Los Angeles, or even San Diego. Anza's original settlement had dispersed, their descendants living on profitable ranches or in more booming towns like San Jose. The presidio was in shambles, with only a few soldiers and their families residing there after the founding of Sonoma. Even the original mission on Dolores Creek was an early failure as disease decimated its neophyte population. Only the commercial activities at Yerba Buena Cove, to the east of the presidio, thrived, and it was there that Mexico organized a formal township in 1834 under the authority of a "Captain of the Port and Bay." So few were the Hispanics in the region that this important position was given to the Englishman, William Richardson. Even though Richardson was a naturalized citizen, known to Mexicans as Don Antonio and married to Comandante Martinez' daughter, the fact was that Yerba Buena seemed to early observors to be little more than a Yankee commercial outpost.

The town of San Francisco was composed of four or five houses, the place being then called Yerbabuena. The town consisted of a store owned by Spear and Hinckley, a billiard room kept by Captain Francis Biochette, a blacksmith and carpenter shop—I do not recall who owned it—and the dwelling of Don Jacob P. Leese and his family.

JOSE ARNAZ, 1840s

There was a Mexican resident in Yerba Buena, the laundress Juana Briones. And a few soldiers remained at the presidio, a few other Mexicans lived near the mission. The center of early San Francisco, however, seemed to be Biochette's billiard room, the "meeting place of captains and supercargoes."

San Francisco, the Spanish frontier town, showed little promise for what it would soon become. It was a rest and recreation center for whalers, it was a safe harbor for ships flying many colors, it was a great and fertile region inhabited by thousands of mission Indians and a mere handful of *gente de razon*. It was not a city, much less a true town. It lacked the elite society of Los Angeles, the magnificent balls of the capital at Monterey. But it didn't lack entertainment. Retired Comandante Martinez provided music and dancing whenever a visitor stopped at his Rancho El Pinole. All the Californios warmly greeted guests at their lonely ranch houses, and Don Mariano Vallejo, descendant of Spanish conquistadors, was said to be hospitable to all those "who are highly respected." Unlike the rest of the province, some of the most elaborate celebrations were given, not on land, but aboard ship by foreign captains. Unlike elsewhere, the invited dons arrived by launch, not mounted elegantly on their silver bedecked pintos. And in Yerba Buena Cove, the Russians were just as likely as the Mexicans to provide the festivities.

. . . a Russian frigate arrived at the port, bringing the governor of all the possessions of Russia in North America. With him came also the Commandant of Fort Ross . . . A banquet was given on board the frigate . . . The dinner was followed by a dance on the same frigate . . . There was much gaiety and the assemblage was numerous and brilliant, especially the women, many of whom were beautiful. The enthusiasm was such that Padre Lorenzo Quijas took part in the dance, exchanging clothes with me, he putting on my frock coat and I his habit. We danced quadrilles together, I in his habit, and the girls laughed uproariously . . . The dance on board the frigate lasted the whole night, and on the following morning the guests departed.

ARNAZ, 1840

By 1841 the Russians no longer threatened California. Economic difficulties, not military battles, forced their withdrawal from the Sonoma coast. As the sea otter had been hunted into near extinction, Fort Ross had tried producing crops. But the foggy valleys of the north coast prevented their success. Then brick-making and shipbuilding were tried, all in order to create an enterprise to pay for the continuation of Fort Ross. Despite such efforts, the community of 400 inhabitants found itself bankrupt. The land was sold to another interloper, the Swiss John Sutter, for $30,000 in wheat, soap, furs, and other goods. Then, abruptly, Fort Ross was evacuated with the

. . . plows left standing in the furrow, oxen left to wander at will . . .

COMMANDER ALEXANDRE ROTCHEV,
1841

If the Russians no longer threatened California, others did. Waves of emigrants were arriving overland, across the Plains and the Rockies, along the Oregon Trail, then down to the Sacramento Valley. They were arriving in increasing, even alarming numbers.

I am afraid we shall see a great deal of trouble in California this year. There are 7 or 8,000 emigrants from the U.S.A. expected . . .

W.D.M. HOWARD, 1846

John Sutter, though Swiss, shared the interests of the American newcomers. From his Sacramento colony called New Helvetia, Sutter sold food and goods to the pioneers—he even built a mill in order to grind the flour they so desperately needed upon their arrival. He encouraged them to homestead, despite its illegality, and to demand rights in this strange but fertile province of Mexican California. He befriended the surrounding Indians, and soon had a force of 300 with him.

It is too late now to drive me out of the country, one step they do against me . . . I will make a Declaration of Independence and proclaim California for a Republic, independent from Mexico.

JOHN SUTTER, 1841
(Vallejo)

Unlike the William Robinsons and Jacob Leeses who married into the finest Californio families, and unlike the Yankee merchants engaged in the hide and tallow trade along the coast, these inlanders were numerous and they had no desire to adapt to local ways. Eventually they would pose the final threat to Hispanic California, a threat already worrying local officials when they founded the fortified pueblo of Sonoma.

I came . . . to ward off incursions from Russia on the one hand and from the people over the Rocky Mountains on the other.

VALLEJO, 1834

It would be in Sonoma that these inlanders would begin the Bear Flag uprising against Mexican authority. Stirred up by U.S. Army officer John Fremont—who, he said, just happened to be in the region enjoying the scenery—these rebels rode into the northern village to demand its surrender. They were a gruff lot, dressed in filthy buckskins, bearded, and well armed. As one of them admitted, anyone "could feel some dread falling into their hands." Unfortunately for General Mariano Vallejo, he became their prisoner along with other members of his family, including his brother-in-law Jacob Leese and his brother Salvador. But the initial encounter apparently wasn't too terrifying, as Leese tried to negotiate the terms of the takeover.

The General's generous spirits *gave proof of his usual hospitality, as the richest wines and brandies sparkled in the glasses, and those who had thus unceremoniously met soon became merry companions; more especially the weary visitors.*

William Brown Ide, 1846

The rebels outside soon tired of waiting and demanded that the general and his family be sent to Sutter's Fort, where they would be imprisoned. As they proclaimed the independence of California, or at least Sonoma, by lowering the Mexican flag, the rebels wondered what to raise in its place. Since the United States had not sanctioned their rebellion, despite the presence of Fremont, they knew the Stars and Stripes would be inappropriate. Instead, they made the flag of the California Republic, crafted out of petticoats and berry juice, and painted crudely with a grizzly bear and lone star on the upper corner. The Bear Flag ruled Sonoma for 26 days, time in which the rebellion spread around the bay, time in which Americans and Mexicans fought and died, time in which the United States navy sailed into Monterey bay, anchored in San Francisco harbor and took possession of California.

One day there came a man-of-war vessel . . . Soon the vessel came to an anchor, fired their guns, lowered their boats, hoisted the American flag . . . What could we do? There were fourteen Indians of us [soldiers], without arms, shoes, or much clothing. The crew then commenced to ascend the hill of the [San Francisco] presidio. Our officers . . . were obliged to put down their arms and surrender.

Lorenzo Venancio, *born 1819 at Santa Cruz Mission*

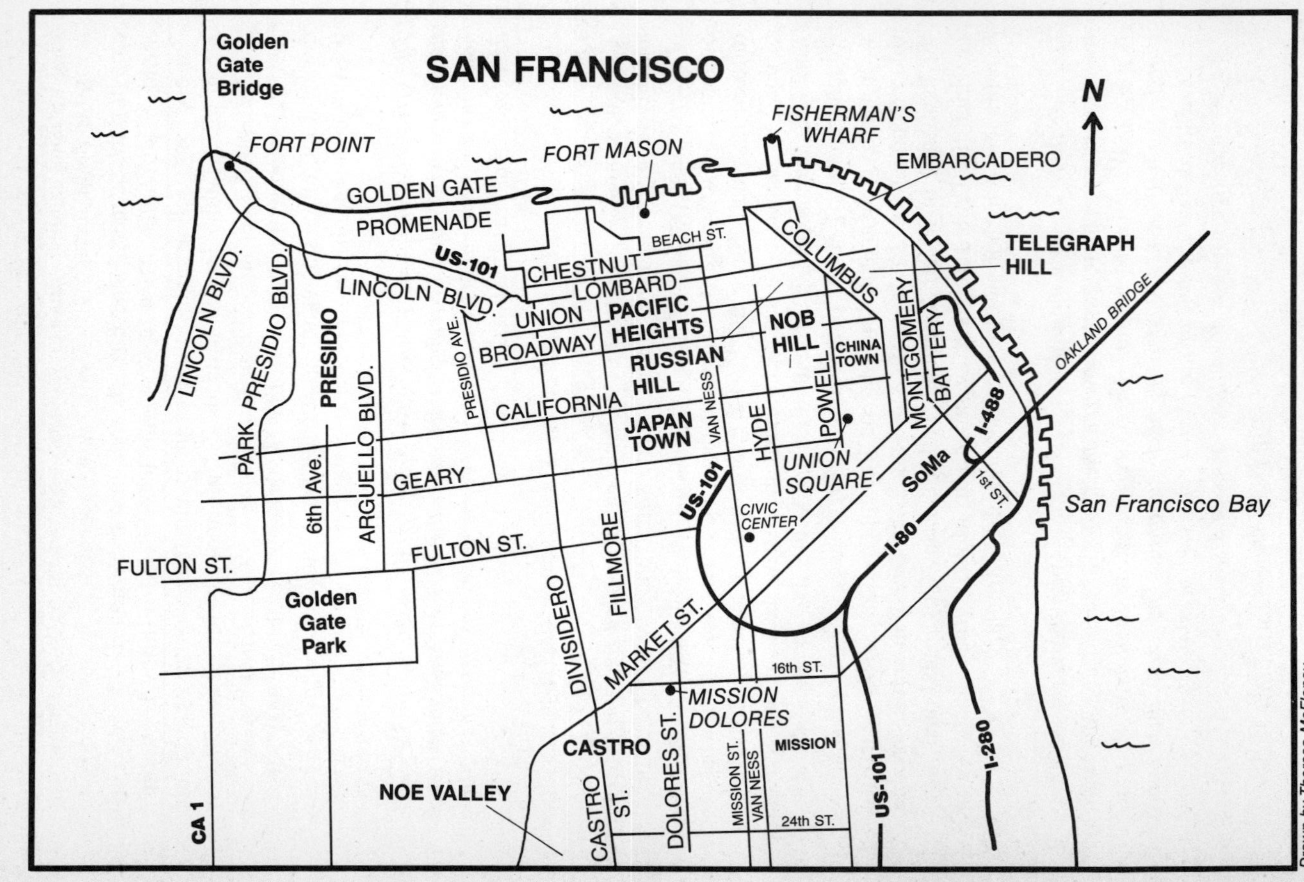

Drawn by Theresa McEleney

San Francisco finally succumbed to nearly two centuries of foreign threats, and General Vallejo, after 48 days in captivity, returned to Sonoma weighing merely 96 pounds.

Tiny Yerba Buena soon would be transformed, its fields of aromatic mint ("yerba buena") lost to the boom of the Gold Rush. Even within the first year of the U.S. takeover, its population doubled when a shipload of 200 Mormans, intent on escaping the jurisdiction of the United States, poorly timed their arrival in the bay. When gold was discovered at Sutter's Mill in 1848, San Francisco's fate was determined. From all over the world, by ship and by land came the forty-niners, hungry for gold. Within a few years, San Francisco's population grew from several hundred to 35,000—more than the entire Hispanic and Indian population in all of Mexican California. As the city, by then called San Francisco, finally complemented the harbor in size, the adobe fortifications at the presidio were replaced by a white picket fence, and Mexican comandantes, Indian soldiers, and Yankee traders were overwhelmed by Germans, French, Irish, Chinese, and, of course, American prospectors. Steamships, built to get prospectors to the fields faster than clipper ships, plied the bay's waters. Yerba Buena had been lost, modern San Francisco born.

It was the winter of 1835–36 that the ship Alert . . . floated into the vast solitude of the Bay of San Francisco . . . Not only the neighborhood of our anchorage, but the entire region of the great bay, was a solitude . . . [In 1859] the superb steamship Golden Gate . . . neared the entrance to San Francisco, the great centre of a worldwide commerce . . . We bore around the point toward the anchoring-ground of the hide ships, and there covering the sand-hills and the valleys, stretching from the water's edge to the base of the great hills, and from the old Presidio to the Mission, flickering all over with lamps of its streets and houses, lay a city of one hundred thousand inhabitants . . .

RICHARD HENRY DANA, 1859

Sights

Earthquakes and the great fire of 1909 may have destroyed most of early San Francisco, taking with them the first plaza of Yerba Buena and the homes of its founders Richardson and Leese, but shops, museums, and parks provide more than ample enjoyments to the traveler. The magnificence of the setting, the views from Fort Point and Golden Gate Promenade in the Presidio area, remain as striking today as they were to the earliest explorers. Silting and land fill may have diminished the bay from its original 700 square miles to 400, but without great bridges spanning it the bay would be as much an obstacle today as it was to Spanish colonists. Whalers would find little comfort in the refinements of contemporary Sausalito, but Mission Dolores has survived, overcoming not only earthquakes and fires but also beer gardens and race tracks to become San Francisco's oldest building. And in the environs of the city, in Pacifica and Martinez, two old ranchos can still be visited.

Although the Camino Real stopped at the great bay and now great city of San Francisco, the old settlements did not. To the north of the bay many sights fortunately remain for excursions, adding their charm and the richness of their history to the beauty of Sonoma's vineyards and rugged coast. At Petaluma is General Vallejo's ranch; at Sonoma, his brother's adobe, the barracks, and mission chapel. At San Rafael there's a replica of the old church. And along the scenic north coast, Chinese porcelains from Cermeno's voyage have been found at Drake's Bay on the Point Reyes National Seashore. Farther north stands the impressive and reconstructed Fort Ross. Other sights can be found to the south of the bay (see ''End of the Missions''), and an excursion inland to Sacramento takes you to Sutter's Fort and back to the days just before the U.S. conquest.

San Francisco

Sand hills, covered with oak scrub and inhabited by rabbits, separated the old presidio from Yerba Buena and the tiny commercial pueblo from the mission. Much of the sand has filled the bay to create the modern downtown, but many hills remain to give the city its character—Nob Hill for example, Russian Hill, and especially Loma Alta, now called Telegraph Hill, from where the Spaniards first viewed the great bay, a view later shared by Bohemian artists and Beat poets. Where the Rezanov expedition found the road between the presidio and mission ''not good for either walking or riding,'' and where the laundress Juana Briones had the only house between the presidio and Yerba Buena (in the North Beach area), paved streets and urban growth long ago unified the old sections of the city into one. Still, the old sections provide a convenient way of organizing your sightseeing. The downtown and Embarcadero sights cover Yerba Buena; the Maritime Museum, Golden

Gate Promenade and the renovated Ghiradelli Square cover the old battery and fort in the north of the city; and the mission stands where it has been for over two centuries, just to the south of Market Street and downtown. Most of these sights lie on or near the *49-Mile Scenic Drive* that winds around the city. (Contact Convention & Visitors Bureau for map.) Yet other sights lie east of the bay and south of the city.

Downtown ☐ Most travelers orient themselves from **Union Square** (Powell and Geary) where they can park their cars underground before shopping in some of the finer downtown stores. But the historic heart of San Francisco is a bit to the north, up Powell to the **Nob Hill** section with its stately hotels on California Street, and then east through most of **Chinatown** (Bush, Stockton, Broadway, and Kearny Streets) to the old Portsmouth Square area (Grant, Clay, Washington and Montgomery Streets). Although the square is the teeming center of Chinatown, with its original population dating back to 1852 when 20,000 Chinese arrived to stake their claims in the gold rush, it also is where William Richardson and his wife, daughter of Comandante Martinez, lived in a tent surrounded by wilderness while they built the first house and general store of Yerba Buena on what is now Grant Street.

. . . an enterprising Yankee, years in advance of his time, had put up, on the rising ground above the landing, a shanty of rough boards, where he carried on a very small retail trade between the hide ships and the Indians.

DANA, 1835

Later, Jacob Leese and his wife, Vallejo's sister, would build the second home, one of redwood, at what is now the corner of Grant and Clay, and in 1844 the Mexican customs house was begun—a little four room adobe facing Washington Street that soon would be taken over by Captain Montgomery of the *USS Portsmouth*. From here, the U.S. flew its flag in 1846 over San Francisco Bay, waters lapping what is now Montgomery Street. With the gold rush, the small Mexican plaza at Portsmouth Square became a typical international port-of-call lined with saloons and gambling halls.

The docks into which we drew, and the streets about it, were densely crowded with express wagons and handcarts to take luggage, coaches and cabs for passengers . . . Through this crowd I made my way, along the well-built and well-lighted streets, as alive as by day . . . and between one and two o'clock in the morning found myself comfort-

ably abed in a commodious room, in the Oriental Hotel, which stood, as well as I could learn, on the filled-up cove [Yerba Buena], and not far from the spot where we used to beach our boats from the Alert.

DANA, 1859

Today the old adobes are gone, the custom house has collapsed, and William Richardson's shop has been replaced by the many high-rises lining Montgomery Street (below Sacramento) that make up the financial district of the city called "Wall Street West." Land fill has buried old wharves as well as hulls of sailing brigs deserted by their crews during the gold rush—under Clay and Sansome is the *Niantic*, under Pacific, Davis, lower Market, and the Embarcadero lie other fine ships, victims to the lure of gold in the Sierra.

Just a few blocks to the north on Montgomery brings you close to the area of the notorious Barbary Coast brothels and dance halls, today handsomely renovated as the **Jackson Square** area (between Washington and Pacific). Here, brick waterfront buildings from the 1850s now stand, landlocked but refurbished, into interior decorator and antique shops (Jackson St.) and professional offices (check Marvin Belli's at 722–28 Montgomery). You might want to stop at the **Wells Fargo Bank History Room** (420 Montgomery St.) with its exhibit of articles from gold rush and wild west days (Mon.–Fri. except holidays 10 a.m.–3 p.m.; free; 369–2619). Just a few blocks east of Jackson Square you come to a modern, but very much tamer version of the Barbary Coast on the Broadway Street boundary of North Beach and at the foot of Telegraph Hill.

North Waterfront □ From downtown at Powell Street you can take a cable car west past the Russian Hill district, and down Hyde Street past that block of Lombard known as "the crookedest street in the world," and on to the waterfront. Here at Hyde Street Pier, within a short walking distance are many of the city's favorite browsing and eating areas, as well as beautiful bay walks and historic museums near the old Spanish battery at Fort Mason.

Scattered along several blocks to the east of Hyde Street, along Beach, are the seafood and Italian restaurants associated with **Fisherman's Wharf** (end of Taylor St. on Pier 45). Along the several blocks farther east, you can explore the magnificent square-rigged *Balcutha* at Pier 41, its below deck restored to show life aboard the clippers near the end of the 19th century (9 a.m.–5 p.m. weekdays; 9 a.m.–10 p.m. weekends; 9 a.m.–9 p.m. summer weekdays; fee; 982–1886).

Back at Hyde Street and the cable car terminal is **The Cannery** with its galleries and boutiques. Straight ahead on the pier is the floating museum, the **Maritime Museum Historic Ships** with a three-masted schooner, a tub and steamship—five ships in all, some boardable (open daily 10 a.m.–5 p.m.; till 6 p.m. May to Oct.; free; 556–6435). Just west on Beach Street you come to the sponsor of the floating ships, the ★ **National Maritime Museum** (at the foot of Polk St.) where you can see old mastheads, ship models, and historic photographs of the Pacific vessels that used to anchor here (open daily 10 a.m.–5 p.m.; till 6 p.m. May to Oct.; free; 556–2904). Across the street from the museum is **Ghirardelli Square,** the renovated chocolate factory now filled with galleries, restaurants, and shops.

From Hyde Street Pier west runs the shoreline **Golden Gate Promenade,** a magnificent walking trail leading past Fort Mason, then along the foot of the presidio, before reaching Fort Point and the Golden Gate Bridge 3½ miles later. **Fort Mason** no longer is the Yerba Buena Battery, but by walking along the bluffs of the promenade (½m from Hyde Street) you can see the view of the Golden Gate that gave the cannon their vantage. No longer the western headquarters for the U.S. Army either, Fort Mason instead is part of the Golden Gate National Recreation Area, with cultural and entertainment events at the **Fort Mason Center** (Laguna and Marina Blvd.; 441–5705) that also houses the **Mexican Museum** (Building D) with its changing exhibits of pre-Columbian and colonial art, as well as contemporary art. (Open Wed.–Sun. noon–5 p.m.; closed holidays; donation; good crafts shop; 441–0404.)

Set above the Golden Gate Promenade and just off the 49-mile scenic drive at Lincoln Boulevard (CA 1) is the **Presidio**. This former Spanish fort now functions a bit as a U.S. Army installation, but more as a park with it's wooded hills fine for picnicking. You can hike around the many historic markers placed on the grounds, or just enjoy the views.

This mesa affords a most delightful view, for from it one sees a large part of the port and its islands, as far as the other side, the mouth of the harbor, and of the sea all that the sight can take in.

Font, 1776

All that remains of the Spanish presidio is part of an adobe, built in 1820 as the comandante's headquarters and now incorporated into the **Officer's Club** (end of parade ground off Lincoln). The 17th-century cannon that once defended the Spanish possession can be seen here as well as in front of the **Presidio Army Museum** (Lincoln and Funston; open 10 a.m.–4 p.m. except Mon.; free; 561–3319) where you can see some photos of the 1906 earthquake and fire that destroyed much of early San Francisco.

Not to be missed for its dramatic location at the foot of the Golden Gate Bridge is ★ **Fort Point National Historic Site** (off Lincoln Blvd.), where the 18th-century San Joaquin Battery stood, and where the city's founders first overlooked the Golden Gate.

The cliff [Fort Point] is very high and perpendicular, so that from it one can spit into the sea. From here we saw . . . the spouting whales, a shoal of dolphins or tunny fish, sea otter, and sea lions . . .

FONT, 1776

Although the old Spanish installation is long gone, the Civil War fort here, abandoned in 1914, has been reconstructed and made into a museum of military history that includes a small exhibit on Spanish forts and one of the battery's original cannon dating from 1684. (Open 10 a.m.–5 p.m.; closed major holidays; free; 556–1693.) *TIP*: Driving to the fort avoid US 101 so that you don't go over the Golden Gate Bridge instead of arriving at the museum. However, the bridge offers exceptional views of the harbor and city, and can be walked as well as driven.

You might return to downtown by taking in some more of the 49-Mile Scenic Drive on the Pacific side of Fort Point where windswept beaches and coves of the **Golden Gate National Recreation Area** (556–0560) can be enjoyed by driving south along Lincoln Blvd. to El Camino del Mar, then on to the Great Highway. A popular stopping point is the **Cliff House** (at Point Lobos Ave., an extension of Geary) with its view over Seal Rocks, a sea lion habitat between September and June, and its comfortable restaurant. Driving a bit farther south on the Great Highway, turn east on Fulton Street for the verdant and magnificent **Golden Gate Park,** now covering the region Font described as ''broken and sandy'' with arboretums and botanical gardens, as well as the lovely Japanese Tea Garden with its footbridges and streams. Here, too, is the **M. H. de Young Museum,** the fine arts museum of San Francisco (fee; 750–3659) with the Avery Brundage Collection housed separately in the **Asian Art Museum** (fee; 558–2993). The park attractions have slightly varying hours though most can be visited 10 a.m.–4:30 p.m., and most are free (Roads closed to cars Sundays; picnicking; 221–1311.)

★ **Mission Dolores** □ In 1776 Fray Junipero Serra, founding father of the original nine missions, realized his dream of a mission dedicated to the patron of the Franciscan order. The **Mission San Francisco de Asis** (16th and Dolores) established next to Dolores Creek, became known over the years as simply the Mission Dolores. Nearby, the creek emptied into a large lake on the shores of which the Anza colonists first camped in San Francisco. The mission, though served by illustrious friars such as San Francisco Palou who wrote the first history of California, struggled as much as its presidial companion on the frontier. Dampness made it difficult for neophytes to overcome the epidemics that swept through their population, and those who were not sick often ran away to the other side of the bay. The surrounding land never was very productive, as one visitor tells us, even though he had just enjoyed a mission dinner of hearty stew and "ordinary quality" wine.

. . . we were conducted to the kitchen garden, which did not answer to my expectations. There was nothing in it but some sort of pulse and culinary vegetables, with a few stunted fruit trees, which scarcely bore any fruit, and most of the beds were overgrown with weeds. The northwest winds, which prevail so much on this coast, and the dry, sandy nature of the soil, are insurmountable obstacles to horticulture.

LANGSDORFF, 1806

When the sanatorium at San Rafael was established, the population of the mission fell from 1800 to 230.

The church, though without the architectural refinements of some of the more successful missions, is massive and strong. Its interior contains a fine 18th-century baroque altarpiece from Mexico and an interesting decorative panel of the Last Supper, though not the painting seen by Langsdorff.

Our Cicerone, Father Joseph Uria, who was, generally speaking, an intelligent and well-informed man . . . understanding that I was a naturalist, took me by the hand when we were in the chapel, and made me take notice of a painting which represented the Agave Americana, *or large American aloe, from the midst of which, instead of a flower stem, rose a holy virgin, by whom, as he assured me, many extraordinary miracles were performed . . .*

LANGSDORFF, 1806

The quandrangle, too, is gone and largely replaced by the towering basilica next door. Where the friary stood is an empty space between the churches, the padres' quarters destroyed years ago for an extension to the basilica that never was built. Even the lake has disappeared, filled in from 15th Street to 23rd, from Guerrero to Harrison, and now a Mexican neighborhood of the city. Yet the church bells still toll during Holy Week. And along with the church you can visit the old cemetery burial place of 5500 neophytes, Governor Antonio Arguello, the first alcalde of Yerba Buena, and of early Anglo-pioneers like James Casey who murdered newspaper editor James King, and then was hanged himself. On June 27th of each year, the mission celebrates the *anniversary* of its founding. (Open 10 a.m.–4 p.m.; 9 a.m.–4:30 p.m. in summer; closed some holidays; donation; 621–8203.)

Other Sights □ While enjoying the waterfront area, you might take a *harbor cruise* or ferry across the harbor to **Sausalito** (546–2810 for information on both) from pier 41. Maybe you'll want to visit **Alcatraz** on a boat tour (contact Ticketron in summer for reservations; 546–2805 for information). Or you might drive or walk the hills of some of the more fashionable historic residential sections of the city. **Pacific heights** is famous for its Victorian mansions, most of which lie between Van Ness and the Presidio bounded by Jackson and Broadway. Two mansions that can be visited are the **Whittier Mansion** (2090 Jackson St.) that houses the California Historical Society with its exhibits on the history of the city (Wed. and weekends 1–5 p.m.; closed holidays; fee; 567–1848) and the Queen Anne **Hass-Lilienthal House** (2007 Franklin St.; fee; 441–3000). Even if you don't want a house tour, a drive around Divisidero near Pacific and Jackson shows the neighborhood at its loveliest, and Union Street between Van Ness and Fillmore takes you to the antique and art galleries, the trendy restaurants and cafes for which the neighborhood is famous. The crest of **Russian Hill** is at the top of Vallejo Street, but you might also want to walk by one of the city's oldest homes (1853) at 1052 Broadway or visit the **San Francisco Art Institute** (800 Chestnut St. at Jones) with its Diego Rivera mural (open 10 a.m.–5 p.m. weekdays; closed holidays; free; 771–7010). **Telegraph Hill** is lovely too with some of San Francisco's earliest homes along Napier Lane off Filbert, and with its winding streets suddenly affording views of the bay. But one of the most stupendous views is from **Coit Tower** (on crest of hill at eastern end of Lombard) where you can also see the impressive WPA depression era murals painted with San Francisco scenes. (Open 10 a.m.–4:30 p.m. daily; closed major holidays; fee; 362–8037.) Although residents of the Beat generation would find the area too expensive today, their traditions live on at the foot of the hill in **North Beach** (certainly not a beach since the time of Juana Briones) at the **City Lights Bookstore** (261 Columbus Ave.) where avant-garde poetry still is published (open 10 a.m.–midnight). Along Market Street, where rancheros once carted their goods to Yerba Buena, is the large **Civic Center** complex (at Hyde St.) with the Opera House, Symphony Hall, Museum of Modern Art, government buildings and the **Society of California Pioneers Museum** (456 McAllister St.) with displays on the history of the state. (Weekdays 10 a.m.–4 p.m.; closed holidays and July; free; 861–5278.)

For *walking tours* of many of these areas contact Architectural Heritage (441–3000) and City Guides (558–3981).

Environs of San Francisco

Oakland □ East of the bay the Peralta ranch covered most of the land now occupied by Oakland, Berkeley, and Alameda. Although none of the Peralta family adobes have survived, there are museums to visit in Berkeley and Oakland. In Oakland a trip to the downtown is definitely rewarded by the ★★ **Oakland Museum** (1000 Oak St. at 10th) with its gardens and art exhibits, but most especially by its Cowell Hall of California History with innovative exhibits ranging from prehistoric through the Spanish and Mexican periods, and all the way to Mickey Mouse and Harley Davidson motorcycles. *Open Wed.-Sat. 10 a.m.–5 p.m.; Sun. noon–7 p.m.; closed major holidays; free; 273–3401. To reach downtown Oakland, cross the Bay Bridge (I-80) and follow CA 17 south to Broadway (10m). The Lake Merritt station of BART brings you here too.*

Berkeley □ The University of California campus can be toured to see its many museums and 720 beautiful acres bounded by Oxford Street, Hearst, and Bancroft Way. The ★ **Bancroft Library** is in the center of the campus and contains many rare books and manuscripts and a world famous collection on the ethnology and history of California. Although the small exhibits here change, usually you can see the fake brass plaque so long thought to have been fashioned by Sir Francis Drake. (Open weekdays 9 a.m.–5 p.m.; Sat. 1–5 p.m.; free.) The ★★ **Lowie Museum of Anthropology** (Kroeber Hall, Bancroft Way at end of College Ave.) contains extensive collections, particularly on North American Indians. Various samples from the collections are mounted into major but temporary exhibits. Call to see if the main exhibit hall is open. (Open 10 a.m.–4:30 p.m. weekdays except Wed.; noon–4:30

weekends; closed holidays; fee; good museum shop; 642–3681.) *Berkeley lies across the Bay Bridge; the campus is a few miles east of I-80 on University Ave. (12m). BART station at Moffit Avenue leaves you near the campus center.*

Martinez □ Although the Peralta ranch covered most of the east of the bay, the polyglot Comandante Ignacio Martinez was able to find over 17,000 acres for his Rancho El Pinole in the Alhambra Valley area now called Martinez.

Among the families that populated the circumference of the bay, that of Lieutenant Don Ignacio Martinez deserves particular mention, on account of his courteous, gay, and festive character. Of the many occasions when I was at Pinole . . . I do not remember a single one when there was not a dance in the evening . . . To arrive at the rancho and to have a fandango in the evening was one and the same thing.

ARNAZ, 1840s

Today Don Ignacio's home is no more, but his son's attractive two-story home, dating from 1849, has been refurbished and can be visited at the **John Muir National Historic Site** (Alhambra Rd. and CA 4) along with a visit to the home of the great naturalist and his orchards. *Open 10 a.m.–4:30 p.m. daily except major holidays; free; picnicking; 228–8860. To reach this pleasant park, follow the Bay Bridge to I-80 north, exit onto CA 4 leading to Martinez and exit at Alhambra Ave. Total distance is 35m.*

Pacifica □ The area to the south of the city, more fertile and benign in climate than San Francisco, attracted early ranches. The earliest was a 1786 outpost of the Mission Dolores founded in what is now Pacifica. Here a quadrangle complete with chapel and living quarters for the *vaqueros,* or cowboys, was established and thousands of cattle grazed in San Mateo County until an epidemic swept through the population of 400 neophytes. The ranch of Francisco Sanchez adjoined the mission branch, and after secularization in 1834 his son took over the mission land that spread miles along the Pacific coast. Don Francisco, a presidio officer and one time alcalde of Yerba Buena, built his adobe on the land next to the mission quadrangle, appropriating some of the old bricks in the process. Today the 1840 **Sanchez Adobe** (Linda Mar Blvd., 1m east CA 1) has been made into a small museum of the early ranching period. Next door can be seen the foundation of the mission quadrangle. *Open Tues. and Sun. 1–5 p.m.; donation; 359–1462. Pacifica can be reached 10m south via I-280 and CA 1.*

Accommodations

Nob Hill, selected by the richest of the rich—the Stanfords, Huntingtons, Hopkins and Crockers—as their hilltop escape from the 19th-century boom town of San Francisco below, retains its elegance in the 20th century as the preserve of some of the city's finest hotels. **The Stanford Court** is a good example of the luxury of these hotels with its circular entrance roofed by a Tiffany dome; its lobby like a private club with warm wood paneling, chandeliers, fresh cut flowers, and comfortable armchairs; its service unobtrusive yet impeccable. Although only 8 stories high, the hotel's location at the corner of Powell and California gives many of its 402 units superb views over the city and bay. The rooms are tastefully decorated with Empire and French provincial style furnishings; the suites are exceptional, many with more than ample drawing rooms and two well-appointed marble baths. Cafe and excellent restaurant; lounges; boutiques and concierge service. Valet parking. ***Very expensive***. Write 905 California, CA 94108; 989–3500, 800–622–0957 CA, or 800–227–4736 within the U.S. Other famous hotels sharing Nob Hill are the **Huntington** (1075 California, CA 94108; 474–5400 or 800–227–4683; ***very expensive***) and the **Mark Hopkins** (999 California St., CA 94108; 392–3434 or 800–327–0200; ***very expensive***).

Union Square, famous for Saks Fifth Avenue, I. Magnin, and Neiman Marcus, is equally well known for its hotels. Dominating the square since the beginning of the century is the **Westin St. Francis** where the ornate lobby bustles with people and the old-world ambience, perfected by violinists of the Compass Rose Room, attracts crowds. The Westin has added a new tower, so that now the 1200 rooms here vary considerably. Four restaurants and coffee shop; lounges; shops. Valet parking. ***Very expensive***. Write 335 Powell St., CA 94102; 397–7000, 800–228–3000. Nearby is **Campton Place** representing San Francisco's recent trend toward small but sumptuous hotels. The lobby is intimate, all soft hues and marble. The bar, excellent restaurant and a rooftop garden complete the common areas. The 125 rooms have a residential ambience and are appointed with all comforts. Valet parking. ***Very expen-***

sive. Write 340 Stockton St., CA 94108; 781–5555, 800–235–4300 CA or 800–647–4007 elsewhere in the U.S.

There are numerous less costly, but nonetheless intimate and finely appointed hotels in the area surrounding Union Square. Offering such traditional hotel amenities as room and laundry service, **The Orchard** has a handsome lobby, designed much like a living room and comfortable for the complimentary continental breakfast offered in the morning, the appetizers with bar service in the evenings. The 96 units, some suites and some with views over a quiet garden, are attractively furnished and the rates are at the ***low end of the expensive range***. Write 562 Sutter St., CA 94102, 433–4434, 800–433–4434 CA or 800–433–4343 elsewhere in the U.S. Other small European-style hotels have lowered their prices a bit further by forgoing some of the traditional services, like room service, but maintaining comfortable decor and amenities in the rooms. **Villa Florence** is one of these hotels, right off Union Square, with a large if somewhat ostentatious lobby, a stylish restaurant, and 177 very attractive rooms (225 Powell St., CA 94102; 397–7700, 800–243–5700 CA, or 800–553–4111 elsewhere in the U.S.; ***just above the moderate range***). The **Vintage Court** is another, with 106 units, complimentary coffee and wine in the lobby, and continental breakfast available in its restaurant (650 Bush St., CA 94108; 392–4666, 800–654–7266 CA, or 800–654–1100 elsewhere in the U.S.; ***just above moderate***).

Although not so magnificently appointed and a few blocks further away from Union Square, San Francisco has some unusually moderate-priced hotels in the center of the city. One is the **Hotel Beresford Arms** with its old-fashioned Victorian lobby and 96 rooms, some suites with kitchens (more expensive). Complementary coffee and pastries served in lobby. Public parking lot next door. ***Moderate***. Write 701 Post St. (at Jones), CA 94109; 673–2600. The **Canterbury-Whitehall Inn** is larger, more rambling and with more services, including some shops and restaurants. Its 250 units vary, but many are large, with refrigerators, and all are clean. ***Moderate***. Write 750 Sutter (near Taylor), CA 94109; 474–6464, 800–652–1614 CA, or 800–227–4788 elsewhere in the U.S.

The **chain hotels** are plentiful; there is a Holiday Inn, TraveLodge, and Sheraton near Fisherman's Wharf and there's a **motel row** on Lombard near Van Ness that includes an Econo Inn and TraveLodge.

Restaurants

San Francisco's dining is renown both for its quality and diversity as well as for its inventiveness, for it's here that California cuisine was born. You may want to dine impeccably at the most established and traditional restaurants such as **Ernie's** (847 Montgomery St. in Jackson Square; daily 6:30–10:30 p.m.; reserve at 397–5969; ***very expensive***) with its classic French cuisine served in an opulent Victorian setting; or **L'Etoile** (1075 California St. in the Huntington Hotel; Mon.–Sat. 6–10:30 p.m.; reserve at 771–1529; ***very expensive***) with its fine French food, polished silver and sparkling crystal; or **Fournou's Ovens** (905 California St. in the Stanford Court; lunch weekdays; dinner daily; reserve at 989–1910) with superbly prepared duckling and rack of lamb served amid 18th-century French provincial antiques. But you'll also want to try the restaurants that have defined new ways of dining, such as **Chez Panisse** (1517 Shattuck Ave., Tues.–Sat. for dinner; reservations required; 548–5525; ***very expensive***), the small restaurant in Berkeley that created what has become known as California cuisine—the freshest of fresh ingredients combined into warm salads, grilled fish with fruit and onion relishes, and duck prepared in such sauces as red wine and fresh figs. The *prix fixe* dinner here usually has choices only for dessert; the menu changes daily. Another innovative restaurant is **Campton Place** (340 Stockton in the Campton Place Hotel; daily 7 a.m.–11 p.m.; reserve at 781–5155; ***very expensive***) with its wonderful interpretations of American cuisine—spiny lobster on blue corn cakes, apple-ham plate, roast chicken stuffed with pine nuts, and delicious desserts including strawberry rhubarb pie and orange pecan pie. The menu changes daily, of course, but the ambience is always intimate, the table settings elegant with Wedgwood china and gleaming silver.

Fortunately you can dine well and experiment, too, at more moderate prices. The **Cafe at Chez Panisse** (open daily 11:30 a.m.–11:30 p.m.; no reservations; ***moderate*** to ***moderately expensive***) not only is far more casual than the restaurant, but its changing menu has numerous choices each day for both lunch and dinner, from appetizers such as pizzetta with eggplant, tapenade, and mozzarella, to entrees like swordfish grilled Turkish style. And although no restaurant quite offers the American cuisine of Campton Place (you might consider breakfast there—try banana hotcakes or poached eggs on biscuits with orange hollandaise and Missouri ham), a fun alternative is the **Fog City Diner** (1300 Battery at the Embarcadero; daily 11:30 a.m.–11 p.m.; reserve if you can at 982–2000; ***moderate*** to ***moderately expensive***). The glimmering chrome of this diner, its seductive Art Deco touches and beckoning neon sign are as pop American as the grilled cheese sandwiches (with jalapeno peppers and red onions) and apple pie. But the lines here are not just for the ambience. The food is good, from the delicious crab cakes to calves liver with tomatoes, leeks, and ginger, and all the way to the desserts.

San Francisco also offers haute Chinese cuisine, and a good place to try it is the **Mandarin** (Ghirardelli Square; daily noon–11 p.m.; reserve at 673–8812; ***moderate*** to ***moderately expensive***) with its crispy and dense smoked tea duck and superb minced quail wrapped in lettuce leaves. And although Italian restaurants are most plentiful in North Beach, two of the finest are located elsewhere. **Lanzone & Son** (Ghirardelli Square; Tues.–Fri. noon–11 p.m.; weekends 4 p.m.–midnight; reserve at 771–2880; ***moderately expensive***; and with Modesto Lanzone's, a branch impressively decorated with art at the Opera Plaza; 928–0400) offers magnificently fresh food on daily changing menus, but the veal is always very good, the pastas excellent, particularly the agnolotti alla crema. **Ciao** (230 Jackson St.; daily 11 a.m.–midnight except Sun. dinner only; reserve at 982–9500; ***moderately expensive***) serves delicious carpaccio and fettucine tuttomare; its sorbets are not to be missed, tangy lemon served in a frozen half-lemon—melon, banana, and strawberry flavors too, all served in frosty fruits.

More casual places, convenient for lunch while you're sightseeing, should be mentioned. In the financial district you can best pick up the local color at **Sam's Grill** (374 Bush St.; weekdays 11 a.m.–8:30 p.m.; reservations for groups over 6; 421–0594; ***moderate***) where the tuxedoed waiters of this lively restaurant serve you a perfectly prepared boned Rex sole, or other seafood if you wish. At Fort Mason you can enjoy a terrific bay view and exciting vegetarian California cuisine at **Greens** (Fort Mason Center, Building A; Tues.–Sat. lunch and dinner, Sun. brunch; reserve at 771–6222; ***moderate***). Many other spots can be selected from neighborhood restaurants (see below), but for snacks consider the ice cream and sorbets at **Gelateria Vivoli** in The Cannery near Fisherman's Wharf and a caffe latte in Berkeley at **Fanny's** (near San Pablo and Cedar, just off University Ave.).

San Francisco is a city of neighborhoods. Although there is no better way to explore the local scenes than to walk around, eating provides one of the easiest ways to introduce yourself to the city. In Italian North Beach, for example, you might want to dine in a restaurant such as the very popular **Caffe Sport** (574 Green St.; Tues.–Sat. lunch and dinner; reservations for 4 or more; 981–1251; ***moderate***), but consider buying an Italian sandwich instead at one of the delicatessens such as **Panelli Bros**. (1419 Stockton), and eating it in Washington Square with all the locals. In Chinatown you definitely should try the variety of dumplings and appetizers called Dim Sum at the **Tong Fong Restaurant** (808 Pacific off Stockton), **Hong Kong Teahouse** (835 Pacific), or **Canton Tea House** (1108 Stockton near Jackson). All three are extremely popular and good; all serve ***inexpensive*** (to ***moderate,*** depending on how much you eat) Dim Sum daily until about 3 p.m. Elegant Pacific Heights definitely requires a less earthy approach, such as dining in a Victorian setting and sampling the seafood at the **Pacific Heights Bar & Grill** (2001 Fillmore St. at Pine; Mon.–Sat. lunch; Sun. brunch; dinner daily; reserve at 567–3337; ***moderate***) or enjoying the authentic pub ambience of the **Balboa Cafe** (3199 Fillmore; 11 a.m.–11 p.m. daily; no reservations; 922–4595; ***moderate***) serving baguette sandwiches and some daily luncheon specials that show the touch of Jeremiah Tower, one of the creators of California cuisine.

Other neighborhoods lie a bit farther away from downtown but offer their own rewards. The Mission area is intensely Hispanic and never more intensely so than along 24th Street east of Mission. As you cruise around here you might consider a freshly prepared burrito, huge and good, accompanied by a fruit *licuado* at **La Taqueria** (2889 Mission near 25th; open daily to 6 p.m.; ***inexpensive***). And the formerly ethnic neighborhood of Noe Valley is quickly becoming renovated by professionals. Its 24th Street (west of Dolores) is lined with shops and interesting restaurants, such as **La Roca** (4288 24th St.; dinner daily except Mon.; reserve at 282–7780; ***moderate***). This small and very pleasant restaurant serves a variety of shellfish in delicious sauces, one a fiery green, another a tomatoey Spanish, and even a savory combination of the two. The food is fresh and flavorful, the prices very good. Another evolving neighborhood is SoMa, a funky and artsy spot south of Market near the Moscone Convention Center. The area is far from yuppified, its old buildings still cheap enough to house experimental theaters, dance clubs like El Rio, and avant-garde galleries. One place to explore SoMa is the **Cadillac Bar & Restaurant** (One Holland Court, off Howard between 4th and 5th; lunch weekdays; dinner every day but Sun.; no reservations; 543–8226; ***moderate***) with its noisy mariachis and Mexican food. Or try the even rarer scene at **Hamburger Mary's Organic Grill** (1582 Folsom; 626–5767; ***inexpensive to moderate***).

Excursions North of the Bay

One of the most scenic trips in California includes the historic sights of the missions at San Rafael and Sonoma, of Mexican barracks at Sonoma and Russian ones at Fort Ross, of an old ranch home built by Vallejo at Petaluma and new ones built in the fertile valleys of Sonoma and on the magnificently rugged coast of the Pacific.

. . . the face of the earth in all those splendid valleys and mountain sides was a mass of clover and the wild oats covered a large section of the country standing more than waist high. All the bays and creeks were literally alive with fish and along the coast and the bay shores, there was no end to the delicious clams and shell fish.

VALLEJO, 1883

You can plan to include all the following sights in a loop through the Sonoma vineyards and then on to the spectacular coast around Fort Ross, heading back on coastal CA 1 past Point Reyes National Seashore and Drakes Bay, before dropping down to US 101 for Sausalito and San Francisco (200m, but you can easily add another 70m by leaving the main roads for some of the sights). Certainly to explore most of the sights, you would want to add an overnight, or even two. Or you can just pick and choose among the sights for a leisurely day excursion to the sea or to valley wine tastings. There's picnicking at Sonoma and its vineyards, at Petaluma and Fort Ross, and along the coast at Sonoma State Beach and at Point Reyes you can both picnic and camp. Many restaurants and hotels can be found along this route, but those in Sonoma, Santa Rosa, and Bodega Bay are most convenient.

San Rafael □ Across the Golden Gate Bridge you find the town that began existence in 1817 as a sanatorium for neophytes from Mission Dolores. The San Francisco mission had been plagued by diseases of epidemic proportions. Its friars thought that a mission branch, complete with chapel and cemetery, founded in the milder climate of what is now Marin County, might help some of the poor neophytes recuperate. So successful was this first of California health spas that it received full mission status, and grew to hold nearly 2000 Indian neophytes, most escaping the fog-ridden Mission Dolores. After secularization the mission buildings, never very elaborate, wasted away until they disappeared. Today a **replica** of the mission chapel (1104 5th Ave., 3 blocks west of US 101 exit for central San Rafael) can be seen at its location near the original site, and you can see some mission memorabilia displayed in the gift shop. (Open 11 a.m.–4 p.m. except Sun. closed during mass; closed some holidays; free; 454–8141.) More rewarding, even if it's more contemporary, is the exceptional **Marin County Civic Center** (1m north of US 101 a N. San Pedro Rd. exit) designed by Frank Lloyd Wright. (Open 8:30 a.m.–4:30 p.m.; free; tour pamphlet, and guided tours—if arranged in advance; 499–6104.) *San Rafael lies just 20m north of San Francisco on US 101.*

★★★ **Petaluma Adobe** ☐ In 1836 Comandante Vallejo began construction on this 67,000 acre ranch. It would not be Vallejo's largest land grant—another would measure 80,000 acres—but the house here would become the center of his vast agricultural estate. With adobe bricks and redwood timber he built a two-story estate around a quadrangle 200 feet square. Inspired by the missions, the ranch was self-sustaining with workshops on the first floor that produced spurs for the vaqueros, clothes for the farmers, and shoes for Sonoma's garrison. And like the missions, Rancho Petaluma could muster 2000 Indians (many originally neophytes at the Sonoma mission) in its quadrangle each morning to receive work orders. Most like a presidio, the ranch house walls were thick, three feet thick.

Sr. Vallejo has so well established and fortified himself at Sonoma that he was given the epithet "little king."

ANGUSTIAS DE LA GUERRA ORD,
1840s

The ranch made a fair income from its thousands of bushels of wheat grown for the Russians; it made even more from its cattle.

Kill all the cattle you want, take all you can use. We do not care how many cattle you kill, but there is one thing we do ask, that is, whenever you kill a steer, hang the hide on a tree or on a fence somewhere so the coyotes cannot destroy it. That is where we make our money; from the hides.

VALLEJO, 1846

The general sold the Petaluma ranch in 1857 for $25,000. Over the years it fell into disuse, but fortunately half of the quadrangle has been restored, the workshops outfitted as they were in the past, the upstairs furnished to the period that the Vallejos used it as a home, and the pastures once again are grazing fields for horses and cattle. The **Petaluma Adobe State Park** (3325 Adobe Rd.) is one of the finest museums dedicated to the great period of Mexican ranching. It becomes even more reminiscent of the past with two **festivals,** the Old Adobe Fiesta the second Sunday in August and the Old California Festival in October. *Open 10 a.m.–5 p.m. daily; fee; picnicking; 707–762–4871. Located amid dairy farms, the adobe is ½m east of US 101 at Petaluma on CA 116, then 2m north on Casa Grande Road.*

A pleasant nearby spot to lunch is on the deck of the **Steamer Gold Landing Restaurant** (1 Water St. in Petaluma; Mon.–Sat. 11:30 a.m.–2:30 p.m.; Sun. brunch beginning at 10 a.m.; 707–763–6876; ***moderate***). While overlooking an old canal, you can enjoy a bucket of steamed clams or other seafood, sandwiches and salads. From the state park, drive west on Adobe Road to E. Washington Street, left over US 101, across the railroad tracks, then left onto the alley-like Water Street after about 3½m and before the traffic light at Petaluma Blvd.

Petaluma is just off US 101, 25m north of San Rafael and 45m from San Francisco. Sonoma lies only 15m east on scenic CA 116 and Stage Gulch Road.

★★ **Sonoma** □ The lovely historic town of Sonoma offers fine scenery, excellent sightseeing, and good wine tastings. The pleasures of the spot were readily apparent to Comandante Vallejo when he first came to Sonoma, known to the local Indians who greeted and entertained him as "the valley of the moon."

. . . my camp was surrounded by about 11,000 Indians who came to greet me. After breakfast I mounted my troops and took them to a spot near the springs known by the name Chicuyen *and now as Lachryma Montis. After eight days of feasting and dancing I finally was freed of so many dancers and proceeded to outline and lay out the new town.*

VALLEJO, 1834

Vallejo founded the pueblo of Sonoma, built the barracks and his Casa Grande where the Bear Flaggers would so rudely intrude, and even replaced the ruined mission church with a parish chapel. His relatives helped populate the region, adding their adobes around the plaza. Today much of the original frontier pueblo has been preserved as the **Sonoma State Historic Park** (First St. East and Spain; open 10 a.m.–5 p.m.; closed major holidays; fee; 707–938–1578). Around the Spanish plaza, still the center of Sonoma, is the two-story ★ **Barracks** (E. Spain near

First St. East), refurbished and with a museum including some interesting items on the pastoral age. Nearby are the servants quarters of the **Casa Grande,** the main house having burnt down in 1860. And across First Street East is the ★ **Mission San Francisco Solano** that has barely survived its burning by revolting Indians and its days when the friary was used as a winery, the church as a barn. But this last of all the missions (founded in 1823), has been carefully restored to include the 1840s chapel built by Vallejo and the original friary, the oldest building in all of Sonoma (dating from 1825) and now housing a small museum. It is from the mission that the annual blessing of the grapes takes place, its one remaining bell (alas, not the one donated by the Russians) announcing the beginning of the **Vintage Festival** with its folk dances, parades and wine tastings. (Usually in Sept., but contact the Chamber of Commerce, 453 First St. East, CA 95476; 707–996–1033.) Other historic buildings can be found around the plaza, ones that aren't part of the state park but survive today as commercial establishments: **Jacob Leese's adobe** (487 First St. West), and **Salvador Vallejo's adobes** (18 W. Spain and 415–427 First St. West) converted into hotels during the roaring gold rush, are some of them. Another spot, the **Blue Wing Inn** (133 E. Spain St.) best typifies the period of the forty-niners when Sonoma grew from an outpost against Russian encroachment into a prosperous, and boisterous, town of saloons and gambling houses. Other later buildings abound in the streets around the plaza; the *Sonoma Walking Tour* brochure (fee; purchase at state park facilities or Chamber of Commerce) can guide you to all of them.

Also belonging to the state park and worth the short detour off the plaza is ★★ **General Vallejo's Home** (just a few blocks west of plaza, follow signs onto Third St. West), named *Lachryma Montis,* or "Mountain Tears," for the springs in nearby mountains. Built in its Gothic and gingerbread styles in 1851, the house today is complete with the general's furnishings and surrounded by 17 acres of his gardens, a wonderful spot for picnicking.

The weeping willow with the green foliage is very, very, very pretty; it gives a nice shade . . . The poplars are beginning to show some green; the orange trees are commencing to throw out new shoots and then the lemon, blossoms.

VALLEJO, 1870

As an historic figure, Vallejo left an enormous legacy in the Sonoma Valley. He also sparked the region's foremost industry when he began cultivating the vineyards of the secularized Mission San Francisco Solano. The missions had long produced sacramental wine, and when they could, as much surplus as possible for trade. Although it wasn't always the most refined wine, tasting too bitter to some, numerous French visitors commented favorably on it, as did others.

An American lady once observed to me, that there were in California two things supremely good, La Senora Noriega, and grapes.

ALFRED ROBINSON (1846)

Not until the Hungarian refugee Agoston Harazthy introduced European varietals to the Sonoma Valley was the California wine industry truly born, however. Yet it was Vallejo who attracted Harazthy to Sonoma, Vallejo who arranged Harazthy's purchase of Buena Vista in 1856, and Vallejo's two daughters who married Harazthy's sons and thus forged a Sonoma viticultural dynasty. Vallejo himself experimented with new varietals and, aging his wines in the cellar of the Sonoma barracks, won numerous prizes. Today Vallejo Harazthy, a fifth generation descendant of the dynasty, is reviving some of the original wines under the M.G. Vallejo label. Some of the profits of these wines will go toward rebuilding the barn at Lachryma Montis and supporting the Sonoma State Park. Also a visit to **Sebastiani Vineyards** (389 Fourth St. East near Spain St.) takes you to the original mission vineyards tended by Vallejo. (Tours every 20 minutes 10 a.m.–4:20 p.m. daily; tasting room 10 a.m.–5 p.m.; closed major holidays; free; 707–938–5532.) And a visit to the **Buena Vista Winery** (18000 Old Winery Rd., 2 m east via Napa St.) takes you into Harazthy's cellars dating from 1862 and allows you to picnic under giant eucalyptus. (Self-guided tours; tasting room; tours of champagne cellars from 10 a.m.–5 p.m. daily except major holidays; free; 707–938–1266.) The ranch lands of Lachryma Montis once extended all the way north to where the **Glen Ellen Winery** (1883 London Ranch Rd.) now welcomes visitors, and where an old adobe winery can be seen. (Open for wine tastings, call 707–996–1066 for hours; free; 1m west of the town of Glen Ellen off CA 12 north.) Many other wineries can be visited (particularly on CA 121 east and on CA 12 north), but note that summer weekends may find the most numerous tasting opportunities as well as the most crowded conditions. September and October are favorite months for a visit, since you can see the grapes being harvested and crushed into wine. (For more information contact Sonoma

County Convention & Visitors Bureau, 637 First St., Santa Rosa 95404; 707–545–1420; and see tour agencies under "Suggestions" below.)

The Sonoma Valley is a fine area to dine, particularly at **John Ash & Company** (Vintners Inn, 4350 Barnes Rd. in Santa Rosa, just west of US 101 near the River Rd. exit; open lunch weekdays, brunch Sun.; dinner Tues. to Sun.; reserve at 707–527–7687; ***moderately expensive***). This restaurant with wine shop not only gives you an excellent opportunity to continue your tasting of local wines, but it also serves them properly accompanied by superbly prepared food in the California style. Although the menu changes daily, the salads are beautiful (such as the tomato, baby greens, black beans, and goat cheese salad) and the entrees ambrosial (such as the boned quail stuffed with veal, walnuts, leeks, and mushrooms, and served with a reduced sauce). Around the Sonoma Plaza, you have a good choice of eating spots. Most refined is the historic **Sonoma Hotel** (110 W. Spain St.; open Fri.–Tues. lunch and dinner; 707–996–2996; ***moderate***) where you can lunch on oriental chicken salad or daily specials such as salmon dijonnaise in a very Victorian dining room or on an outdoor patio. **La Casa** (121 E. Spain St.; daily 11:30 a.m. through dinner; 707–996–3406; ***inexpensive to moderate***) serves good Mexican food, such as a very flavorful cheese soup with tomatoes, lime, and cilantro in a rich broth, in a most attractive setting. And even more casual is **The Cheese Factory** (2 W. Spain St.; daily 9:30 a.m.–5:30 p.m.; ***inexpensive to moderate***), a wonderful store stocked full of picnic supplies—its own Sonoma cheddar and Sonoma Jack cheeses, prepared pasta salads, sandwiches, local wines, and the like. And you don't have to go far to picnic since the store provides tables on an outdoor terrace.

Overnight accommodations can be enjoyed in Sonoma at small inns like the **Sonoma Hotel,** built in the 1880s, refurbished as a stagecoach inn by Sebastiani in the 1920s, and recently restored to its turn-of-the-century character with an old wooden bar in the lounge, and attractive Victorian furnishings throughout. The 17 rooms (some with private bath) are furnished with antiques, one with a bed frame that belonged to General Vallejo's sister. ***Moderate.*** Write 110 W. Spain St., CA 95476; 707–996–2996. In Santa Rosa, you can enjoy a country-style inn that takes its position in this valley seriously enough to surround itself with vineyards. The **Vintner's Inn** offers very ample modern units decorated with French provincial furnishings, many with fireplaces and balconies or patios. ***Expensive*** rates include a full breakfast. Write 4350 Barnes Rd., CA 95401; 707–575–7350 or 800–421–2584 CA. Other small establishments in Santa Rosa, and farther north in Healdsburg can be contacted through **Wine Country Inns of Sonoma County** (Box 51, Geyserville 95441). More plentiful rooms and fuller facilities can be enjoyed at the **Sheraton Round Barn Inn**. The 252 units here are all oversized, with desk area and very comfortable furnishings; those with pool views are particularly fine and have furnished terraces. Restaurant and lounge with entertainment. Lap pool, Jacuzzi, jogging path, and access to an unusual 18-hole golf course with a Japanese-style setting, including a pagoda. A very good buy at ***moderate*** rates. Write US 101 & Mendocino Ave., Santa Rosa 95401; 707–523–7555, 800–833–9595 CA, or 800–325–3535 elsewhere in the U.S.

Sonoma can be reached most rapidly from San Francisco on US 101 to Novato, then east on CA 37 to CA 121/12 north for a total distance of just less than 50m. Santa Rosa is on US 101, 53m north of San Francisco. But the backroads offer more interesting routes. From Petaluma follow CA 116 and Stage Gulch Road east for 15m to Sonoma. Between Sonoma and Santa Rosa follow the vineyard route of CA 12, for a total of 20m.

Bodega Bay □ The cove at Bodega Bay provided one of the few sheltered anchorages along the rough north coast. From here the Russians found they could steal their way to the Farallones or San Francisco Bay, then safely return with their bounty—seal and, better yet, otter skins. Over five years only 1000 otters were captured in contrast to over 8000 seals. But the sought after otter pelts were worth any effort, fetching as they did prices of $120 in China for just enough fur to trim a silk robe. After 1818, the Russians relied on other enterprises to generate income, farms just inland from Bodega and brick-making on the bay here that they called Port Rumiantzov. Though nothing remains of this industrious community, an early traveler has preserved it for us.

Well-made roofs, houses of elegant form, fields well sown and surrounded with palisades, lent to this place a wholly European air.

A. Duhaut-Cilly, 1828

Today you can just enjoy the bay, fishing its waters, and resting at the few hotels here. It's a good spot to overnight or even weekend while exploring the coast and the inland country roads leading off of the town of Bodega. You can picnic or camp at the foot of some steep dunes at the **Sonoma Coast State Beach** (just 4m north of Bodega Bay) or you can seek out some of the restaurants in the Bodega area, such as the French-California cuisine offered at the **Sonoma Coast Villa** (16702 Coast Hwy; lunch Sun., dinner Wed. to Sun.; 707–876–3226; ***moderately expensive***). Run by the owners of San Francisco's Blue Boar Restaurant, the dining here varies with the daily menu, but you can usually count on Sonoma delicacies like goose and duckling as well as seafood. The restaurant is located 5m south of Bodega Bay. Another restaurant, more continental, but still emphasizing local seafood and poultry is the popular **Bodega Gallery Restaurant** (17110 Bodega Ln.; open Thurs. to Sun., lunch, dinner, and Sun. brunch; 707–876–3257; ***moderate to moderately expensive***). Located in the charming 19th-century Potter School building, the gallery restaurant also offers art exhibits and, with dinner, classical guitar music. To reach this restaurant, just head 1m south of Bodega Bay, turn east to the town of Bodega, and after another mile look for the cupola of the school house. If you just want views of Bodega Bay and some seafood (or if you find yourself traveling during the week when the other restaurants are closed), just cruise the waterfront for one of the restaurants here, such as the pleasant **Lucas Wharf,** 595 Coast Hwy.; daily 11 a.m.–9:30 p.m.; 707–875–3522; ***moderate***) where I found the food uneven, but the simpler dishes, such as fried calamari and steamed clams, are fine. For accommodations, the Best Western **Bodega Bay Lodge** has a tranquil location with good views of the bay and wildlife on the marsh pond. This motel offers a number of amenities including many rooms furnished with kitchenettes, balconies with sea views, and fireplaces and courtesy coffee. No dining facilities for the 64 units, except for a very good complimentary continental breakfast. Pool, whirlpool, fitness room with sauna. Access to horseback riding and golf. Parking. ***Moderate to expensive.*** Write to them at Coast Highway at Doran Beach, CA 94923; 707–875–3525, 800–368–2468 CA, or 800–368–2468 elsewhere in the U.S.

★★★ **Fort Ross** ☐ Along the precipitous coastal road north of Jenner, you come to understand just how out of reach this Russian establishment must have seemed. With each mile of crashing surf, steep cliffs, and curving road, you can sense the isolation they must have felt, an isolation that one visitor found made him feel melancholy, even somber. Yet others, arriving after months of travel and privations, found Ross "almost European" in its hospitality.

The governor of Ross, Alexander de Rotchev, his wife, nee Princess Gazarin . . . exerted themselves at all times to make our visit at their settlements agreeable . . . Anyone who has led the dreary life of a trapper . . . or has been pursued by the yells of savages, can fully appreciate the joy of a choice library, French wines, a piano, and a score of Mozart.

EUGENE DUFLOT DE MOFRAS, 1841

Within the redwood palisades visitors found a well-appointed commanders house, officers' barracks, storehouses and many-sided blockhouses, as well as a redwood chapel surmounted by a Greek orthodox cross. Today, replicas of these buildings where the officers and "better class" of Russians lived can be visited at the **Fort Ross State Historic Park** (19005 Coast Hwy., Jenner 95450), where the setting alone is worth a stop. The Commander's House (1836) belonging to Rotchev is the oldest original building at the park and offers a display on the Russian presence in California. The barracks and "Old Commanders House" offer period displays as well. Outside the palisades lived the Russian peasants and Aleut hunters, who along with Pomo Indians constituted a population that some estimate at 500. These hunters, laborers, and farmers also acted as soldiers, spending nights on guard duty and holidays "in gun and rifle practice." The visitor center has attractive exhibits on Ross, from Pomo Indian times through Anglo-ranching days. (Open daily 10 a.m.–4:30 p.m.; closed major holidays; fee; free tour brochure and 45-minute self-guided audio tour for fee; picnicking; 707–847–3286).

The fort is located 12m north of Jenner, 25m north of Bodega Bay, and nearly 100m north of San Francisco on Coast Highway 1. (Beware of night driving on this tortuous road.) In Jenner, right where the Russian River meets the sea, is the **River's End Restaurant** where you might stop for some steamed clams or dine on continental cuisine, or decide to stay awhile—cabins available. (Restaurant open Fri. from 4 p.m. on; weekends 11 a.m.–through dinner; 707–865–2484; ***moderate.***)

Point Reyes National Seashore □ In 1579, Francis Drake became the first Englishman to sail around the world. However, this historic feat was achieved from less than honorable purposes, since he was avoiding capture in the Atlantic after robbing a Spanish galleon of its 30 tons of silver and gold. While escaping in the Pacific, he ran low on fresh water and pulled into what is now called Drakes Bay, where he remained a month.

How unhandsome and deformed appear the face of the earth itself! Shewing trees without leaves and the ground without greeness in the months of June and July.

DRAKE EXPEDITION (1628)

While making repairs on the *Golden Hind,* Drake had considerable time to observe the Miwok Indians who paid him repeated visits. Not sure of their intentions, a fort was built. And not till later did Drake feel adequately safe with the Miwok to accompany them to some of their villages, the first such European exploration of California. Although the pirates grew to enjoy the company of the Miwoks, the same cannot be said of the Miwoks who gave every indication—mourning and crying—of believing these Europeans, the first ever seen, were returned spirits of the dead. Indeed the Miwoks treated them respectfully, even fearfully, but they must have been greatly relieved at their departure, not sorrowful as the Englishmen thought when the Miwok "ranne to the tops of the hills to keep us in their sight as long as they could."

Although Spain had already claimed the California coast and had explored a good part of it even farther north than Drakes Bay, Drake took the opportunity to take possession of the land for Elizabeth of England, calling it Nova Albion.

Before we went from thence, our generall caused to be set up, a monument of our being there: as also of her majesties, and successors right and title to that kingdome; namely a plate of brasse, fast nailed to a great firm post; whereon is engraven her graces name, and the day and yeare of our arrivall there, and of the free giving up, of the province and kingdome, both by the [Miwok] king and the people, into her majesties hands.

DRAKE EXPEDITION (1628)

Incredibly the "plate of brasse" was discovered in the 1950s—at least that's what was believed until recently. The brass plate was "found" toward San Francisco Bay, giving rise to speculation that Drake had discovered that bay, not the smaller one to the north. Also when Cermeno anchored at Drakes Bay in 1595, he made no mention of remnants of Drake's fort or debris from his month-long stay. Archaeologists have recovered shards of Oriental porcelain proving the presence of Cermeno's galleon from Manila, but still no finds have been made to confirm exactly where Drake landed. Nonetheless, most scholars believe Drake landed in the bay named after him, or even in Tomales Bay, but definitely not the great bay to the south.

Today the "original" fake brass plaque that caused such a stir is housed in the Bancroft Library at Berkeley, and Drakes Bay is surrounded by the 70,000 acres of the **Point Reyes National Seashore** where you can hike and camp, bicycle and ride horses (permits required for all; reserve campsides), or swim at **Drakes Beach** (15m west of headquarters) where even in colder weather you can just beachcomb, picnic, or look at the historical display. From above **Point Reyes Lighthouse** on a dramatic tip of the peninsula (almost 20m from headquarters), you can whalewatch from December to February. (A climb down to the lighthouse is not for the faint-hearted.) To get permits, maps, and information on the hours and weather conditions for all parts of the park, make sure you visit headquarters first and take in the replica of a **Coast Miwok Village** nearby. Headquarters and the visitor center are 1.5m to the left of the access road. Picnicking supplies are very good at **Perry's Deli** and next door is the **Knave of Hearts Bakery** with cappuccino and good homemade pizza. Both are 1m to the right of the access road and on the way to the village of Inverness with its restaurants and inns, and further on the way to Drake's Bay. (Headquarters open 8 a.m.–4 p.m., till 5 p.m. in summer; for more information on the extensive wilderness facilities here, write Superintendent, Point Reyes National Seashore, CA 94956; 663–1092.) *WEATHER NOTE*: Fog and winds can sweep the beaches in summer while rains affect the inland areas in winter. Here spring brings the balmiest weather.

Point Reyes headquarters lies just off the Inverness exit from CA 1, just above the town of Olema. About 40m north of San Francisco, the park can be reached via the Golden Gate Bridge to Sausalito, and on US 101 to the Stinson Beach exit for CA 1, justly called the Panoramic Highway here. Along this road there're fine beaches (try Muir Beach), artistic communities (Stinson Beach and Bolina), and parklands: **Muir Woods National Monument** with its stately redwoods and easy walking trails (open daily through sunset; free; 388–2595); and **Mount Tamalpais State Park** for its hiking and bridal paths and winding road up to spectacular views of the San Francisco Bay area (open daily through sunset; free; 388–2070). *Both are about 15m north of San Francisco and just above Stinson Beach. North of Point Reyes you skirt Tomales Bay and continue 30m through farmlands and hills with grazing horses and sheep, to Bodega Bay.*

Other Excursions

To consider the capital of California in Sacramento as a mere excursion from San Francisco may be inappropriate, but in fact many tours leave from the bay area to take you along the historic American River Pathway on a Gold Rush era tour, a period beyond the scope of this book. However, if you plan to make the 90m trip into the interior capital, plan a visit to ★★ **Sutter's Fort** (28th and L sts.) containing that Swiss pioneer's home dating from 1839 and with elaborate displays on life in the 1840s. (Open 10 a.m.–5 p.m. daily, closed major holidays; fee; 916–445–4209.)

Suggestions

Directory □ The zip code varies throughout the region, but the 415 area code is constant except when otherwise specified, or for 800-toll free numbers. ★ The *San Francisco Convention & Visitors Bureau* has excellent maps and information materials at its location on 201 Third Street, Suite 900, CA 94103; 974–6900, but the Visitor Information Center is more conveniently located at Market and Powell, on the lower level of Hallidie Plaza. ★ There's a 24-hour events and information tape at 391–2001.

Getting Around □ San Francisco is a good walking town, although you may be more comfortable walking its hills in sturdy shoes. ★ The **cable cars** make the hills fun, not tiring, and they run along Powell and Hyde, Powell and Mason, and California (all intersect on Nob Hill at Powell and California). Purchase tickets before boarding at the self-service machines along the lines. ★ Municipal buses also help you get around; for these MUNI routes check the Yellow Pages or call 673–MUNI ★ **BART** rapid transit trains link the city with the East Bay area, helping you avoid the traffic congestion on the Bay Bridge (788-BART). ★ There're taxis, of course, and car rentals, too. ★ If *driving,* you should know that the law here regarding parking on hills requires both the emergency brake and parking gear to be engaged AND that you curb your wheels, turning them towards the street when facing uphill, toward the curb when facing downhill. ★ The tour agencies range from the bus tours of **Gray Line** (896–1515), the van tours of **Maxi Tours** (563–2151), and the custom tours of **Creative Sightseeing Tours** (863–5868) to the champagne and limo service of **Classic Fantasy** (687–

5466). All these agencies tour Sonoma and Marin counties as well as the city.

Arriving □ The San Francisco International Airport lies 14m south of the city and is reached by taxi, car rentals, the **Airporter** bus with regularly scheduled runs from hotels (495–8404), **Bay Area Super Shuttle** vans with 24-hour personalized service (558–8500), and limousines (397–LIMOS). ★ There are also airports in San Jose and Oakland with connections between the three provided by **Airport Connection** (885–2666). ★ **Amtrak** trains provide service to the bay area from the Transbay Terminal (First and Mission; 982–8512; USA-RAIL). ★ Also at the Transbay Terminal is **Trailways** (982–6400) while the buses of **Greyhound** operate from 50 Seventh Street (433–1500).

Weather □ The peak season for travel certainly is the summer season through October, and hotel prices often are higher at this time. ★ The very clearest and best weather is in October, a time when the Sonoma area to the north is beautiful, too. ★ The inland areas are easily 10 degrees warmer than the bay and coastal areas on any given day. ★ San Francisco rarely reaches a temperature above 70° F or one lower than 40° F. ★ Summer mornings are foggy, the afternoons usually sunny, but still spring-like, and the evenings cool and foggy. ★ Rains fall December through February. ★ The average high temperature in January is 55° F; the low is 45° F. ★ The average high in July is 64° F; the low is 53° F. ★ Year round, sweaters or light coats are necessary for the evenings, and sometimes for the day, too. ★ Although Berkeley and the northern areas are appropriate for casual attire, the city is more business-like in dress.

PRACTICAL TIPS FOR CALIFORNIA TRAVEL

WHEN TO GO The coastal area covered by this guide has mild weather throughout the year, with temperatures warmer in southern California than northern, but still rarely extremely hot. Summers are warmer than winter, but in California the main difference between the seasons is wet and dry, not hot and cold. Summers here mean dry, despite the early morning fogs which can persist longer in the day in the north; and winters mean wet, particularly during January and February, although southern California receives very little rain even then. Inland from the coast, the weather in the valleys is more seasonal with summer bringing temperatures 10 to 20 degrees warmer and winter an occasional frost and, sometimes, snow. In the mountains, the summer air may remain mild, but winter snowfalls are frequent.

Although the coast has year round temperate weather, it still has its peak seasons for travel. The summers are popular throughout the state, but particularly in the south, from Santa Barbara to San Diego, where the beach culture reigns supreme. But although September to June are off-season in southern California, many find sunny skies and the mild temperatures warm enough for pool swimming, a way to pleasantly escape winter weather elsewhere. In the north, the air usually is too brisk, the sea too turbulent to promote a beach culture. Instead, travelers enjoy the rugged coastline from Big Sur north to Oregon by camping, surfing, picnicking, and just beachcombing—as well as enjoying the cultural sights of the region—from summer through the good weather in the fall, when the clearest skies and warmest temperatures prevail. The fall is also harvest time at the vineyards, and from Monterey through Sonoma, tourists flock to wine tastings and festivals. But winter, more so than in the south, is off season.

For more information on local variations in weather, check the temperatures given under "Suggestions" at the end of each destination chapter. *CLOTHING TIP*: Summer clothes are appropriate in the south during June, July, and August, but rarely in cooler San Francisco where a light-weight coat can always be useful. Sweaters can be needed anywhere at any time of year, particularly in the evenings.

PLANNING AIDS Although hotel, restaurant, and festival listings can be found in later chapters, you may want to obtain the most up-to-date prices, the exact festival date for a given year, or a more comprehensive listing of hotels if you're traveling during peak season. There are a number of excellent sources of free information and brochures.

Travel agents can facilitate reservations for you at hotels and can arrange flights, car rentals, and tours. Their computers provide them with the latest prices. They also have listings of special package tours that might make your trip less costly and more convenient. Travel agents receive their fees, not from you, but through discounts provided by their network.

The state tourist office issues many brochures, including a good road map, calendars of events, and camping and accommodation listings:

California Office of Tourism
1121 L Street, Suite 103
Sacramento, CA 95814
916–322–1396

The local chambers of commerce and convention and visitor bureaus often have even more information on hotels and local festivals. Their addresses and phone numbers are listed under "Suggestions" in the appropriate destination chapter.

If you really prefer to do your own research for a trip, make sure you check the "Suggestions" section under your destination for the listings of the tour operators, airlines, and other transportation. Also, you can check current prices by contacting hotels, airlines, and car rental agencies through their toll-free 800 telephone numbers. Just check the nearest urban Yellow Pages and, for example, for the hotels, look up "Hotels and Motels—Out-of-Town Reservations." Or call toll free information at 800–555–1212.

TRANSPORTATION How you decide to travel within California should be determined by what you plan to do once you're there. If you're just going to a resort, say in Santa Barbara, then you may want to rely on taxis, not a rental car. And the same would be true for a visit to San Francisco or Monterey, both of which are good walking towns, unlike

San Diego and Los Angeles. For day excursions you could arrange either a tour or car rental. Traveling extensively along the coast does require that you bring a car, rent one, or limit yourself to the sights along the route of Amtrak, Trailways, Greyhound, or tour agencies. (For the operating areas of these train and bus lines check under ''Suggestions'' in the destination chapters.)

If you decide to fly and then rent a car, check with your travel agent about special airline packages called ''Fly and Drive'' that often include discounts on car rentals. Also, remember that there usually are extra charges for not dropping your car off at the same town where you picked it up. If at all possible, you might want to plan a loop tour. Or if you plan to travel extensively with one of the bus or train lines, contact them in advance for information on any discounted ticket arrangements that might be available. And last, but not least in terms of cost, if you are arriving in California by plane, make sure you reserve your ticket as far in advance as possible, since often there are discounts available that won't be on spur-of-the-moment travel.

CAMPING Many scenic campgrounds are mentioned in the various regions, but for those primarily on a camping trip, more information will be necessary. Before setting out on a trip where you plan to stay at national and state parks, it's best to write for complete listings and up-to-date procedures. Many of these campgrounds operate on a first-come, first-serve basis, but others permit advance reservations. Because the public campgrounds are either free or inexpensive, they fill up early in the day during peak travel seasons. Also, campgrounds, especially in the national forests, vary from wilderness conditions to those with full amenities. To help plan your trip, write to the California Office of Tourism for their state parks brochure, or check with some of the organizations below.

California State Parks
Department of Parks and Recreation
Box 2390
Sacramento, CA 95811
916–445–6477

National Park Service
Western Region Information Office
Fort Mason, Bldg. 201
San Francisco, CA 94123
415–556–0122

U.S. Forest Service
630 Sansome Street
San Francisco, CA 94111
415–556–0122

BED & BREAKFASTS Every year more and more homes are opening up in this new form of guesthouse. Some are excellent alternatives to hotels, well located and intimate, and often moderately priced. Although a few are mentioned in the destination chapters, more often you are referred to a bed and breakfast association that has more knowledge as to whether the home has appropriate insurance and state permits. In addition, the California Office of Tourism has a B & B brochure available.

HOSTELS The number of lodgings available under the American Youth Hostel Association is quite extensive in California, including some in the cities, such as the conveniently located one in the Fort Mason area of San Francisco. These low, budget-priced facilities are also near popular parks and monuments, such as the one at Point Reyes National Seashore. Though age no longer matters, lodge use is restricted to members and, most often, to those arriving on their own steam, like bikers and hikers. Each "lodge" (or Victorian home, or whatever is used) normally has separate dorms for men and women, and shared kitchen and bathroom facilities. If this is your chosen method of travel, write:

American Youth Hostels
680 Beach Street, Suite 396
San Francisco, CA 94109
415–771–4646

HOTELS California offers sumptuous resorts, wonderful inns, fine old ranches, and just about all other kinds of accommodations you would expect to find in the United States. The listings in this book emphasize those hotels that are special to the region, and though often these are expensive, you might find them the best place to visit, if not stay, for local ambience or dramatic views of the coast. Also listed is the location of the local motel row where you can find well-known examples of national chains, such as Super 9, TraveLodge, and Holiday Inn. The appearance and services at these hotels usually require no description for the traveler of U.S. highways. These national chains (except for Motel 6) are listed in urban-area Yellow Pages with toll-free numbers for making reservations. If you make your reservations well in advance for peak season and holidays, you should have no trouble finding accommodations. If not, you might want to contact the local chamber of commerce, a travel agent, or even try some of the guides to cheap motels sold in bookstores.

BUDGET TIPS Even if you don't like camping or fast food chains, there are some ways to cut back on costs while still enjoying some of the finest accommodations and restaurants available. For resort hotels, off season travel often permits you to stay at the hotel of your choice at considerable savings. And just about any time of the year, you can find substantial weekend discounts at city hotels that rely on business people to keep them full during the week. In many towns, some of the finest restaurants reduce their prices for what is called ''Early Dinner Specials'' between 5–6:30 p.m. on weekdays. You can discover whether the restaurant of your choice participates by calling, or by looking at the ads in the local weekly paper or tourist pamphlets.

Other less self-indulgent options include arranging for your own breakfasts and lunches by buying from bakeries and delicatessens, and preparing them either in your hotel room, or better yet, at picnic facilities. And if you don't feel it's a vacation if you're cooking all the time, look for a good Mexican restaurant where the prices are usually surprisingly low.

To cut back on transportation costs, make sure you contact the bus, train, or airlines in advance to take advantage of discounted passes and rates. And if you'll be visiting the national parks often, check into the benefits of an annual pass (National Park Service, Office of Public Inquiries, Washington, DC 20402). Other discounts are available to special groups: students who belong to the Council on International Education Exchange (312 Sutter St., Suite 407, San Francisco 94108; 415–421–3473) receive a travel catalog and reduced hotel rates, while senior citizens often receive museum and hotel discounts; other senior discounts are available through the National Park Service (see address above) and by membership in a variety of associations, such as the American Association of Retired Persons.

GUIDE TO THE MISSIONS

Mission	*Location*	*Founding Date*	*Founding Position*	*Star Rating*
La Purisima	Lompoc near Santa Barbara	1787	11th	★★★
San Antonio de Padua	Jolon, north of San Miguel	1771	3rd	★★
San Buenaventura	Ventura	1782	9th	★
San Carlos Borromeo	Carmel	1770	2nd	★★★
San Diego de Acala	San Diego	1769	1st	★
San Fernando Rey	San Fernando	1797	17th	★★
San Francisco de Asis	San Francisco	1776	6th	★
San Francisco Solano	Sonoma	1823	21st	★
San Gabriel Arcangel	Los Angeles	1771	4th	★★
San Jose de Guadalupe	Fremont	1797	14th	★
San Juan Bautista	San Juan Bautista	1797	15th	★★
San Juan Capistrano	San Juan Capistrano	1776	7th	★★★
San Luis Obispo	San Luis Obispo	1772	5th	
San Luis Rey	Oceanside	1797	18th	★★★
San Miguel Arcangel	San Miguel	1797	16th	★★
San Rafael Arcangel	San Rafael	1817	20th	
Santa Barbara	Santa Barbara	1786	10th	★★★
Santa Clara de Asis	Santa Clara	1777	8th	★
Santa Cruz	Santa Cruz	1791	12th	
Santa Ines	Solvang	1804	19th	★
Soledad	Soledad	1791	13th	

SOURCES

Jose Antonio Anzar in Zephyrin Engelhardt's *Mission San Juan Bautista,* Santa Barbara, 1931.

Jose Arnaz, "Memoirs of a Merchant," translated by Nellie Van de Grift Sanchez. *Touring Topics,* XX, September-October, 1928.

Faxon Dean Atherton, *The California Diary of Faxon Dean Atherton,* 1836–39. Edited by Doyce B. Nunis, California Historical Society, 1964.

Hubert Howe Bancroft, *History of the Pacific States,* volumes XIII-XIX, San Francisco, 1884–90.

Arturo Bandini, "Navidad," *California Illustrated Magazine,* 1892. Reprinted in 1958 by California Historical Society, Suzanna Bryant Dakin, editor.

Frederick William Beechey, *An Account of A Visit to California 1826–27,* reprinted by Grabhorn Press in 1941.

Horace Bell, *Reminiscences of a Ranger,* Los Angeles, 1881.

Herbert E. Bolton, *Anza's California Expeditions,* 5 volumes, University of California Press, 1930.

Brigada Briones, "A Glimpse of Domestic Life in 1828," reprinted in *Sketches of Early California,* Donald De Nevi, Chronicle Books, 1971.

William Ide Brown, in Fred Blackburn Rogers' *William Ide Brown, Bear Flagger,* John Howell Books, 1962.

Edwin Bryant, *What I Saw in California,* 1849 Appleton edition reprinted by Lewis Osborne, 1967.

Juan Cabot in Zephyrin Engelhardt's *San Miguel Archangel,* Santa Barbara, 1929.

Cabrillo Expedition, "Diary" in Herbert E. Bolton's *Spanish Exploration in the Southwest,* Charles Scribner's Sons, 1908.

Edward D. Castillo in "The Impact of the Euro-American Exploration and Settlement," *Handbook of North American Indians,* volume 8, Smithsonian Institution, 1978.

John & Laree Caughey, *California Heritage,* Ward Ritchie Press, 1962.

——— *Los Angeles: Biography of a City,* University of California Press, 1976.

Richard J. Cleveland, *Narrative of Voyages and Commercial Enterprises,* 1842. Third edition 1850 printed by Charles H. Peirce.

Sherburne F. Cook, *Conflict between the California Indian and White Civilization,* University of California Press reprint, 1976.

Peter Corney, *Voyages in the Northern Pacific,* H.I.T.G. Thrum, 1896.

Miguel Costanso, *Diario,* translated by Frederick J. Teggert, Publications of the Academy of Pacific Coast History II, 1911.

——— *The Narrative of the Portola Expedition of 1769–1770,* edited by Adolph van Hemert-Engert and Frederick J. Teggart, Publications of the Academy of Pacific Coast History I, 1910.

Leonardo Cota as quoted in Dora Crouch et al., see below.

Juan Crespi in Herbert E. Bolton's *Fray Juan Crespi,* 1927. Reprinted 1971 by AMS Press.

Dora P. Crouch, Daniel J. Garr, and Axel I. Mundigo, *Spanish City Planning in North America,* MIT Press, 1982.

Richard Henry Dana, *Two Years Before the Mast,* 1840 with 1869 addendum as reprinted by Modern Library 1936.

William Heath Davis, *Seventy-Five Years in California,* 1909. Reprinted 1929 by Lakeside Press.

Drake Expedition from *The World Encompassed by Sir Francis Drake,* 1628, as quoted in Lawrence Kinnaird's *History of the Greater San Francisco Bay Region,* volume 1, Lewis Historical Publishing, 1966.

Eugene Duflot (de Mofras), *Travels on the Pacific Coast (1840–42),* edited by Marguerite Eyer Wilbur, Fine Arts Press, 2 volumes, 1937.

A. Duhaut-Cilly, "Account of California in the Years 1827–1828," translated by Charles Franklin Carter in *California Historical Society Quarterly,* volume VIII (1929), issues 2, 3 and 4.

Samuel F. duPont, *Extracts from private journal-letters, 1846–48,* Ferris Brothers, 1885.

Narcisco Duran in Zephyrin Engelhardt's *Missions and Missionaries* (see below).

George Washington Eayrs in Irving B. Richman (see below).

Zephyrin Engelhardt, *San Buenaventura: The Mission by the Sea,* Santa Barbara, 1930.

——— *San Carlos Borromeo Mission,* Santa Barbara, 1934.

——— *Missions and Missionaries,* 4 volumes & Index, James H. Barry Company, 1913.

——— *San Diego Mission,* James H. Barry Company, 1920.

——— *Santa Ines Mission and Mission La Purisima Concepcion,* Santa Barbara, 1832.

Jose Maria Estrada as quoted in Z. Engelhardt's *Santa Ines Mission* (see above).

Pedro Font, "Diary of an Expedition to Monterey," in Herbert E. Bolton, volume IV (see above).

Juan Bautista Gancho and Pedro Cabot in Zephyrin Engelhardt's *Mission San Antonio de Padua,* Santa Barbara, 1929.

Maynard J. Geiger, *The Life and Times of Fray Junipero Serra,* Academy of American Franciscan History, 1959.

——— *Mission Santa Barbara 1782–1965,* Heritage Printers, 1965.

Congressman Giles as quoted by Howard Zinn in *A People's History of the United States,* Harper & Row, 1980.

J.M. Guinn, *Historical and Biographical Record of Los Angeles and Vicinity,* Chapman Publishing Company, 1901.

George P. Hammond, *The Larkin Papers,* 10 volumes, University of California Press, 1951.

Teresa de la Guerra Hartnell in Suzanna B. Dakin's *The Lives of William Hartnell,* Stanford University Press, 1949.

William Hartnell in Suzanna B. Dakin (see previous entry).

L.W. Hastings, as quoted in Thomas Larkin below.

Prudencia Higuera, "Trading with the Americans," *The Century Magazine,* volume 41, 1890.

W.D.M. Howard in John Hawgood's "The Patterns of Yankee Infiltration in Mexican Alta California," *Pacific Historical Review,* February 1958.

C. Alan Hutchinson, *Frontier Settlement in Mexican California,* Yale University Press, 1969.

George Heinrich von Langsdorff, *Narrative of the Rezanov Voyage,* Thomas C. Russell, private press, 1927.

Jean Francois Laperouse in *The First French Expedition to California (1786),* edited by Charles N. Rudkin, Glen Dawson, 1959.

Thomas Larkin, *The First and Last Consul,* edited by John A. Howgood, Pacific Books, 1970.

Fermin Lasuen, *Writing,* edited and translated by Finbar Kenneally, 2 volumes, Washington, DC, 1965.

Fernando Librado in Thomas C. Blackburn's *December's Child: A Book of Chumash Oral Narratives,* University of California Press, 1975.

Jose Longinos (Martinez) in Lesley Byrd Simpson's *Journal of Jose Longinos Martinez, Notes and Observations of the Naturalist,* John Howell Books, 1961.

Fernando Martin and Pasqual Oliva in Z. Engelhardt's *San Diego Mission* (see above).

Archibald Menzies, "Journal of the Vancouver Expedition," edited by Alice Eastwood, *California Historical Society Quarterly,* II (1924).

Felipe de Neve in Edwin Beilharz' *Felipe de Neve,* California Historical Society, 1971.

Angustias de la Guerra Ord, *Occurrences in Hispanic California,* 1878; translated by Francis Price and William H. Ellison for Academy of American Franciscan History, 1956.

Francisco Palou, *Historical Memoirs of New California,* edited by Herbert E. Bolton, 1926. Russell & Russell reprint 1966.

——— *Life of Junipero Serra* (1787), translated by George Wharton Jones, Pasadena, 1913.

Mariano Payeras, see Z. Engelhardt's *Santa Ines Mission* above as well as his *San Gabriel Mission.*

Antonio Peyri, as quoted in Zephyrin Engelhardt's *San Luis Rey Mission,* James H. Barry Co., 1921.

Jose Ramon Pico, "Christmas Before the Americans Came," in *Christmas in California,* California Historical Society, 1957.

Pio Pico in Martin Cole's edition of *Narracion Historica,* Arthur Clark Company, 1973.

Hugo Reid in Suzanna Dakin's *The Scotch Paisano,* University of California Press, 1939.

Nikolai Rezanov, *Voyage to Nueva California in 1806,* Thomas C. Russell, private press, 1926.

Irving Berndine Richman, *California Under Spain and Mexico,* Houghton Mifflin Company, 1911.

Antonio Ripoll in Zephyrin Engelhardt's *Santa Barbara Mission,* James H. Barry Co., 1923.

Alfred Robinson, *Life in California,* 1846. Reprinted 1969 by De Capo Press.

Alexandre Rotchev in *Russian California,* Emil T. Bunje, et al., Berkeley, 1937. Reprinted by Rand E. Research Assoc., 1970.

Jose Senan in Lesley Byrd Simpson's *The Letters of Jose Senan, OFM, Mission San Buenaventura 1796–1823,* John Howell Books, 1962.

Junipero Serra in Antoine Tibesar's *Writings of Junipero Serra,* 4 volumes, OFM 1955–66.

William Shaler, "Journal of a Voyage between China and the North-Western Coast of America Made in 1804," *The American Register,* volume III, 1808.

George Simpson, *Narrative of a Journey Round the World in 1841–1842,* London, 1847.

John D. Sloat, as quoted in Bancroft (see above).

Francisco Suner and Josef Barona in Zephyrin Engelhardt's *Mission San Juan Capistrano,* Los Angeles, 1922.

Pablo Tac, "Indian Life and Customs at Mission San Luis Rey [1835]," Minna and Gorden Hewes, editors, *The Americas: A Quarterly Review* 9:87–106, 1958.

——— "Conversion de los San Luisenos," *Proceedings of the 23rd International Congress of Americanists,* pp. 635–48, New York, 1928.

Estevan Tapis, see Z. Engelhardt's *Santa Ines Mission* above.

Baynard Taylor, *Eldorado,* George P. Putnam & Son, 1850. Reprinted 1854.

Theodore E. Treutlein, *San Francisco Bay: Discovery and Colonization,* California Historical Society, 1968.

Guadalupe Vallejo, "Ranch and Mission Days in Alta California," *The Century Magazine,* volume 41, 1890.

Mariano Guadalupe Vallejo in *The Vallejos of California,* Madie Brown Emparan, Gleeson Library Associates, 1968.

George Vancouver in Marguerite Eyer Wilbur's *Vancouver in California,* Glen Dawson Press, 1953.

Lorenzo Venancio in H.A. Torchiana's *The Story of Mission Santa Cruz,* Paul Elder & Company, 1933.

Sebastian Vizcaino, "Diary," in Herbert E. Bolton's *Spanish Exploration in the Southwest,* Charles Scribner's Sons, 1908.

Charles Wilkes, *Narrative of the United States Exploring Expedition,* volume V, Philadelphia, 1845.

Oscar Osburn Winther, *The Story of San Jose,* California Historical Society, 1935.

GLOSSARY

Alcade	Mayor
Alta California	The Spanish province that currently is the state of California. It was called ''alta,'' or upper, to distinguish it from its neighbor, Baja.
asistencia	A mission outpost with permanent buildings including a chapel.
atole	Porridge
bark	3-masted sailing vessel
brig	2-masted, square-rigged sailing ship
Californio	A non-Indian California-born person
Camino Real	Royal, or, more properly, public road. Also known in California as the mission trail and the king's highway.
convento	A wing of the mission quadrangle containing the friars rooms, refectory, and kitchen.
don	Spanish title for a gentleman
dona	Spanish title for a lady
fray	Friar
gente de razon	The so-called rational people; used on the Spanish frontier for anyone, including non-mission Indians, who lived in the European manner.
gentiles	Non-Catholics; heathens
hacendado	Land baron; owner of a ranch or hacienda
league	Usually 2.63 miles
matanza	Slaughter
merienda	Picnic, cook-out
New Spain	Mexico
padre	Friar, priest
presidio	Fort
ramada	Thatched shelter
rancheros	Ranchers

ranchos Ranch

secularization Civil control of the missions; in effect, the end of those religious institutions.

tamale A leaf-wrapped concoction of corn meal, meats, and perhaps chiles.

vaquero Cowboy

INDEX